John Button is a Professorial [...] Melbourne, a part-time colu[...] *Morning Herald*, and an excursionist into the realms of trade and business. He was Industry Minister in the Commonwealth Government between 1983 and 1993.

Flying the kite

TRAVELS OF AN AUSTRALIAN POLITICIAN

JOHN BUTTON

RANDOM HOUSE

A U S T R A L I A

Random House Australia Pty Ltd
20 Alfred Street, Milsons Point, NSW 2061

Sydney New York Toronto
London Auckland Johannesburg
and agencies throughout the world
First published 1994
Reprinted 1994 (three times)

National Library of Australia
Cataloguing-in-Publication Data

Button, John, 1933– .
  Flying the Kite.

  ISBN 0 09 182872 4.

  1. Button, John, 1933– —Journeys. 2. Cabinet officers—
  Australia—Travel. 3. Australia—Foreign public opinion.
  4. Australia—Foreign economic relations. 5. Australia—
  Foreign relations—1976–1990. I. Title.

327.94

Typeset by Midland Typesetters Pty Ltd, Victoria
Printed by Griffin Paperbacks, Adelaide
Production by Vantage Graphics, Sydney

Contents

Acknowledgements

When it comes to using a word processor, I'm certainly not a New Age Guy. This book was written by hand, and I'm grateful to Mickey, Loretta and Pat, who deciphered the handwriting (described by one of them as like 'the scratchings of a chook') and typed the manuscript. Members of my former staff, some of who stoically travelled with me, have tolerated my phone calls to check my recollection of events. My wife, Dorothy, put up with me gazing at the wall behind my desk, on Saturdays and Sundays, when we might have been doing something more interesting. She also jogged my memory about events and incidents which occurred when we travelled together. Some foolhardy people, including my sons Jamie and Nick, encouraged me to keep going. I owe them all my thanks.

Australia's fatal shore?

I t is a big country. Historians have evoked powerful images of vast distances and tired feet. Television commercials constantly remind us—big country, big thirst. How many urban Australians are conscious of it, is a different question. But you understand it flying to Jakarta, Singapore or Bangkok. It takes nearly half the flight to get out of the place: hours of flying over red, dry land. Drysdale and Fred Williams country. Australia in the mind of the artist.

For Americans and Europeans it is still a great distance away. The First Fleet took eight months to get here: a destination, a country, chosen for its remoteness. Today jet aircraft help underpin the idea of a global village. But for Europeans accustomed to short flights to London, Zurich or Madrid, the contemplation of more than twenty hours in an aeroplane creates a threshold in the mind. Technology expands the opportunities and defines the imagination.

Australia is also an island—a fact dramatically realised on Qantas Flight 27 from Tokyo to Sydney when the flight attendants, like hospital nurses, wake you in the early hours of the morning. You stir grumpily, wondering if it's designed for your good health or has something to do with their rosters. Raising the blind and looking out the window, you see the dawn coming up over a vast ocean. Then there is a glimpse of a dusky-blue haze of coastline at the edge, some emerging beaches, and the muggy spires of commercial Sydney. You struggle with mixed emotions.

Australians make about two-and-a-half million overseas trips each year, of which about half are holidays and a quarter visiting relatives in other countries. My former colleague, Senator Peter Walsh, a stern man and dedicated Finance Minister, considered this outrageous because of its effect on the balance of payments. He once suggested a departure tax so high that it would deter almost everyone from travelling abroad. Two hundred years after the First Fleet, some of us found the symbolism of this proposal chilling. The 'Fatal Shore' indeed.

Like most of these travelling Australians, I enjoy being overseas and I'm always glad to be back. The returning tourists at Australian airports loaded up with duty-free; with videos, cameras and grog, scarcely disguise their excitement at being home. One imagines video nights in hundreds of suburban houses: Mum at the top of the Eiffel Tower, Fred in front of the Taj Mahal. The image of the picture nights is supplemented by overheard anecdotes of the deprivations suffered by foreigners: grey pebbly beaches; no news about Australia; and the Colosseum, old, but tiny compared with the MCG.

There is, of course, nothing particularly Australian about this. It would happen in Canada, or the American Mid-West, or with British tourists returning from Spain. Overseas travel is a 'high-touch' activity; a desire for direct experience and to see it with one's own eyes. It is a complement to TV images or maybe just a sentimental journey to places of cultural origin. But sometimes one might query the quality of the experience and the value of the perspectives, and the absence of recognition that all countries have strengths and weaknesses and that many of them do a lot of things better than us.

Travel, it is said, broadens the mind. As Dr Johnson put it: 'All travel has its advantages. If the passenger visits better countries, he may learn to improve his own, and if fortune carries him to worse, he may learn to enjoy it.' Australian parliamentarians should have broad minds, and perhaps have a better opportunity than most to improve their own country with the knowledge derived from travel. So they enjoy travel entitlements to overseas countries and compete vigorously for membership of parliamentary delegations and 'fact-finding' missions. Sometimes they produce reports which are seldom read. But while friendships are made between members of parliamentary delegations overseas, often across Party lines, they don't seem to talk about their experiences much when they return to Canberra. The occasion when Barry Jones told me that the milkshakes in Buenos Aires were the best in the world stands out in my mind as a rare one in which a government Minister or parliamentarian generously shared an observation about overseas travel. There were others, of course; gossip about peccadillos, Australian crassness or tensions between members of a delegation. And Gerry Hand as Immigration Minister vividly describing his visits to refugee camps.

It is not surprising that there is not much debate in the Australian Parliament which could be described as 'informed' by overseas experience, or attempts to relate what might be relevant in other countries to Australia's problems and opportunities. One suspects a certain coyness about this, a fear of being labelled as a travel junketeer or an eccentric variety of 'tall poppy'. The value of travel is assumed. Without it discussion might be worse. More importantly perhaps, the history of Australian politics has been characterised by the same derivativeness which has until recently affected much of our intellectual and cultural life. Historically, this has been captured in symbolic 'one-liners' such as 'British to the bootstraps' and 'All the way with LBJ'. Moods, evocations of longstanding loyalties, and political 'trends' abroad have achieved greater significance than empirical evidence based on close observations of similarities and differences.

So the search for convenient overseas role models has been singularly persistent, irrespective of their appropriateness to Australian circumstances and conditions. It is as if we could take 'off the shelf' instant and cosy solutions for this country. For decades, for example, sections of the Australian Left wasted emotional and intellectual energy seeking a relevant role model in the Soviet Union. Similarly in the 1980s 'Thatcherism' in its various manifestations became the 'light on the hill' for the Australian Conservatives. The posturing remained so until 1992, the year in which a former Thatcher minister, Ian Gilmour, pointed out in his book *Dancing with Dogma* that the late and early Thatcher economic policies had little in common except self-congratulation.

Politicians were not alone in their seemingly uncritical acceptance of overseas models. In the 1960s and 1970s Australians dithered over comfortable allegiances to Britain or the United States. We became inverse victims of the 'not invented here' syndrome. The cringe was not confined to culture. Imported European, American and later Japanese products were assumed to be better. They usually were, but not much thought was given to 'Why?' Imported ideas were thought to provide the secret to success. It became fashionable, for example, to advocate the introduction of legal remedies such as class actions and highly regulatory product liability laws copied from the United States. The relevance of their application in a country of sixteen million people was hardly considered.

Australian 'tall poppies'—whether they were intellectuals, scientists, artists or businesspeople—were treated with scepticism and indifference. Visiting tall poppies, however mediocre or irrelevant, were regarded with deference and acclaim. They brought, like mail steamers to the colonies, suggestions of a different kind of good life—more sophisticated, culturally and economically vibrant, and intellectually aware. Many of Australia's youngest and brightest took the hint. International challenges and opportunities beckoned. The brain drain became an endemic Australian disease.

There was something pathetic about a country which in those years accepted that it did almost nothing particularly well. We did provide good soldiers in Malaysia, Korea and Vietnam. We grew high quality wool and dug up good iron ore. We won a lot of cricket and we had good tennis players and golfers. These things were thrown up by nature, lifestyle and environment. But they became the symbols of the Australian image—easygoing, good-natured, sporty and mediocre. The idea of excellence, where it existed, was narrowly based with shallow roots. This was something for others: not for us. In industry the notion of aspiring to world best practice was two decades away. As late as 1980 we were still being encouraged to believe that the resource industries would provide us with yet another Nirvana.

A lot of this happened because Australians had an underdeveloped sense of difference. In the 1960s and 1970s we hadn't worked out that we were different in history and experience from Europe and North America, and desperately different in our geographical location. Allegiances, which had served us with mixed success in the past, were mulled over in the hope that they would provide a key to the future. Conservative politicians who overflew Asian countries in these two decades seeking warmth and comfort in London and Washington were merely displaying the powerful instincts and inferior vision of cave bats seeking the light. In fact the development of the European Community, the emergence of Japan as an economic power, the growing independence and single-minded pursuit of national economic objectives in various countries in Asia were all indicating that Australia's world was becoming polycentric.

To thoughtful Australians and many overseas critics and observers Australia seemed set in a morass of tired and borrowed ideas. The country's political leaders exuded the scent of middle-aged grey power. 'How come,' people asked, 'a country with Australia's wealth and natural resources doesn't perform better? Why does this young country have none of the vigour and enthusiasm of youth?' Australia's economic performance had never matched its rhetoric, said Singapore's Prime Minister Lee Kuan Yew. And in Australia people were troubled too. The concerns were reflected in the titles and contents of influential books like Donald Horne's *Lucky Country*, Max Walsh's *Poor Little Rich Country*, Peter Robinson's *Australian Capitalism in Crisis* and later *Australia and Argentina on Parallel Paths*.

Australia in the 1970s was changing, but at its own leisurely pace. Migrant communities were starting to enrich the cultural and restaurant life. The abolition of the White Australia Policy led to governments of both political persuasions administering sensible and relevant immigration policies. The country began to acquire a multiracial complexion. As a political leader, Gough Whitlam still paid some deference to kings and potentates. But he challenged the cult of mediocrity and worked to a wider agenda; recognising China and embracing the realities of the emerging countries of Asia. His later remark 'When I opened China to the world ... ' was a characteristic mix of self-congratulation and self-deprecating humour. And yet it was largely right.

Australia's tragic involvement in the Vietnam War was a huge catalyst for change. The Vietnam generation was more questioning of comfortable assumptions, more sceptical about the 'wisdom' and motives of the United States and less 'Eurocentric' than the generation before. And in the 1970s new pockets of excellence began to emerge. The Australian film industry abandoned its endearing hillbilly image, Australian dance and pop music developed a character of its own, and Australian writers caught up with the painters in exploring new themes and experiences.

What wasn't much realised in these two decades was the

extent and pace of economic change in the rest of the world. The failure to recognise this became the focal point of Australian insularity. There was growing recognition of the emergence of Japan as an economic superpower. The Australian mining industry acquired a superficial expertise in negotiating with the Japanese. Australians who travelled to Singapore noted the changes which were taking place. There was talk about the 'Asian Tigers', which prior to the Marcos regime included the Philippines. China seemed a sleeping economic giant sedated by communism and racked by nightmares of political and regional tensions. Europe pursued its path towards the European Community, grew richer and behaved with characteristic egocentricity. The Common Agricultural Policy was regarded by Australians as not only economically reprehensible but rather unfair.

And in the mentor nations, from which we traditionally borrowed ideas, nothing much happened. Britain was in decline. Successive governments at Westminster shuffled the deckchairs. The United States was preoccupied with Vietnam and the rising industrial competitiveness of Japan. The most dramatic changes were of course taking place in countries like Korea and Taiwan, the vigorous city-state economies of Hong Kong and Singapore, and in the remainder of the Asian Tigers. In Australia their relative economic success was often attributed to a variety of alien and rather sinister institutions from MITI in Japan to authoritarian governments in Korea, Taiwan and some of the countries of South-East Asia.

The period of real economic change in Australia began in the early 1980s. The need was dramatised by Treasurer Paul Keating's 'Banana Republic' reference in 1985. But ministers in the Hawke Government elected in 1983 had a strong commitment to internationalising the Australian economy. As time passed its critics would say it moved too slowly; its traditional supporters would argue it moved too fast. One of its first acts as a government was to sign the Close Economic

Relations Agreement with New Zealand, a small hesitant step in the right direction. CER had been worked on and negotiated by the Liberal Government which held office between 1975 and 1983. This government had contemplated general reductions in tariffs and rejected them. It had commissioned and received a major report on financial deregulation.

The Hawke Government acted on both those matters. Financial deregulation, the floating of the dollar and phased reductions in tariffs set Australia on a new course, from which there was no turning back. When Alan Bond's syndicate won the America's Cup race in 1983, it was perhaps the last occasion on which Australian self-esteem would be allowed to rest on the narrow basis of sporting achievement. For better or worse Australia was becoming part of the world and the 'global economy'. 'Constant change', as a date pad epigram reminds us, 'is here to stay.' There was the possibility of Australians developing a new confidence and sense of self-awareness.

'History', said a philistine of international renown, 'is bunk.' I don't wish to argue the point. History is about events and ideas and recorded experiences. Events change rapidly. Attitudes change more slowly. A mixture of technology, experience, and new national aspirations in the three decades following the Second World War resulted in a period in which the world changed more rapidly than ever before. Australia did not change very much in this period; certainly not in ways which were perceptible or demonstrable to the rest of the world. In the late 1970s and the 1980s the process of change became more obvious. The speed increased, but the memories and perceptions of Australia as it was lingered on. So did some of the habits.

This is essentially a book about the 1980s. It was, however, a decade which had to be seen in the context of what had gone before, and which is understood better with the wisdom of hindsight. In the 1970s I travelled overseas as a Member of Parliament. On the first occasion I went to the United Kingdom; on the second to the United States. In each case I was a guest of the government of the country I visited. In each case I was the recipient of one of the travel grants made available to help win the hearts and minds of 'promising' political leaders abroad. In Britain they were provided to Commonwealth countries; in the United States to Third World countries and some others, including Australia.

I had lived and worked in Britain before, and grown to appreciate its cultural and intellectual life and its traditions of tolerance and free speech. There in 1975, I was largely in the hands of officialdom, represented by people who were philistine; transfixed by the rigidities of the class system and its attendant snobbery, and mesmerised by Britain's 'glorious' past. They seemed to regard Australia as a loyal outpost of 'their values' and Australians as a collection of country yokels who occasionally produced good cricketers or a political luminary like Sir Robert Menzies, who understood 'their' system. In the United States in 1978 I had my first experience of regularly meeting people who didn't know where Australia was and, in that huge, diverse and insular society, of understanding the comparative irrelevance of a country of sixteen million people.

Travelling to various countries in the 1980s was a little different. As a minister people make appointments for you, doors are opened, you stay in good hotels, and you exchange business cards and diplomatic handshakes with the members of political and bureaucratic elites. To some it sounds glamorous; sometimes it was. But for every meeting which produced some positive outcome or a smattering of intellectual excitement, there were half a dozen dominated by the traditions of the 'courtesy call': exchanging banalities and regrets, searching for common ground, waiting with a perceptive eye for the signal that the discussion would have to conclude. In this milieu of people, who spend their lives jetsetting between interminable meetings, the glimpse you catch of the country you happen to be visiting tends to be one dimensional: a view from the top. Frequently it is a jaundiced view compounded by jet lag, itineraries, sleepless nights and airline schedules. The danger signs emerge when you commence a speech by saying 'It's nice to be here in Rome ... ' when you're actually in Paris.

The treadmill is hard to get off. In many countries, it's made worse by security problems. Out for a short walk in Milan one day I turned into a cobbled street full of boutiques and started to 'window-shop'. A plain-clothes policeman stood at each end of the street. A third one followed me about six paces behind. When I stopped he stopped. When I moved he moved. Finding no pleasure in window-shopping, I returned to my hotel. On another occasion, in an Asian capital, as a guest of the government I was provided with a bodyguard called Mr Toh. When I went to bed at night he dozed in a chair outside my room. When I woke in the morning he was there. If I spoke to anyone he was standing a foot away; 'Toh to Toh', as he became known. If I spoke to him I had to choose the right ear. The other one had a microphone in it. Australians and Australian public figures are not used to this. That is something for which we ought to be very grateful.

Ministers travel overseas as representatives of Australia. In part it is an information-gathering exercise. But the bottom line is selling the place: promoting investment and trade, encouraging knowledge and understanding. In the 1980s it was hard work; largely because of fixed, frequently outdated and strongly held negative perceptions about Australia. It was said that it was too far away to think about seriously. The market was too small. The country was an unsophisticated producer of raw materials: nothing else. Unions provoked a constant climate of industrial unrest. The people were lazy. Inflation was too high. By the mid- to late-1980s, having explained the changes taking place in Australia to a German business audience, it was slightly galling to be told that Australian wages were too high. In Britain, having outlined the improvement in the Australian industrial relations climate, it was depressing to be told that the unions were ruining Australia. In Germany wages were much higher than Australian wages. In Britain industrial relations were worse.

In the case of Japan there were strong and understandable perceptions of cultural difference. Japanese industrialists, worried about the small size of the Australian market and about poor labour relations, asked for investment incentives. European textile manufacturers complained about the management and poor customer-response of the Australian wool industry. In Italy at a meeting with representatives of the Italian leather industry, I expounded on the benefits of collaboration between Australian hide producers and Italian leather producers. They listened politely. Then the chairman said: 'We agree with you. We've been writing to your producers about this for years. But they never reply.' Many of these complaints were self-serving or misinformed. Nonetheless they were real. Perceptions lingered on. The image of Australia was like the reflection of a distorting mirror in a run-down fun fair. It was fat and lazy.

These images from a comfortable past only served to complicate and prolong the attempts Australia made in the 1980s to shift from an insular resource-based economy to one which was more open and diverse in its productive and export-earning capacity. Australia's wealth had accumulated on the basis of its capacity as an exporter of raw materials. Australians, however, had no developed tradition of international trading and marketing. The agricultural and mining industries properly congratulated themselves on their efficiency, but in their period of highest growth operated in predominantly sellers' markets. Strong demand for their products reduced the need for cultivating long-term marketing sophistication. Manufacturing and service industries were inward-looking. Marketing for them was about knocking off your competitor in a small domestic market. They had little feel for the challenge of international competition. The culture was to ask the government to protect them from it.

Throughout the 1980s a series of government policy decisions pushed Australia into the international marketplace. But it was not as easy as it seemed. Rural industries slowly confronted the realities of restricted market access as overseas governments yielded to the pressure of their own environment with nervous apprehension. Technocrats, who for sound reasons advocated internationalisation of the economy, had little practical appreciation of the day-to-day impact on Australian businesses. At official levels there was little understanding of the experience and ineptness of Australian managers in understanding the sophistication of overseas markets.

The pace of technological change and its impact on international competitiveness was not 'factored in' to the thinking of Australian economists. 'I see no signs of the "digital culture" in Australia,' the vice-president of a multinational electronics company told me in 1984. 'Unless you understand that, you will have a lot of problems.' A few understood it, but not many. Australia clung desperately to its membership of the OECD, a predominantly European club of wealthy nations. There our representatives exchanged Australia's performance indicators with other members. We gained little insight into the high-performing economies of the Asia Pacific region. Some, pontificating from the sheltered enclaves of Australian institutions, thought them to be a temporary aberration. For others it was all too hard. As in the 1970s, so in the 1980s we pursued liberalisation of trade in agricultural products. It was a worthy pursuit but it was too frequently naively motivated; seeking to return Australia to a world which had already passed us by.

Throughout the decade Australia's population mix continued to change. Industrial relations improved. Wage levels, relative to other developed countries, became more realistic. The importance of good technology to competitiveness was better appreciated. We started to embrace a digital culture. Management began to be more professional. But Australia's international image changed more slowly. The process was not helped by the general quality of the country's international representation. With some notable and outstanding exceptions, Australia's diplomatic and trade representatives continued to project an unchanging public face of Australia. In some places it was almost expected of them. It was much more comfortable to deal with an up-market Les Patterson than a hardheaded and professional Australian advocate, constantly pursuing trade and business opportunities. And for those who applied themselves to the task there were the continual frustrations of sending back cables which were filed rather than acted on.

The institutional mechanisms and corporate awareness of government bureaucracies were inflexible and unfocussed. The ball game was changing, but not the players.

As a travelling Minister I had moments of despair when I encountered diplomats and trade representatives incapable of answering relatively simple questions about the country in which they lived. Enjoying a lifestyle to which few of Australia's high-achieving citizens were accustomed, they were more confident in the milieu of cocktail party gossip, pecking orders in the embassy and membership of local golf clubs, than in a realistic appraisal of Australia's external relationships in a changing world. At a function in Switzerland one evening I shocked a senior Australian bureaucrat by suggesting that international subscriber dialling and the fax machine made traditional diplomatic practices redundant. 'Maybe,' I implied, 'there should be a complete reappraisal of the diplomatic role.' He looked at me in disbelief. Then the expression on his face relaxed into its usual complacency. I realised he'd concluded that I had gone mad.

It is of course an artificial distinction to talk about the

1980s as a discrete period. The process of change operates as a continuum. Images of the 1970s blur into images of the 1980s. Many of the challenges of the 1980s are being responded to in the 1990s. And as Australia and its relationship with the rest of the world changes, so other countries are changing too: sometimes more rapidly than us. The art of predicting likely directions of change is as eluding as economic forecasting. We can only guess at broad possible scenarios. This is a lesson we have hopefully learnt from the 1980s. Listening in Red Square in 1985 to Mikhail Gorbachev making his first public speech as Leader of the Soviet Union, I did not understand a word of what he said. But I did think he sounded authoritative, charismatic and businesslike. What I also didn't understand, and perhaps he didn't either, was where his leadership was destined to take the Soviet Union and the world.

Similarly as a visitor to Germany in the 1980s I began to understand the qualities which had made it the economic powerhouse of Europe. Few people could have predicted the impact which changes in Europe's Eastern Bloc were to have on the economy and politics of Germany in the 1990s. In 1989 I made an official visit to India. I left there with a sense of hopelessness and frustration. Yet by 1993 the Indian economy, sheltered for forty-four years by bureaucratic controls, was opening up to the rest of the world. Investment was being encouraged, unnecessary regulations removed and a new mood of economic rationality was starting to develop. There were now signs of hope. In Vietnam, with a business delegation in 1990, I saw the first signs of economic reform and of a new country opening up to the world. Poverty and the absence of technical administrative skills made me think it would take a very long time. Returning early in 1993 I was surprised at the progress which had been made.

It's not a bad thing for Australians to understand that other countries in the 1980s and early 1990s were also undergoing rapid and difficult changes. Frequently it was happening in countries where poverty was endemic and the quality of life of the more fortunate sections of the population, poor. In these countries the motivation for modernisation and improving living standards was strong. In Australia relatively high living standards and a much envied lifestyle made it more difficult to understand the necessity for change. It was not easy to explain that we could not stop the world and that we could not get off.

For some the search for new directions in a changing world environment became something of an obsession. In 1991 a visiting professor from Harvard, Hirotaka Takeuchi, warned Australians of the dangers of 'paralysis by analysis', and of seeing themselves as victims of change. Victims, he pointed out, tend to blame others for their problems, and are reluctant to respond pro-actively to their circumstances. Fortunately this syndrome is not a universal Australian trait and Australia is not alone in confronting new circumstances. This sense of loneliness, if any, comes from Australia's past where there were always comfortable alliances to support us: umbrellas under which we could shelter: walls to protect us from the outside world.

Travel, to paraphrase the words of Doctor Johnson, helps us to appreciate our own country and enables us to learn from others. Because of its vastness and relative remoteness, overseas travel for Australians has a unique quality about it. Ministers and parliamentarians are usually engrossed in the daily hurly-burly of politics. Travel provides them with opportunity to see their world with fresh eyes: and to get a better understanding of how others see us.

In the 1980s I was another Australian travelling abroad. I went to a number of countries not mentioned in any detail in this book. I visited China five times apart from Shunchang. I had the advantage, and sometimes the disability of seeing things from a privileged position. On many overseas visits nothing much happened which could be described as positive or particularly encouraging. From other visits to the United States, Vietnam, Indonesia, Malaysia, and sometimes Japan, I returned home with a sense of some achievement. In those countries where I achieved little, I nearly always learnt something, as travellers do, and I have retained impressions, sometimes coloured by experiences which I found frustrating and bizarre. Perhaps those experiences were nonetheless valuable. Perhaps they help to clarify my images of Australia: past, present and future.

At the end of the decade and in the early 1990s a few things happened which made me think that the image of Australia amongst those who observe us from outside was becoming clearer and more precise. In 1989 the British Secretary of State for Industry complained wryly to me that Australian companies in China were becoming a bit too competitive. From the mid-1980s Australian manufactured exports grew rapidly. A number of technically innovative and enterprising new firms emerged, looking outward to the world as their marketplace. There were signs of a new and vibrant digital culture. People overseas seemed more aware of the quality and uniqueness of Australian films and literature. German industrialists talked to me about Australia as a convenient export base for Asia: an idea 'we didn't buy five years ago'. A group of ASEAN ministers commented in 1991 on the growth of high quality Australian exports to the region. 'We see it happening. Do Australians know about it?' they asked. Probably not, I thought. But they should.

Australians will best succeed in the 1990s if they have confidence in their own capacities: and perseverance. Otherwise these positive signs could be straws in the wind. The story of Australia's involvement with the world is a cautionary tale. Some countries decline and others progress, sometimes in relative terms and sometimes absolutely. In 1994 I like to think that there are good reasons for optimism, because from the shadows of an insular past Australia is coming out.

Captain Jones's
England: 1975

The British are right. London to Sydney direct is a long flight. In 1975 it was longer, with three refuelling stops on the way. Then for an hour or so passsengers paced the airport concourses at places like Bahrain, Bombay, and Singapore—blearily contemplating the offerings of duty-free goods, with glazed eyes and minds like bubble gum.

Sydney to London took just as long. Australians are right about that. Whichever way you travel, what's waiting for you at the end has some effect on your minimal capacity to think positively about anything on a long flight. This time I was travelling first class on British Airways. For two weeks I would be a guest of the United Kingdom Government: the lucky beneficiary of a program designed to foster appreciation amongst Commonwealth 'opinion makers' of British institutions and the British way of life. I would be met on arrival by a Mr Harold Jones.

For some reason, which I never understood, Harold was waiting for me in the basement car park at Heathrow Airport. A British Airline official told me where to find him. It was 6 a.m.

'I'm Harold Jones,' he announced formally as he stepped out of the shadows. 'Captain Harold Jones, retired. I'm an escort officer with the Foreign and Commonwealth Office. I will be responsible for you during your stay as a guest of Her Majesty's Government.'

He was a plumpish florid-faced man of medium height, dressed in a dark pinstriped suit and a bowler hat. I was dressed in corduroy trousers and a pullover. He looked at me disapprovingly: 'I'm sorry,' I said. 'It's been a long flight.' 'Can't be helped,' said Harold. 'I've got a bit of a hangover myself. We'll get you to your hotel and you can smarten yourself up.'

Harold organised the luggage and in a few minutes we were in a chauffeur-driven Bentley on the way to London. 'Ever been in a Bentley before?' he asked. I said 'No, never.' Harold nodded sagely. I detected a further note of disapproval, and went into a jet-lagged decline. For some time we travelled in silence, interrupted only by the chauffeur pointing out an occasional landmark. But there weren't many. London, like most cities, displays nothing of particular interest in the outer suburbs. Harold seemed relieved of a burden when he finally checked me into my hotel. 'Clean up and get some rest,' he advised. 'Tomorrow we will start work in earnest.'

The next day we met for a briefing session at the Foreign and Commonwealth Office on the South Bank of the Thames. It was a new building, which gave the impression of having been occupied by civil servants for a thousand years. People kept clocking 'in' and 'out', men with manila folders under their arms minced up and down lengthy passageways, tea-ladies trundled trolleys in and out of office doors. Even in the toilet there was no relief: each sheet of toilet paper was stamped with the words 'Property of Her Majesty's Government'. I felt this had some symbolic importance and stuffed a few sheets into my coat pocket.

In the briefing room I sat down on one side of the oblong table in the centre of the room. 'No, Sir,' said a hovering clerk, 'I'm sorry, you're on the other side.' He gestured towards two milk bottles on the table, one containing a plastic Australian flag and the other a British flag. I rearranged myself behind the Australian flag. A few minutes later a man, who introduced himself as Major Cartwright, and two others entered the room and sat on the other side of the table, followed by Harold, who sat discreetly behind them.

'Well,' said Major Cartwright, 'welcome to the Department. Indeed welcome to Britain. We've studied the summary of your background and interests and have decided what we think you should do in the course of your study tour here in Britain. Suggestions only, of course. We would welcome additional suggestions from you. Are you interested in the cricket, by the way? I'm sure Captain Jones could arrange something at Lord's,' He smiled knowingly. 'Harold has excellent contacts. The theatre too. Harold is good with theatre tickets. But that's all on the lighter side. On the business side we begin this evening with a cocktail party at the Commonwealth Association. Hopefully we'll get a couple of members of the House of Commons to meet you. I also note your interest in the media, which suggests a visit to the BBC and the Press Club. Harold has contacts there.'

He studied the papers in front of him, 'Hmm ... town planning, the arts, architecture, the environment ... diverse interests ... We're not so strong in these areas. But I think something could be arranged: perhaps a visit to the Barbican complex and a couple of the "new towns" out of London. The arts? There's a thing called the Arts Council. I think we've got people in there before.' 'Yes, that can be arranged,' interrupted Harold, 'a former adjutant of mine is working in the administrative office.' Cartwright studied his papers again. 'I don't think there's much else, but if we might impose on you a little, we would suggest very strongly that you make a visit to Bristol to see the Concorde aircraft—a triumph of British engineering and ingenuity.' He smiled again—'Supplemented by some minor assistance from our French cousins.'

Cartwright leaned back in his chair and folded his hands across his stomach. 'I think that will fill in the time pretty well. But perhaps we've overlooked something you'd like to follow up.' I said I thought it sounded an interesting program. I made some suggestions about other organisations I would like to visit. Cartwright nodded slowly: 'I don't think those places are on our list, but you will have free time in which to make your own arrangements and the chauffeur will take you wherever you wish to go.' 'Would it be possible,' I asked, 'for me to meet some ministers in the Wilson Government or some officials in the parliamentary Labour Party?' Cartwright raised his eyebrows. 'I'm not sure that we could help with that sort of thing.' 'No,' said Harold. 'I'm afraid not. We don't have any contacts there at all.'

The next morning when I woke up there was a telegram which had been slipped under the door of my hotel room:

At 1100 hours there will be a forward movement to the Royal Ophthalmic Hospital at Ryde. Chauffeur will meet in hotel foyer. Please confirm by phoning Whitehall 918-2345: Harold Jones.

I phoned the Whitehall number. Harold was not in and I spoke with a secretary. I told him I had received the telegram. I said I was a bit confused; there was no mention of this visit in the program discussions yesterday. 'I am, of course, happy to go but I'm not sure about its relevance to the program.' 'The hospital,' he said tersely, 'does some of the most advanced eye surgery in the world.' 'I'm sure,' I replied, 'but I'm not particularly interested in eye surgery. I don't think I could ever learn how to do it.' There was a long pause at the other end of the telephone, and a faint rustling of papers.

'I think I'll phone you back,' he said. Ten minutes later he phoned back. 'I'm sorry, Senator, but Captain Jones has been very busy and seems to have mixed you up with an eye specialist from Uganda who is also on our books. We will have to cancel the day's program.'

The next morning on the way to the House of Commons Harold congratulated me effusively for having taken the initiative in what he described as 'the case of the misdirected telegram'. 'No such luck with that Ugandan chap, I'm afraid. I was too late to stop him going to the Arts Council.'

At the House of Commons, Harold announced triumphantly that he had captured two Members of Parliament for lunch with us on the terrace overlooking the Thames. We arranged to meet at noon and in the meantime I was placed in the charge of a guide for a tour of the building. At lunch the two members turned out to be Conservatives from rural constituencies in the south of England. I had heard of 'backwoods peers' but this was my first meeting with backwoods commoners. One of them told me that he'd almost gone to Australia during the Second World War. The other informed me that he had. 'I recall Sydney vividly. The wharf labourers were on strike because the showers were too hot. At the time it seemed to suggest a high standard of living.' The conversation floundered, like a primary school geography class, in a morass of mutual ignorance. But on the terrace the sun was warm, there was plenty to eat and drink and the movement on the river created a pleasant diversion. As Harold picked up the bill, he whispered to me, 'Splendid chaps these two: always willing to have lunch with foreign guests.'

Harold handed me over to a Royal Air Force officer for the drive down to Bristol to see the new Concorde aircraft. It was a boys' day and we clambered over the plane like kids in a toy shop. We sat in passenger seats, had our photos taken by an official photographer and sat in the flight deck in front of the awesome instrument panels. An engineer explained the benefits and problems of supersonic flights, and the contributions of the British and French to the creation of this marvel of technology.

Meanwhile, back in London, Harold was 'pulling strings' to arrange tickets for the theatre and various other visits. For the theatre he assembled a small party from 'the office' to accompany us. Within a few minutes of the curtain going up Harold was fast asleep. At supper afterwards he contributed to the discussion of the play by glaring menacingly at his subordinates and saying, 'I don't care what you people think. That sort of thing is not my cup of tea.'

When I arrived at the Arts Council for a prearranged appointment I was told that Harold's 'contact' had taken the day off. I presumed he was exhausted by his meeting with the eye specialist from Uganda. In the circumstances I was given a pile of brochures, with the suggestion that a further appointment might be made when the situation became clearer. As a concession to my expressed interest in architecture and town planning, visits were arranged to the new Barbican complex, and to two of the 'new towns' on the outskirts of London. Harold made a point of declining to accompany me on the visit to the 'new towns'.

'Those places,' he said, 'are swarming with socialists.'

In between these segments of the official program, and in my allocated 'free time' I wandered happily around London, visited some friends and made a few arrangements of my own. 'I can't seem to meet anyone I really want to talk to,' I complained to a visiting Australian diplomat over a cup of coffee. 'Perhaps,' he suggested sympathetically, 'you might like to talk with the Prime Minister's private secretary. He's a friend of mine and would be happy to talk with you.' And so I found myself gleefully instructing the chauffeur one morning to take me to No. 10 Downing Street. There, overcome with a sense of occasion, I shook hands with an astonished policeman at the door, and then enjoyed a lengthy discussion about what was actually happening in Britain. Harold found out about this visit from the chauffeur. He responded with a mixture of indignation and amazement, 'I'm supposed to be running this show,' he remarked, huffily. 'And we've never got anyone in there. Never!'

Arrangements were made for me to go to a one-day cricket match at Lord's between Australia and the West Indies. I was told to go to the Pavilion and ask for the Hon. Penleigh-Jones, described to me as a cricket expert. It was a warm, sunny day when I arrived at Lord's and found my host for the day. He reminded me of a highly agitated Bertie Wooster. Seated in the sunshine, he managed to look like a traditional village idiot by wearing his white, peaked hat back-to-front. He asked after Harold, and told me that they had known each other well in India during the war. 'I'm afraid,' he said, 'that Harold was never much good at cricket. We used to get him to bring out the drinks—always managed to top them up with a couple of bottles of gin. A good man, Harold.'

The game had more than its quota of cricket excitement. Penleigh-Jones talked incessantly between overs, lapsing into reverent silence the moment the bowler took the ball for a new over. 'You know', he said, 'I sat in these identical seats in 1938 when Bradman scored a century on this ground. I must say that I think your people badly misjudged Jardine. I was only a lad at the time, but I remember my father telling me about it.' I remarked that there were two sides to every story. 'Of course,' he said, 'I have to admit that; it's like cricket itself, two sides.'

In the course of the day, Penleigh-Jones regaled me with details of who scored what in which match (test or county), the best dismissal, the outstanding performances of left-handed spin bowlers and right-handed black batsmen, the fastest man between wickets, why Boycott would never be Captain of England, and the most outrageous offences of incompetent umpires. I longed to ask him if he actually wrote the cricket almanacs or just read them; then when he told me he'd never missed a single match at Lord's since the war, I decided that he might just have an extraordinary memory. My head ached with cricket information. I feared an oral exam at the end of the game. In the afternoon tea-break I tried to change the subject. 'Do you,' I asked hesitantly, 'have a family of your own?' A family, old boy,' he replied, 'I have ten grandchildren and there's one more in the oven.' He pondered reflectively, 'We'll soon have a side.'

On the second last day of my visit Harold set up a lunch at the London Press Club. In the car on the way to the Press Club he told me it would be indiscreet to mention the name of 'your chap Murdoch' during the lunch. 'He's trying to move in here and we don't like it much.' I assured him I would be careful.

Harold had assembled two professional journalists to introduce me to the mystery of the British press. When we arrived at twelve noon, they had obviously been in the bar for some time. Harold was in an expansive mood as he bought drinks and introduced me to his two friends. The first, whom he called 'Bunny', worked on 'County Jottings' for the *Daily Telegraph*. The second, whose name was Holton, was a feature writer for the *Yorkshire Post*. We spent an hour at the bar before lunch, taking turns to buy rounds of drinks. Harold told an Irish joke. Holton told a joke about Americans.

'Did you hear this one?' asked Bunny. The conversation slowly degenerated into a succession of Irish, French and American jokes until the whole world outside our small group began to seem extraordinarily droll. 'Tell us a Rumanian joke,' Bunny said to Holton. 'The *Yorkshire Post* is the world's leading authority on Rumanian affairs,' Harold explained, 'all because of Holton—he's the expert.' Holton said there were no Rumanian jokes.

Later I asked Holton what was the basis of his interest in Rumania. 'It's really quite simple,' he replied. 'Rumania is the home of Count Dracula. My major interest is in cyclical research. No better place for that than Rumania. I go to Transylvania every year and have written five books on cyclical research.'

When we left the Press Club, after a long lunch, everyone was a little the worse for wear. Harold's face reminded me of an overly decorated Christmas pudding with two bright-red cherries stuck in it. Holton looked like Count Dracula and Bunny looked like a fat white rabbit. There was an effusive round of farewell handshakes and promises of further lunches. Harold stuck his bowler hat on his head at a dangerous angle, a farewell gesture greeted with roars of laughter. I imagined future lunches—'Do you remember the day Harold stuck his hat on crookedly . . . ?'

'Why did you bring those two to lunch?' I asked Harold, as we drove away from the Press Club. He told me that he had known them since the war. 'They're part of my network,' he said. 'They're the network into the Press Club. In fact I met Bunny in rather unusual circumstances. We were in Burma and a bloody Jap sniper got me—right through the right tit as a matter of fact. I fell backwards. Bunny was there behind me and I fell into his arms. We've been friends ever since.'

In the car driving back to the hotel, Harold turned round from the front seat and gazed at me with a benign, if somewhat bleary, expression on his face. 'There is something I want to say to you—something I'd like to get off my chest.'

I felt apprehensive. 'What is it?' I asked. 'Well,' said Harold, 'I've been a bit uptight about your visit to Britain and being assigned to arrange your program. The fact of the matter, old boy, is that I can't stand your rotten socialist lot—Wilson, Whitlam—all that crowd. Terrible people, and of course you're one of them. I've never had one of your lot before; usually I get Canadians or Africans. Canadians are a piece of cake and I know how to handle blacks—not your lot. But in fact you've turned out to be quite a decent chap.' 'Thank you, Harold,' I said, and meant it.

Harold saw me off at Heathrow Airport. I was catching a plane to Israel and we arrived early because of the strict security procedures. It was a warm, sunny day. As we walked into the airport building Harold excused himself and ran back to the car and rummaged in the boot, emerging with a tightly furled black umbrella. 'What on earth do you want that for on a beautiful day like this?' I asked him. 'It's a symbol of office, old boy.' He pointed to the crowded passenger lounge. 'You watch, we'll go through this lot like a packet of salts.' And we did. Harold pointed with his umbrella, twirled it like a drum major, used it horizontally like a rifle to push back crowds, and somehow we got to the front of the queue. 'See,' he said, 'it works.'

As we said goodbye, I inadvertently reached into my pocket and found some English pounds. 'Harold,' I said on the spur of the moment, 'this money is no longer of any use to me. Would you take it and buy yourself a drink?' Harold looked at me sadly as if his worst fears had been realised. 'I'm sorry,' he said, 'under no circumstances would that be possible.' 'Good God,' I thought to myself, 'what a fool I am. Heathrow Airport two weeks later. And we've gone back to square one.'

I scuttled through the gate to board the plane. Harold stood stiffly at the gateway, his bowler hat planted firmly on his head, his 'symbol of office' clutched in his right hand. For me he was an unforgettable figure: a complex relic of England's 'finest hour'.

You ought to go to America: 1978

In a favourite film, *Casablanca*, everyone who came to Rick's Bar wanted to go to America. True, it was a film in which refugees played a prominent role. The torch of the Statue of Liberty beckoned to them, as it had to generations of Europeans fleeing from oppression of one kind or another. In the late 1960s and 1970s the United States took on a degree of fashionability as a place for Australians to visit. People used to say 'you ought to go to America'. It was as if the old reliable springs of Europe were slowly drying up. We weren't quite ready to be told we should go to Asia, or more particularly, Japan or Malaysia or Indonesia. But America was suggested as the place where the future lay: everything was bigger and better than anywhere else. It was not a sanctuary, but a Mecca. When you asked these pursuers of the American Dream for particulars, they talked about Disneyland, the Grand Canyon, the magic of New York, and California as a bubbling cauldron of latest trends. Americans got things done. They were friendly, good at business and custodians of the good life. 'You ought to see it for yourself.'

I always resisted these suggestions. America did not attract me. It seemed too big, too confident, too egocentric; a bit 'awesome'. Perhaps because I'd never had a big brother, I rejected the type. I recognised the huge contribution the United States had made to the world, and Australia, in the Second World War; and during the long, dark years of the

Cold War. But I didn't like their clumsy 'bull in a china shop' behaviour in international affairs. A country which produced McCarthyism, and specious and wrong-headed justifications for involvement in the Vietnam War had something seriously wrong with it. One looked at the public face, ignored the complexity behind it, and reacted unfavourably.

American culture seemed powerful and homogeneous. The worst of it intruded into our living room with television. European countries provided an easy and interesting differentiation. You could enjoy the differences: French, British, Italian, German, whereas the American product seemed too much of the same. I thought of America as a place of magnificent myths and mediocre reality. It seemed a country with a split personality. So much confidence and self-esteem and so much poverty, violence and inequality; it produced instant millionaires, and great literature but it was usually escapist or depressing.

On the other hand, I'd usually liked Americans. Those that I'd met seemed friendly, decent, likeable people. My encounters with them went back to childhood days. United States servicemen came in droves to the military camp in the provincial city of Ballarat, on recreation leave from the Pacific War. Some of them came regularly for meals at our home. One of them, an army padre, abhorred physical exercise. My father used to ask him if he'd like to go for a walk. 'I'm tempted', the padre would drawl, 'but if you don't mind I'll lie down until the temptation wears off.' To us this seemed very bold; almost heretical. Another, an officer in the Marine Corps, wrote in my autograph book: 'To a young lad, who would make a fine marine.' At the time we both thought this was a splendid compliment. 'What do you think of Melbourne?' we would ask. 'Half as big as the New York Cemetery and twice as dead,' was the standard reply. Perhaps my ambivalence about America went back a long way. Trying to synthesise it all in my head in the mid-1970s, I decided what I liked least about America and Americans was the style and quality of American 'bullshit'. Australian 'bullshit' is usually agnostic and sceptical. Leg-pulling is part of the national sense of humour. Nobody is expected to believe it, the perpetrator least of all. American 'bullshit' is serious stuff. It's earnest. They tend to believe it themselves. It's a mistake to laugh at it.

'Why don't you come to America?' suggested the State Department in 1978. It was the third invitation to visit as a guest of the United States Government, on what they called a 'leadership grant'. My ambivalence about America seemed no excuse. I accepted, although with less enthusiasm than I might have shown for such a generous offer.

I touched base, as it were, in Honolulu. At the airport there was a bus from the plane to the terminal. The woman driver instructed the passengers through a public address system: 'Watch your step when you alight from the bus. I'll say it again; watch your step when you get out of the bus. And have a nice day.' It sounded efficient: and friendly. I glanced at a seasoned Australian visitor next to me in the bus. 'You're in America now,' he said. 'Everything works here. The only things you'll miss are larrikins and cynics.' Like all generalisations it had its shortcomings, but as I was to discover, fewer than most.

The flight from Sydney to Honolulu had not been totally uneventful. Thirty minutes out of Sydney the senior flight attendant approached me and said she was moving me from economy to first class. 'If the United States Government doesn't know how to treat an Australian Senator, then I assure you sir, Pan Am does.' She smiled as she said it, which made it sound less pompous. I mumbled my thanks and moved to first class.

Three Australian men seemed to be occupying a fair amount of the cabin crew's time. 'Have a drink,' one advised me. 'It's the only way to travel by air.' They were members of a film crew, on the way to the United States to shoot a commercial. They seemed intent on setting an example. I told the producer how I'd been upgraded to first class. 'I know,' he said, 'We fixed that. Gave the blonde lady a bit of "bullshit".' 'Thank you,' I said. 'No worries. It was easy. Everything is PR in the US.'

We had dinner. My travelling companions kept drinking champagne. They became the subjects of special, but good-humoured, attention. 'Ladies and gentlemen,' said the flight attendant over the PA system. 'We're about to enter a patch of turbulence. Please fasten your seat belts .. that includes Mr Dixon: now Mr Dixon will you make a special effort?' In the dawn light as we approached Hawaii, the cabin crew collected the glasses from Mr Dixon and his friends. I last saw them asleep on benches at Honolulu Airport.

A young man from the State Department met me at the terminal, rushed me through customs and bundled me into a cab. At the hotel the porter, whose name was Pedro, told me he'd been to Melbourne on a holiday last year. 'How was it?' I asked. 'Amazing, man, it was amazing. The way they make you wear seat belts down there. I can't get over it.' In the elevator a woman asked me where I came from. When I told her, she took a few seconds to collect her thoughts. 'Australia,' she said. 'OK; I have a friend who used to be a missionary in Fiji and Australia.'

There seemed to be a festival of some sort. I watched a procession in the main street. It began with an interminable display of jogging by people of all shapes and sizes, and advanced years. They wore outlandish clothing and T-shirts embossed with slogans like 'Middle-Aged Marathons', 'Honolulu Health Clinic' and 'Old Joggers Never Die'. I felt less confident about this, they looked very unfit. Prudently they were followed by an ambulance. Then came a large number of handsome horses ridden by Hawaiian 'princesses' in Spanish-

style equestrian costumes, floats, contingents from the army
and navy bands, the Sacramento City High School marchers
and the Ohio Baptist Tabernacle marchers for Jesus. 'The
girls march well,' I said to a young woman sitting next to me,
in an effort to compensate for my dislike of marching girls.
'Yes, they're well trained,' she said expertly. 'Did you note
the marines? They march out of phase.'

I went to Waikiki Beach. The surf was flat. The beach was
so crowded it was almost impossible to find a place to sit.
Eventually I found a spot with a metre's space on either side
of me. Within minutes the fattest woman I've ever seen in a
bikini plonked herself down in one of the spaces. She attracted
some attention from nearby sunbathers and gave me a winning
smile. I imagined people saying 'What a lovely couple', and
dashed into the sea. She'd gone when I came out of the
water. I looked around at the people on the beach and there
seemed to be a lot of fat people. I sat down and pondered on
the world's distribution problems. If fat people were thinner,
I thought, then they would be healthier and the fat could be
distributed amongst the world's undernourished. I called my
theory: 'The theory of fat dynamics'. I noted it in my diary:
Waikiki Beach, Sunday, 11 June 1978.

Hawaii was an aperitif, it was time to get down to drinking
in the full American experience. On the plane to continental
America, I began to study an alarming array of facts and
figures about the United States. The State of California alone
had an economy twice as big as Australia's. Five other states
each had an economy bigger than ours. The country boasted
the most millionaires per capita. Fifty percent of black
American children were illegitimate. The United States had
the world's tallest building, the longest bridge and the biggest
canyon. The population was highly mobile and there were
an estimated twelve million illegal immigrants. The information seemed endless: a litany of great achievements and
big problems.

I spent a night in Los Angeles in a hotel which seemed to be situated between two runways at the airport. Jets shot past the windows of my room like sharks in an aquarium; the building shook and rattled. The following day I caught one to Washington where my first engagement was a briefing from State Department officials.

The briefing was a relaxed affair. In Washington they would arrange visits to the White House and the Congress. I would be taken to a concert, to a meeting with the Chief Executive of the Public Broadcasting Corporation, and a law firm with special relationships with Australia. Suggestions were made about places I should visit in and around Washington. I was asked if I would like to be a guest in the homes of American families in the evenings. Foolishly, and probably because of tiredness, I said 'no'—I was destined to spend quite a few nights in hotel rooms. After four days in Washington I would set out to see as much of the United States as possible in the available time. We settled on an itinerary which included New York; Boston; Chicago; San Francisco and Phoenix, Arizona. Phoenix was chosen as a sample, if not particularly representative, of a southern State city. That night I was taken in a group to a concert. After half an hour I fell asleep. At interval I excused myself and went back to the hotel.

I had an impression of the history of Washington from the novels of Gore Vidal. Like most capital cities it has an impressive public face: grand monuments and public buildings, good open spaces laid out with parks and lakes, a pleasant central business district, and chic inner suburbs like Georgetown. The summer climate is said to be oppressive; the city had been built on swamplands. Like Canberra, Washington was built as an artificially created capital of a federal system of government; in its own patch of federal territory. As an older city it has more sense of history and charm than Canberra but less natural beauty. Both cities have the ubiquitous bureaucratic buildings, the legislature and national library. Washington is the home of the United States Supreme Court; the National Gallery; memorials to Lincoln, Jefferson, and Roosevelt; the Arlington National Cemetery; the Martin Luther King Memorial Library, and the great museums of American History and Achievement.

In 1978 Canberra was about to have the necessary National Gallery and an unnecessary High Court building. The proposed Museum of Australia was a gleam in the eye of a visionary dreamer of national capitals, perhaps never to be realised. The only public building of historic and symbolic national significance in Canberra was the National War Memorial. It was a tale of two cities and two nations. Washington was older and the capital of a powerful nation; but its public face symbolised American achievement, success, and pride in the great figures of American history. In Canberra the National War Memorial stood as a lonely monument to Australia's glorious failures: seemingly the only physical evidence of achievements which Australia as a nation recorded with pride.

I was later taken to the White House on a guided tour. Young men built like rugby half-backs, with blazers and crew cut hair, shepherded a group of us round the building. 'My name is David Johnson. I'm a member of the United States Secret Service. Please do not touch anything and remain at all times within the group.' It sounded cool and understated. He meant to say 'Step out of line and you're in trouble'. We gazed at the artefacts of a long line of presidents. Mr Johnson told us about Mrs Carter's preferences in table settings. From the Oval Room we watched a helicopter taking off from the garden. 'That's the President on his way to Panama. There are a few problems down there.'

When I visited the Congress legislation was being debated which provided appropriations for public works. I listened as one speaker after another described a particular project in his home town or State which merited special national attention. Congressmen wandered round the floor of Congress and chatted in conspiratorial groups. No-one seemed to be listening to the speeches, other than the Speaker of the House, Tip O'Neill, who occasionally called for order or chided the speechmaker for excessive hyperbole. One sensed that the real action was somewhere else.

I was taken to meet some congressmen 'interested' in foreign visitors. The conversations were friendly, but slightly ethereal. Most of them, I suspected, were a bit vague about where Australia was. Senator John Glenn, the former astronaut, was a notable exception. I was told he specialised in the South Pacific region. He signed some autographed photos for my kids and asked some questions about Australia and Indonesia. He had not been to Australia, but professed great affection for Australians. 'I'll never forget the people of Perth,' he told me. 'They turned on all the lights when I flew by. Yes,' he said, 'very warm friendly people.'

The civil servants, particularly from the State Department, and the professional staff of congressional committees were different from most of the congressmen I met. They impressed with their knowledge and efficiency. Those whose business it was to know about the South Pacific region and Australia knew what they were talking about. Informal questions about the internal politics of the Australian political parties found me floundering for adequate answers. United States bureaucrats seemed more easygoing and willing to embark on critical analyses of government policies and programs than their Australian counterparts. This, I suspected, followed from the regular turnover of personnel in civil service positions: exchanges between industry, universities and the public sector. A change of administration meant a change in high-level advisers. The think-tanks of the civil service are changed and renewed.

In discussions with United States businesspeople in Washington, New York and Chicago, the informational level about Australia varied from total ignorance to a sophisticated awareness amongst those with specific investment interests or subsidiary companies in Australia. In New York, at a business lunch, I was treated to a highly entertaining, if bemused, description of recent visits to America by premiers of Australian States seeking to raise loan funds. Sir Charles Court had inspired a New York Chamber of Commerce luncheon with heady rhetoric about the new frontiers of Western Australia: 'It was mainly crap, but everyone loved it.' Neville Wran had impressed them. President Carter and the United States Government were out of favour in business circles. The outlook was regarded as gloomy: 'Could we borrow that guy for a year or two?' I was asked. Later I was to have a similar experience in California. There I was told that Don Dunstan had given a brilliant luncheon address to the Chamber of Commerce. I asked what he had talked about. 'He talked about something called industrial democracy. He made it sound very interesting. But thank Christ it's way down there in South Australia.'

Washington is a tourist city for foreigners and Americans. They visit the White House, the Congress, the National Gallery and the monuments. Like Paris or London it contains many of the historic treasures of the nation. It is about American achievement and the pioneers, statesmen and heroes who have made America great. In the Smithsonian Institute—a series of museums—there are permanent and imaginatively displayed exhibitions of American art, cultural life and folk history: a rich pageant of American persistence, ingenuity and inventiveness from the time of the early pioneers to the present day. Wandering through the galleries of the Smithsonian you felt a sense of how it had all happened over the years, and in the brilliantly conceived Aeronautical and Space Museum, how it was still happening in 1978. There one could follow the history of human flight from the first primitive aeroplane of the Wright brothers to a model of the rocket which took the first man to the moon. Like the museums devoted to the early history of the country, it was a monument to American ingenuity, to the belief in progress and 'know-how' as the catalyst of human achievement.

On a Sunday, responding to a suggestion made at the briefing session, I took a tour bus down to Mount Vernon; George Washington's home in Virginia. The passengers on the bus were almost exclusively foreign tourists. I sat next to a black African dressed in a yellow hat and a flowing robe of many colours. 'Where do you come from?' he asked. I told him I came from Australia. He gave me a blank look. 'Oh,' he said, 'is it nice there?' We lapsed into silence. Then I asked, 'Where do you come from?' 'Liberia,' he replied. I gave him what must have been a blank look. I could not remember where Liberia was. So I asked, 'Is it nice there?' We fell into a further silence of mutual ignorance. Then as we approached Mount Vernon we began to talk again. He didn't know where Australia was and I didn't know where Liberia was. But we both knew about George Washington—the boy who cut down the cherry tree and grew up to be the General who fought the British and later became the first President of the United States. Mount Vernon sits on a hill looking down on the Potomac. I wandered round the old house looking at relics of Washington's life, and through the spacious and well-tended gardens. I listened to American tourists talking about 'their' history. It was the same week in which a house in the Melbourne suburb of Fitzroy was demolished. It was the house in which Australia's second Prime Minister and one of its greatest, Alfred Deakin, was born.

From Mount Vernon the tour bus took us to the Arlington National Cemetery. Tourist buses were lined up outside the gate disgorging their passengers, who raced up the hill to the graves of Jack and Bobby Kennedy. Most of them were Americans. They stood at the gravesides looking more like pilgrims than tourists. Many of them wept. Sentiment and history are both part of the American dream. An hour or so later we were at the Jefferson Memorial. The crowds were smaller, but there was a similar sense of awe. 'We hold these truths to be self-evident,' the man standing next to me read aloud to himself. 'Now isn't that really something.' He was a Chinese American.

In New York and Boston I was a solitary imbiber of the American experience. A visit to the United Nations head-quarters and the Brookings Institute were programmed, mandatory events. Apart from these educational experiences, I went as a tourist to the Statue of Liberty, Central Park, the Metropolitan Museum of Art and the Empire State Building. In Boston I visited Harvard and the monuments to the Pilgrim Fathers. In New York I began to understand why people said New Yorkers were different. I'd become used to the instant affability of America, where even a cup of coffee is accompanied by 'There you go now, have a nice day'. In New York the cheerful politeness seemed to be carried to extremes, as if to compensate for the misanthropic suspicion of most New Yorkers. A telephone inquiry about theatre tickets produced a polite explanation and 'Thank you for calling. It's been a pleasure to be part of your day.' I hung up in a mild state of shock: cultural shock, I suppose. American intimacy and distance go hand in hand.

I went to Chicago with my head cluttered with film world images of the 1930s: black cars cruising the streets with machine-guns poking out the windows, warehouses stashed with illicit booze, 'Untouchables' loitering in hotel lobbies. I found instead a stylish city of opulent buildings, grand public spaces, a dignified capital of the thriving economy of the Mid-West.

David Goss, the Australian Consul in Chicago, had set out to see that I got the most out of my visit to the city. His guests at a dinner party on the first night of my visit included a federal court judge, the Director of the Art Institute of Chicago, the manager of a nuclear power station, and the principal of an all-black school on the South Side. Each of his guests invited me to visit the institution where he or she worked. So I sat in on the judge's court for an hour. I went to the power station, where my ancient watch set off an alarm and became an object of fascination at the security post. At the black school I gained a glimpse of the other side of America—disadvantaged and struggling: the walls decorated with life-size murals of successful black athletes; early symbols of the black power movement. In the Art Institute of Chicago my eyes feasted on the sumptuous collection of nineteenth century French paintings. 'How did you come to get all these paintings?' I asked, and was told that in the late nineteenth century the cattle barons of the Mid-West used to holiday in Paris. They picked up many of these paintings quite cheaply in small galleries and street exhibitions. Later they were donated to the Institute.

In Chicago the Australian Trade Commissioner gave a small party attended by a few Chicagoans who'd been to Australia and a small group of expatriates: representatives of banks and one or two government instrumentalities. There was a discussion of what manufactured goods Australia might sell in the United States and the opportunity which existed in the huge market of the Chicago region. In my whole time in the country I'd seen only one Australian product; kids drinking cans of Fosters at a baseball game in a park in Georgetown, Washington. I'd been deeply moved: almost homesick. Australians, it was said at the party, lacked marketing skills. I talked to an Australian trying to establish a market for clothes hoists in Chicago. I thought of the fierce Chicago winter and the relatively short summer. I suggested he try the Sunbelt States in the South and market them as a cost-free, energy-saving, clothes drier. 'Head south,' I advised him as I said goodbye. It was easy advice to give. I was heading south myself.

In Phoenix, Arizona, I was the house guest of an American

couple who made a point of looking after visitors from overseas. They met me at the airport. My luggage didn't turn up. They bought me a pair of swimming togs, so I could swim in their pool—it was forty degrees centigrade; clear dry heat. They took me to a restaurant for dinner, where the waiter brought in a birthday cake; somehow they'd found out it was my birthday. They drove me round and showed me the sights of Phoenix, and the husband Bert went back to the airport at midnight to collect my baggage. They were the kindest hosts. It was a teasing isolated sample of American hospitality.

I went from Phoenix by bus to the Grand Canyon. It was a long, hot journey through small-town Arizona, but worth it to see the world's biggest canyon. I'd seen the tallest building, the biggest canyon; in San Francisco I would see the largest bridge.

In the *San Francisco Chronicle* of 3 July 1978 Benjamin Hooks, the Executive Director of the National Association of Coloured People, was reported in the following terms:

> There's a sickness in America today. There's a sickness that comes about because people who are making good salaries have no sense of compassion or empathy for those who have been disenfranchised by life and who cannot make it. We see a neo-conservative blanket that quietly but steadily creeps over our nation.

The 'neo-conservative blanket' took a big creep forward with the election of Ronald Reagan as President in 1980. In 1978 the United States was moving into one of its more conservative moods. There was disenchantment with the presidency of Jimmy Carter. The divisions between rich and poor remained stark. The scars of the Vietnam War involvement were still being licked. There were concerns about the growing industrial might of Japan. The world seemed ungrateful to America.

Yet, the use of the word 'sickness' implied a cure. There was always hope of a cure. Americans sustained themselves through difficult times with powerful myths. Whatever 'America' was, Americans believed in it. There was some soul-searching, but it was never allowed to interfere with pride in past achievements, a belief in American capitalism and a tremendous faith in technological solutions to every problem. Always one encountered confidence in 'American know-how' as the key to the future. When I asked politicians and people in the nuclear power industry about safety issues and nuclear waste disposal, the replies seemed almost apologetic. Sure there were problems, but they were technical ones. They'd been a bit slow about applying themselves to these issues; but once they did, solutions would be found.

Americans are, on the face of it, a religious people. They go to church, indeed to a myriad of different churches and denominations. Belief in God, however, seems subordinate to the belief that mankind's problems can best be solved by human ingenuity; by the technological dynamic of American society.

This confidence is a subset of the unique phenomenon of American patriotism. They believe in their system of government and the natural superiority of their democratic tradition. History provides the cement of their beliefs. The Pilgrim Fathers found the Promised Land, Washington repelled those who might take it from them, Jefferson and others laid down the truths which they hold to be self-evident. Lincoln, Roosevelt and the Kennedys built and reinforced powerful illusions. So the shrines of American achievement and achievers were appropriate places to visit: Mount Vernon; the Smithsonian; the graves of the Kennedys ('the Holy Family' as Gore Vidal called them); and the Jefferson Memorial.

I tried to absorb all this. Inevitably I compared America with Australia. America is a large and powerful country: Australia is not. America has a longer history of European settlement. But the mythology, the beliefs, the traditions can be fairly compared. Americans cling strongly to their symbols of nationhood: Australians do not. It is hard in Australia to identify folk heroes of the past who form part of the national sentiment and mythology. In America they are part of the civic landscape. It is hard to imagine Australians crying at the grave of a deceased Prime Minister or revering the words of an early statesman. In America 'the only thing you'll miss are larrikins and cynics', my travelling companion had told me at Honolulu Airport. I had begun to miss them, it was time to go home.

I spent the fourth of July in San Francisco. On the fifth I left America to return to Australia. I had a bit of a 'hangover'. There are no available statistics, but I suspect a lot of Americans had the same problem. July the fourth is a holiday and a great national celebration. It commemorates the day on which Americans rejected colonialism and established their independence. As the plane climbed over the Pacific Ocean west of San Francisco, in those minutes when the airline passenger is caught emotionally between two cultures, I thought about Australia's numerous 'national' holidays.

Ronald Conway had called his book about Australia *The Land of the Long Weekend*. I wondered, for Australians, if any of these holidays amounted to anything more than that. Australia Day, the anniversary of the landing of Phillip's First Fleet, landed with rejects from British society; Anzac Day, sometimes described as commemorating the day Australia became of age, but didn't; Queen's Birthday, a reminder of a colonial past and a neo-colonial present; Labour Day, more honoured in the breach than in the observance; Melbourne Cup Day, time off for a horse race. Each of these holidays might have some marginal historic or sentimental significance for a section of the Australian population. Most commemorate sadness or absurdity, possible division rather than unity or remind us of the quirkiness of Australian history.

The fourth of July is a different festival. The day that America established its independence, Americans were on their own, and they knew it. They would continue to absorb people and influences from other countries, but they would not be a derivative society subservient to the Old World. And from Independence Day the process of building a nation began; a process in which the actors, the myths, the sense of history and achievement became important; so important that they embraced all newcomers and transcended the differences of a diverse society. In America there were many natural advantages: of resources, wealth, population and talent. But like most countries they were intent on making their own history. In Australia there were still too many signs, a lurking feeling, for some a hope, that it is made elsewhere.

An innocent
abroad: 1984

I n November 1983 the Secretary of my Department suggested that I should make an overseas trip. Officials could draw up an itinerary for me. It was felt that I should visit industries and study government policies in Europe and the United Kingdom.

The idea of an overseas trip had not really occurred to me. In November 1983 I was not thinking much further ahead than Christmas. It had been a busy and difficult year. The economy was still suffering the effects of the recession. As Minister for Industry I'd been preoccupied with the problems of the steel industry. There was a lot of gloomy discussion about the future of manufacturing in Australia. Some people thought that the recession would go away if industry had higher levels of protection. This would minimise uncertainty about the future. It didn't seem quite right to me. I was interested in the question of why some manufacturing economies did so much better than others. What were the ingredients of success? In other countries it didn't seem to have much to do with protection.

I talked about these issues with the Secretary of the Department and other officials. I was told that the government had been asked to send a minister to the European Management Forum in Davos, Switzerland. 'Davos', a high profile international business conference where international trade and industry issues were regularly discussed, would provide an opportunity to learn first-hand about the approaches adopted by other countries. It would be interesting to visit the United Kingdom, which provided the highest level of investment in Australian manufacturing.

I could meet with some counterpart industry ministers in other countries and renew acquaintances with some European industrialists I had met in the course of their visits to Australia. I said I would like to visit Sweden. I had an impression of Sweden as a country where social harmony coexisted with efficient and high quality manufacturing. Volvo, Saab, Electrolux and other Swedish brand names were fixed in my head. It seemed a contented, well-ordered place. The idea of an overseas trip of this kind began to take on a new appeal. At first in November 1983 it had seemed a bit burdensome, but as time passed I became increasingly interested.

Tentative arrangements were made. Several drafts of the itinerary were submitted. It was suggested that I should not visit a couple of countries en route, because an announcement I was about to make on tariff issues might offend their governments. I deleted a possible visit to Tahiti from an early draft. It had crept into the itinerary from computer records of previous ministerial trips; ministers had 'rested' there on the way home.

'Could I,' I asked when the first draft itinerary arrived, 'have at my own expense a few days skiing holiday in the middle of the trip?' This, it was said, was an unusual request. It would at least require approval from the head of the Prime Minister's Department. Certainly ministers sometimes took 'breaks' whilst travelling overseas. In the interests of proper records of international visits a gap in appointments was not, however, considered desirable. In this case the Prime Minister gave his approval, because he asked me to attend the European Management Forum at Davos. It was summer-holiday time in Australia and I would not necessarily be working if I had been at home. However, it was not to be seen as a precedent.

The underlying political and public service culture of the time was still based on the assumption that somehow foreign travel was nothing but an indulgence. Australia was still a sheltered and isolated place. 'Overseas' was for 'holidays', not business enlightenment or work.

Draft itineraries went back and forth until finally it was decided. I would go straight to Europe, stopping only at Bangkok on the way, and Singapore on the way home. The final itinerary provided for visiting ten countries in twenty-three days, including four at the meeting of the European Management Forum.

In Bangkok I had asked for lunch to be arranged with the Governor of the Bank of Thailand, Dr Snoh Unakul, an old student friend from Melbourne University. Studying the itinerary on the plane from Melbourne to Bangkok, I noticed that the Governor of the Bank was described as 'Dr Nukul'. I made a mental note to tell the Department that although Thai names were difficult, they should in future make an effort to get them right.

In spite of my friendship with Dr Snoh, I was overawed by the prospect of meeting with a senior official of a foreign government. My knowledge of banking was confined to regular adversarial meetings with the manager of my local bank. So I spent the morning studying statistics on exchange rates, relative growth in the Thai GDP and other unfathomable mysteries in preparation for the meeting.

At 12.30 p.m. on my way out to lunch, I picked up a copy of the *Bangkok Post* at the desk in the hotel foyer. The headline said 'Governor gets tough with Commercial Banks'. Underneath there was a large picture of the Governor of the Bank of Thailand. It was not my friend Dr Snoh. Rather it depicted a man with a stern face; a man who indeed looked tough. Somehow the picture induced a sense of terrible panic. 'Here I am,' I thought, 'on my first official visit overseas, I can't remember the exchange rate and I've got the wrong guy. He'll think I'm a fool, everybody will think I'm a fool.

He might get tough with me as well as the banks.' I briefly contemplated cancelling the appointment, taking ill, returning to Australia. Then I thought 'What the hell?' and decided to keep the appointment. In the car on the way to the bank I discussed the problem with the Australian Ambassador to Thailand, Gordon Jockel. A shrewd and experienced diplomat, he told me not to worry about it. He implied that over many years of diplomatic service he'd become accustomed to politicians stuffing things up.

Dr Nukul received me in a large and elegant anteroom. He smiled warmly: 'I'm delighted to meet you. Indeed, I've asked a couple of ministers in our government to join us for lunch.' 'Tough guys,' I thought, 'are often charming when you first meet them.' I decided to come clean. 'I think,' I said, 'that I've made a mistake.' 'Yes, yes,' he replied, 'I understand. Your friend Dr Snoh left the bank three months ago and is now in another position. I will take you to see him later. I was also at Melbourne University, but two years before you. Let's go and sit down.' The Colombo Plan, I thought, had not been a good idea.

During our lunch Dr Nukul talked about his time at Melbourne University. He seemed genuinely interested in what was happening in Australia. I was just beginning to relax when a minister asked me a question about 'push–pull' inflation. Fortunately a Thai official who'd been to school at Geelong Grammar answered it before I'd got my thoughts together. I began to feel even more at ease. My ordeal, however, was not entirely over. Struggling with chopsticks, I managed to send a slippery meatball shooting across the green tablecloth with the velocity of a snooker shot, into the lap of the Minister for Finance. The Governor smiled. The Minister hinted that this was a common occurrence: almost a sophisticated party trick. A Thai waiter moved quickly to retrieve the errant meatball. I began to realise that Thai hospitality embraced tolerance as well as lunch.

In the afternoon we visited Dr Snoh. Something of a 'guru'

as an economic adviser to successive Thai governments, he was nonetheless relaxed and informal. We sat in the sun on the steps outside his office and chatted about Thailand's long-term economic planning. It was not a concept with which, as an Australian, I was particularly familiar; but it seemed to make sense. From time to time, he told me, he became tired of the day-to-day demands of his work and retreated to a Buddhist monastery. There he refreshed his spirit and thought things through. Reflecting on the frenetic pace of Canberra politics, I decided it was a wonderful idea.

I left Dr Snoh to sample the different culture of the 'Sundowners Club', a Friday evening drinking session of expatriate Australian businessmen and officials working in Bangkok. Like similar clubs in many overseas cities at that time in Australia's history, it was an authentic transplant of an Australian pub scene in Balmain or Carlton. There was plenty of beer and backslapping, jocular mateship, cricket talk and very few women. I was presented with a pewter mug. A man told me it would be useful: 'Look in the bottom of the pewter pot, and see the world as the world is not.'

In Europe our first stop was in Amsterdam where I had arranged to meet Mr Jeelof, a Vice-President of Philips, the giant transnational electronics firm. Jeelof had visited me during one of his frequent trips to Australia. I'd been impressed with his wide knowledge of international business and overawed by his descriptions of how large multinationals operated in a global marketplace. Concepts such as cutting back production in one country and pumping it up in another because of an exchange-rate movement were new to me. In Amsterdam I learnt a lot about the realities of international manufacturing in an industry like electronics. At the Amstel Hotel over a dinner comprising seven courses of salmon—each cooked in a different way—I began to develop a hazy appreciation that life at the 'big end' of international business was hard; on the stomach as well as the nerves.

In London my first meeting was with the Minister for Industry and Information Technology. He had some of the mannerisms I associated with a typical Conservative politician. Polite rather than friendly, he began by exploring the possibility of common ground with some remarks about cricket. I had the feeling that he knew little about Australia and was not particularly interested. He seemed comfortable talking about cricket, but I wondered how long the conversation could be sustained. I began to get worried. What if some persistent journalist asked me what I'd discussed with the Industry Minister? So I asked him what was going on in British industry.

He seemed relieved and launched into a lengthy exposition of British ingenuity, their new-found mastery of computer technology and the second Industrial Revolution which Britain was about to have. It would come from computers and the forces unleashed by the privatisation of British Telecom. Britain was ahead of the world in Information Technology. It consumed twenty-nine percent of Europe's microchips compared with twenty percent in Germany. France was even further behind. Australia might, he suggested in a kindly way, hook onto the coat-tails of the New Age by carefully investing in British technology. In ten years time a breathless world would be panting to catch up.

I asked what all this would do to alleviate the high unemployment in Scotland and the north of England. He said this was a problem which would take time to deal with. But it would be accommodated by the Thatcher Government's economic policies, the privatisation of Telecom and the new age of technology. British management was on the move and he spoke of miracles at British Leyland. He asked no questions about Australia. It was as if I'd come for a tutorial rather than a conversation. When my questions became more specific he said that if I wanted to know more about government support for the emerging trends in industrial innovation, I should discuss the details with his parliamentary Under-Secretary. He was, I felt, going through the motions. I thought he had other things on his mind. Ministers, I was to learn in time, often do. A visit from an overseas minister plays second fiddle to a forthcoming Cabinet meeting, a domestic argument or a political crisis of one kind or another.

The Under-Secretary had a fresh pink face and a regimental tie. A backbencher, a part-time magistrate and an officer in the Royal Marines Reserve, he had seen service in Malta. He seemed anxious to please, although his pink face assumed a pained expression if a question probed the outer limits of comfort. He preferred to talk about small business. He had lots of figures in his head. I referred to the Minister's views on the revolution in British technology. 'What,' I asked, 'is the government doing about venture capital for new firms?' 'Ha, ha,' he said, 'we have a new pamphlet on that,' delving into the bottom drawer of his desk. 'You will be one of the first to have one.' 'And protection of intellectual property?' His pink face beamed at me. 'I knew you'd ask that question. We have a pamphlet on that too.' He rummaged in the bottom drawer. 'And small business finance?' Again he returned to the bottom drawer. There was a generous subsidy available for installing robots and machine tools. However the pamphlet was temporarily out of print. 'How,' I asked, 'do these economic programs sit with the free-market philosophy of the Thatcher Government?' The Under-Secretary smiled and leaned forward as if to embrace me in a warm Anglo-Saxon conspiracy. 'We,' he said, 'believe totally in the free market, but in some areas we have to steal a march on our competitors in Europe. Sometimes it is better if the right hand does not know what the left hand is doing.' He sighed theatrically. I am sure he would have wished it all to be simpler.

A number of people, including the Minister, told me that British Leyland was a place I had to visit: an example of the new management and industrial dynamism. And so I went there for a lunchtime meeting. I was assured that the company was being turned round by new management and would soon recapture its rightful place as a leader of the world automotive industry.

At night I was the guest at a Savoy Hotel dinner of about twenty British industrialists and officials hosted by the Minister for Industry. I had never been to the Savoy before. I had been hoping for a good meal and was disappointed, although the wine was plentiful and excellent. The Minister made an elegant little speech of welcome extolling the exciting prospects for British industry and suggesting, obliquely, that although I was Australian and Labor I seemed a decent sort of chap. Then over dinner we got down to the serious talk. It seemed to revolve round the question of how British investment and equipment could save Australia from a fate worse than slow death. Would I be able to intervene with the Queensland Government to ensure that a British company was successful in a tender for the Queensland railways? Would I be able to persuade Australian companies to buy British equipment? Would I put in a good word with so and so? I wondered if it happened this way in Britain. I thought not. The evening slipped away into a haze of polite misunderstandings.

I made arrangements to visit the headquarters of the British Labour Party. I arranged private talks with the Deputy Parliamentary Leader, Roy Hattersley, and the Shadow Minister for Trade and Industry, Peter Shore. At the Party headquarters there was a prevailing atmosphere of gloom. Tensions between rival factions seemed more important than the prospect of winning government. There was a lot of talk about Tory plots to decimate the trade unions. Ideological disputes in the Party branches were turning away traditional supporters. There seemed little hope for the future.

I met Peter Shore and a member of his staff in a small office at the House of Commons. A well-regarded former minister, he too seemed dejected and without hope. He spoke in a desultory manner about international trade and at one stage turned to his assistant and asked, 'What is the other thing I'm responsible for?' 'Industry,' replied his assistant. 'Oh yes, industry—that's something which I'm not particularly interested in.' I tried to engage him in a discussion about prospects for the future, and the possibility of Labour's return to power. His mind, however, was fixed doggedly in the past. What, I asked, did he think about Britain's new industrial order? He said he knew nothing about it. I left with a better understanding that going in to government is better than going out.

My arrangement with Mr Hattersley was even less successful. I was to meet him at the Reform Club at six o'clock in the evening. I arrived on time and was shown into a comfortable lounge room by a butler, who offered me a drink. Mr Hattersley, it was explained, would be a little late. His train was caught in a snowdrift outside London. I sat down in a brown leather armchair and studied the members of the Reform Club sipping gins, dozing in armchairs, exchanging distant greetings and reading the *Times*. It reminded me of a 1950s movie—any moment I expected to see a friendly face of someone I felt I knew; like Alec Guinness or Alistair Sim or Robert Morley.

A man came over and asked if he could join me. He looked like Alistair Sim. I explained that I was waiting for Roy Hattersley. 'Interesting chap, Hattersley,' he drawled, 'a very interesting chap,' in a manner in which one might describe a species of cobra. 'Might I buy a drink?' He sat down in the chair next to me and told me of his affection for 'Orstralia'. He said he had been to Australia many times because of some business interests, but mainly for the sailing on Sydney Harbour. It was the best sailing in the world.

'Don't know much about politics,' he said, 'but I did meet a man who seemed to know what it was all about; a man with an Italian type of name.' 'Santamaria,' I suggested. 'Yes, that's right: Santamaria—an interesting sort of chap.' He launched into an entertaining and detailed history of the Reform Club. In the nineteenth century there had been a division in the Club which had split, as a result, into two: 'Brooks' and 'the Reform'. At Brooks, he told me, they had a tradition of sitting for lunch at a long table with whomever might be present on the day. 'I was there quite recently,' he said. 'There was an opinionated chap talking at length about "Orstralia". Another quiet chap at the end of the table interrupted him at one point and said "I don't think that's correct." "Have you ever been to Orstralia," said the first man. "Yes," said the quiet man, "my name's De L'Isle. I was Governor-General." Pretty good story, heh?'

An hour and a half passed. I decided Roy Hattersley was destined to spend the night in a snowdrift and I decided to leave. I met my wife and went to the theatre to see a play called *Steaming*. Jet-lagged, I fell asleep.

Westland Helicopters, a supposed jewel of British industry, had its main manufacturing plant in Somerset. The following morning we set out from London for Somerset in a company helicopter. After a quick tour of the factory we sat down to lunch. While we ate, the Deputy Chairman, Sir Basil Blackwell, and his management colleagues explained the benefits which would flow to the Australian Navy if it purchased the company's helicopters. 'In my opinion,' said the Deputy Chairman, 'the three greatest events in British history were the Battle of Agincourt, the ascension of Queen Victoria to the throne and the retaking of Port Stanley in the Falklands war.' He looked at me with a penetrating stare. 'And remember, Senator, our helicopters were there.' I tried to imagine Westland helicopters at the battle of Agincourt, but he intercepted my indulgence. 'I mean,' he said, 'that our helicopters were right there at Port Stanley. They are,' he repeated several times, 'the most recently battle-tested helicopters in the world.' It was a golden opportunity for Australia.

On the helicopter trip back to London we were accompanied by a director of the company, who was a former admiral in the British Navy. As we approached the centre of London through squally rain and scudding clouds, he became increasingly agitated. This did nothing for my morale as an infrequent flier in helicopters. I was glad when we touched down on the helipad on the River Thames. Then I realised the cause of his annoyance. He took me aside, looked at his watch and said, 'I'm terribly sorry about this, Senator. I promised to have you on the deck at 1600 hours. It's six minutes past. That is not good enough. Definitely not. It reminds me of the days when I was commander of the aircraft carrier, *Eagle*. We had a rendezvous with a destroyer in the South Atlantic ... five days steaming time for each ship. The destroyer arrived twenty minutes late. Not good enough. So I flashed the Captain a signal saying "You're late." Do you know what happened?' he asked me. I said that I had no idea. 'Well,' said the ex-Admiral, 'the cheeky young bugger flashed me back a signal saying "request time check, Sir?" I had to hand it to him. I thought to myself this young chap will go a long way.'

One way or another the aircraft industry seemed to be anxious to display its wares to a Minister in the new Australian Government. Two days later I found myself at Toulouse in the South of France at the manufacturing centre of Airbus Industries. Here we saw some samples of the latest French rocketry—fascinating for a Defence Minister, but less so for me. I inspected the assembly line for the new Airbus. Sitting in the pilot's seat of a new 320, I was told that the plane could technically fly without a pilot. It was a promise which I found less than comforting.

In Paris, a few days later, I was invited to lunch with an International Marketing Director of Airbus. A red-faced, ebullient and hyperactive man, he had a sales pitch which left the hypothetical used-car salesman for dead. As I entered the room where we were to have lunch, he was deftly opening a magnum of champagne. 'We will start,' he announced, 'with some traditional French hospitality. Later we shall talk bizness.' I told him that I did not drink champagne. I saw immediately that his worst fears had been realised, but he recovered quickly.

'*Alors,*' he said, '*ça fait rien.* I will drink the beautiful champagne—you perhaps will have a viskey.' He then poured me half a tumbler of whiskey and commenced the rapid demolition of the magnum of champagne. He watched anxiously as I took occasional sips at the whiskey. He fixed me with beady eyes. I made a guess at what he was thinking: 'This Australian yokel has a fat chequebook in his pocket. If I can get him full of grog he'll take out his Parker pen and sign up for ten aircraft.' He finished the champagne and poured himself a stiff whiskey. 'Now,' he said, 'we'll drink viskey together.'

At lunch I tried to explain that any decision to purchase aircraft for Australia would be made by the Cabinet after full consultation with the airlines. He asked me when Cabinet would meet. I picked a date two or three months ahead. This produced a careful examination of his diary. 'On that date,' he said, 'I am supposed to be in America signing up a contract for twenty aircraft. But if necessary I will change that appointment and come to Australia.' He wrote something in his diary. 'I think it might be better if . . . ' I began. But my host was sniffing the bouquet of an expensive bottle of claret and extolling its virtues as another fine product of France.

As I left the lunch an official from the Australian Embassy handed me a note from the Secretary of my Department in Canberra. I can't remember the exact words of the note. They included something about 'due process'. The tone, however, was quite clear: 'We're frantic about your unscheduled lunches. Ministers should not be let out on their own without officials. Make no commitments! Would you please phone as soon as possible?' I returned to the hotel to phone him. A young

Australian customs officer, stationed in Brussels but temporarily resident in Paris, was waiting to see me. He'd been told to make sure I called the Department. An expert on the dumping of cheeses and butter, he seemed bemused by the whole incident. I finally caught up with the Secretary at the Commonwealth Club. I think I reassured him. But it was a long time before I travelled on my own without an accompanying official to make notes and keep the corporate diary.

In the afternoon I had a meeting with Mr Laurent Fabius, the Industry Minister, later to become the Prime Minister of France. He was young and charming. He received me in a gracious room in an eighteenth century palace. In Paris, ministers work in an environment of elegance and style, as their predecessors have for centuries. There are not many high-rise office blocks. While we talked, competent and well-trained young bureaucrats glided in and out like courtiers in the time of Louis XVI. One French Empire seems to slip easily into another. We sat underneath a large crystal chandelier facing each other across a marble-topped desk and talked about new technology and its effect on employment. We were both struggling to come to grips with a new and contemporary problem. The conversation interested him and he seemed in no hurry. I became fascinated by his long, thin and expressive hands—Paul Keating hands, a Paul Keating sort of man.

In the evening I returned to the Plaza Athene Hotel. The brother of the King of Saudi Arabia was in residence with a retinue occupying two floors of the hotel. It was not an inconspicuous visit. Stretch-limousines were lined up outside in the street. A lot of the other guests in the hotel were Arabs. A number of them were standing around the foyer with suspicious bulges under their jackets. I wondered if they had any suspicion that an Australian minister and his adviser were upstairs on the top floor stowing away in their luggage, cakes of expensive designer-brand soap from the hotel bathrooms.

Later I looked into the hotel dining room. It was empty except for a young Australian businessman sitting at a table on his own. I went over to talk to him and we discussed our recent experiences in France. He was there on a selling mission for his British-owned engineering company. I asked where he thought his company would be in five years time. What would it be doing? What was planned? He said, 'I can't discuss that now, I'm preoccupied with this cheeky little Armagnac. I'm delighted to have found it. It's a wonderful surprise.' The following morning I found a note from him under my bedroom door. 'That's a good question you asked me last night,' it said. 'Maybe we should think about it.'

The history, the elegance and the street life of Paris combine to make it a city one is always reluctant to leave. But this time I was going to Rome, which has its own quite different charm. There is less sense of empire and more sense of Pope and Church. The history is very different. There is less rampant chic and intellectual fashion. The people and the climate are a degree warmer; it's not an offence to speak their language badly. Nobody works at the weekends. And I was going to spend the weekend in Rome.

The manager of the Bernini Bristol Hotel in Piazza Barbarini was waiting to welcome us when we arrived There was an Australian flag flying over the entrance to the hotel. The Australian Ambassador to Italy and the Trade Commissioner were there to brief us. There was not too much to say. The weekend was free. We settled for a day of walking round Rome and a Sunday drive to Hadrian's catacombs. On Monday I was to meet with the Italian Industry Minister. There would be a dinner at the Australian Embassy in the evening. The Ambassador was light on information about Italian industry, implying that it was not his field. The Trade Commissioner stepped into the breach and gave me the information I needed to sustain an informed discussion.

On the Monday morning the Australian Ambassador insisted

on accompanying me to the meeting with the Industry Minister. This time the meeting was in a Roman palazzo-like building of some antiquity. The Minister, Mr Artisinea, was one of the younger breed of Italian politicians. He had the professional manner of the technocrat. He talked about Italian politics and apologised for his inadequate knowledge of Italian industry. He had only been in the job for a couple of months. 'You should understand,' he said, 'that with our system of government the average tenure of an Industry Minister in Italy is only eight months.' The Ambassador, who had remained silent up to this point, seized the opportunity to ask a question, 'I'd be interested to know,' he said, 'whether that creates any difficulties for long-term planning?' The Minister sighed and leaned back in his chair. He studied us with a look of great sympathy. 'Yes,' he said, 'it does,' and went on with the simpler description of the hazards of Italian politics.

That night at the Ambassador's residence, a group of Italian businessmen, officials and their wives had assembled for dinner. I have no clear recollection of the conversation at dinner. I remember we were waited on at table by two black Africans from Ghana, who wore uniforms and white gloves. It seemed that they went with the house. The Italian guests were surprised to find that a Minister from a distant country like Australia could speak Italian. They asked questions to confirm in their minds my affection for Italy. In the Italian manner they exchanged reminiscences about other occasions on which they had encountered the phenomenon of non-Europeans who spoke Italian. Some of them even gave me vocabulary lessons. There was a friendliness and warmth about it all. It was just as well; the following morning I was leaving for a cold country.

Cold climates: 1984

We staggered cold, wet and dishevelled into the warm foyer of the Imperial Hotel in Vienna. It was 11.00 a.m. The hotel manager, dressed in tails, looked us up and down with an air of total disapproval. My private secretary, Philip Clark, took an instant dislike to him. He spent some time during our short stay trying to take the mickey out of 'the snooty-nosed bastard'.

Outside, the solemn-faced burghers of the city strolled along the snow-covered footpaths in fur hats and fur-lined overcoats. They looked as solid and comfortable as Christmas puddings. 'This,' I thought, 'is the country of "haves" and "have nots": those who have fur coats and those who don't.'

The fact that we were cold and wet was, of course, my fault. I had insisted on going out to try to find the apartment I had lived in as a student, twenty-five years before. When we finally located the place on a street called Momsengasse, we stood reverentially in the street and gazed up at the shabby, grey building. It had all the charm of a housing commission high-rise. Passers-by looked at us suspiciously. We must have looked like a couple of stragglers from Napoleon's Army in Russia. I felt no emotion: only cold. The route from Momsengasse 6 to the Imperial Hotel marked my upward social mobility in Vienna. I guessed that the hotel manager understood where I really belonged.

Austria for most of the 1970s and early 1980s had been one

of Europe's quiet achievers: a steady, prosperous economy with low unemployment and sensible industrial relations. The Australian Commercial Counsellor, a noted Mozart scholar happily situated in Vienna, had arranged appointments for me. They were with Mr Anton Benya, President of the Parliament and President of the Austrian Confederation of Trade Unions, and Dr Norbert Steger, the Austrian Vice-Chancellor. Benya, a respected international figure, talked about the success of the consultative process in Austrian employer–employee relations over many years. In Australia the experience had been very different. We'd only recently embarked on the process of the wage accord. We had, it seemed, a fair way to catch up.

Steger, an urbane and stylish politician in his early forties, told me that the Austrian Government had just commissioned a wide-ranging survey of their country's 'image' in the United States. Seventy per cent of the respondents had confused Austria with Australia. Sixty percent thought Austria was the home of the kangaroo. We agreed that we had a mutual problem. I'd come a long way to hear about it. But Steger was generous with his time and we had a long discussion about Austria's successful industry sector. This success had been based on high quality mechanical engineering. Economies, he argued, should have a balance of high-tech and conventional industry. About thirty-five percent of Austria's manufacturing production could be classified as high-tech. Australia, he thought, should try to achieve this sort of balance. And would I remember that Austria did not like our import restrictions on high-priced footwear.

I was grateful for the shortness of our stay in Vienna. That winter it seemed like the coldest place on earth. We flew from Austria to Zurich. From the air, we looked down on the Austrian countryside blanketed in heavy snow.

My memories of Zurich were not warm either. Years ago, while hitchhiking through Europe, I'd spent two sleepless nights there in a hostel for homeless men. It had been cold and full of crazy people. I remembered an alcoholic waking me in the middle of the night. He wanted to borrow a hat. He said his head was freezing. This time we were picked up at the airport in Zurich to be driven up the alpine road to Davos. The car, an Audi, had heating in the passenger seats. It was something I had not experienced before. I approached Davos with a warm inner glow.

Davos, a beautiful alpine resort, has been the home of the annual conference of the World Economic Forum (previously the European Management Forum) for many years. The conference lasts for several days and the delegates pay handsomely for the privilege of attending. They are comfortably housed in a number of hotels at the resort. It is all a triumph for the Swiss tourist industry.

The methodology of managing the conference is simple. A number of high profile figures are invited as guests: presidents; prime ministers; ex-prime ministers; ministers for industry, finance and trade; former ministers; and an assorted collection of political, economic and business gurus. Sometimes there is a special delegation from a particular country. Topics are selected for introduction by 'keynote' speakers. Then the invitations go out to businesspeople around the world. They respond in large numbers. It is implied that they will have the opportunity to rub shoulders with the great; to talk with political leaders on an equal basis.

The Director of the Forum, Professor Klaus Schwab, runs it, not surprisingly, with the precision of a cuckoo clock. The hotel and transport arrangements are impeccably managed. There are plenary sessions, seminars on particular topics, break-out groups, workshops and tutorials. There is even a 'World Leaders Forum', where prime ministers, ministers, and other dignitaries are whisked away to a chalet on the mountains. There they take part in a sort of VIP group therapy. They exchange views about the world's trade and business future.

Professor Schwab is assisted by a number of bright young managerial types who handle the day-to-day organisation of the conference. Ministers, I discovered, with an inclination to sleep in or disappear for a few hours on the ski slopes are reminded of their obligations to be in the right places at the right times. It is very efficient. The joys of a resort are tempered by the discipline of a holiday camp.

In 1984 the high profile figures at Davos included: Raymond Barre, a former French Prime Minister and perennial right-wing candidate; the prime ministers of Turkey, Malaysia, Portugal, Belgium and the Philippines; the Crown Prince of Jordan; the fashionable German Economic Minister, Count Lamsdorff; a Vice-President of China; the Japanese Deputy Foreign Minister and senior officials from the US Treasury, Department of Agriculture, and State Department. There was also a large contingent of international civil servants including the Secretary General of GATT, the President of the World Bank, the Secretary of the OECD and the Chairman of the International Monetary Fund. And in business, amongst the leaders, there was the opportunity to meet with the chief executives of ICI, Nestlé and Hewlett-Packard.

A touch of glamour was to be provided by the presence of the Prime Minister of Canada, Pierre Trudeau. His participation in the forum had all the panache of the Scarlet Pimpernel. He dazzled the hundreds of guests at the cocktail party following the opening ceremony by a fleeting appearance with a young blonde on his arm. She wore a skin-tight dress. He wore a dinner jacket. Amidst the sea of grey business suits they glittered briefly like a kaleidoscope of coloured lights. Then they disappeared.

At that moment I found myself standing in the crowd next to a manufacturer of aluminium window frames, from Kuwait. He was not quite sure why he'd come to Davos. He said he couldn't understand many of the other participants. He hoped that Mr Trudeau and his Lady would re-appear. He was destined for disappointment. I doubt if many participants saw Mr Trudeau again. At the 'world leaders' meeting in the mountain-top chalet he was supposed to open the discussion. He did not appear. Messages were brought in indicating that he was running late and I imagined Professor Schwab's organisers frantically searching the hotels in the resort. Finally he arrived, gave us a short burst on structural adjustment in the Canadian textile industry, and disappeared. Later there were rumours that he had been 'sighted' ski-ing on a remote slope with a young woman. But by this time he'd passed into the folklore of Davos.

The Australian participants at Davos comprised a small group of Commonwealth public servants and about twenty businessmen from major Australian companies. It was complemented by a small delegation from Tasmania, led by the Premier, Robin Grey. At the time, Tasmania was the only Australian State with a non-Labor government. The Tasmanian delegation was small, but not inconspicuous. They wore sweatshirts embroidered with a map of Tasmania and bearing the caption: 'Tasmania, the last bastion of free enterprise.' At the conference sessions they handed out Tasmanian apples. Fortunately, most of the predominantly European forum participants had no idea where Tasmania was. Some thought it was just south of the Falkland Islands.

At a special Tasmanian presentation the Premier extolled the benefits of investment in his State. People coming to invest in Tasmania would be given free air tickets. 'See that man over there—' he said, pointing at the Tasmanian Industry Minister. 'He's got the tickets in his pocket.' The Minister dutifully patted the pocket of his jacket. The small audience seemed rather bemused. After all it was a long time before the airlines began marketing 'mystery flights'. But perhaps the Tasmanians had the last laugh. A Swiss newspaper report of the Symposium said there were participants from forty-nine nations. Tasmania was mentioned. Australia was not.

On the second morning of the conference I was not feeling too well. It was, I'm afraid, my own fault. I'd forgotten that I had to get up early to participate in a BBC television program. I went, as instructed, to a small breakfast room in the hotel. In the middle of the room a table had been set for breakfast. It was surrounded by television lights and cameras. A strange collection of people had been assembled. The Prime Minister of Turkey, the Japanese Deputy Foreign Minister, a Vice-Minister from China, an Arab Sheik from one of the Gulf States and me.

The producer, a fussy man in a velvet jacket and bow tie, explained the purpose of the program. It was designed to introduce to a British audience the different and exotic foods eaten at breakfast in various countries round the world. We were instructed to sit at the table, enjoy a cup of coffee, relax, and be perfectly natural. The compere would introduce the topic, then ask us each in turn what we would have been eating for breakfast if we'd been at home on that particular morning.

The cameras began to roll. The compere introduced the topic in a precise, deliberate BBC voice. Then he turned to the Japanese Deputy Foreign Minister; 'Minister, if you were in Japan this morning what would you be having for breakfast?' The Foreign Minister smiled politely and said, 'Almost certainly, I would be having bacon and eggs.' The compere looked a bit flustered. He cocked an eyebrow and said, 'Bacon and eggs?' 'Yes,' said the minister, 'bacon and eggs.' The compere turned to the Sheik from the Gulf States: 'And you, sir, in your country?' The Sheik said 'Eggs, but no bacon; definitely no bacon.' 'Very interesting,' said the compere with an air of forced nonchalance. 'We're able to see that in two different countries, each far from the British Isles, people eat eggs for breakfast—not quite what we'd expected but . . . ' He was interrupted by the Turkish Prime Minister. 'This is very interesting,' he said. 'I too am very fond of bacon and eggs.'

The producer called out, 'Right, gentlemen, we'll stop there for a minute.' The cameras stopped. The TV lights were turned off.

I overheard the producer and compere whispering in the corner of the room. 'Which idiot,' hissed the producer, 'chose these people?' I knew that I was participating in a performance which would never go to air. I knew that I had been expected to be the bacon and eggs man. After a few minutes the producer said, 'OK, gentlemen. Won't keep you much longer. We'll run quickly through to the end.' The compere turned to me, 'Senator, if you were having breakfast in Australia this morning . . .' But he could hardly keep a straight face. 'The way I feel this morning,' I replied, 'I'd probably be having an Alka-Seltzer.'

The Davos Forum is what you make it. The resort is situated in a valley in the mountains facing a popular ski slope called 'Jacobshorn'. There are social events as well as working sessions. The ski slopes are a constant temptation, which I for one could not resist. On a bright, sunny afternoon I took Philip Clark on a series of chairlifts to the top of Jacobshorn. He had never skied before. He snowploughed slowly down, his progress punctuated with a series of spectacular soft landings and long slides on his bottom. When we returned our skis to the ski-hire shop the man in the shop said, 'Vat hav you bin doin? Zee sun is shining. Zer is no schnowing but you look like a snowball.' Philip looked highly offended. 'Don't mock me, my friend,' he said. 'Today I have known real terror.'

Generally there was not much terror; although, as an innocent, I felt a touch of it as we drove up a mountain road to the chalet where the world leaders' informal gathering was to take place. I had a sinking feeling in my stomach. What if they asked for contributions in alphabetical order by country? Australia would come first. What would I say?

Fortunately it didn't turn out that way. The more experienced attendees took the running: Arthur Dunkel, the Secretary General of GATT; Raymond Barre from France; Count Lamsdorff from Germany. The discussion turned to economic growth, world trade and the need to reduce tariff protection and other inhibitions on trade. Somebody pointed out that this was not as easy as it sounded. Politicians had electorates to consider—if countries were to specialise in particular industry sectors jobs would be lost in other sectors. There was a need for adjustment-policies which had to be explained to the community. The media was criticised as unhelpful. A social safety net had to underpin industry change. One speaker called it 'a hard mattress'. Count Lamsdorff criticised MITI in Japan: companies should compete internationally, not nation states. MITI had damaged world trade by its refusal to accept this view. The Japanese Deputy Foreign Minister seemed to agree. Departmental rivalries run deep in Japan as everywhere else.

Unemployment, it was said, was not caused by imports but by failure to promote exports. Everybody seemed in agreement as to why things were going wrong, but were less sure about how they might put the problems right. The discussion made me feel more at ease. Nobody had any brilliant solutions. They were talking about issues which were to dominate political and economic debates in Australia in the 1980s, although I didn't fully comprehend this at the time.

I became bold enough to point out that most of the contributors were from wealthy manufacturing and service industry economies in Europe and the United States. There had been no discussion of Asia and the Pacific and no discussion about resource-based economies.

Some countries like South Korea classified as underdeveloped were in fact powerful industrial economies. It was inaccurate to put countries in simple classifications. There had to be more detailed perspectives on different countries round the world. I was unsure about the response I would get: maybe silence or a change of topic. But a Mr McNamara from the United States Treasury said he agreed. And Dr Mahathir, the Prime Minister of Malaysia, strongly supported what I had said. I felt I had some mates. At the conclusion of the meeting I talked with Dr Mahathir. We were both conscious of coming from a different and distant part of the world. In outlook we were not European. We developed a rapport which was to stand the test of time.

On the last day at Davos I hosted a lunch for the Australian delegation and a number of invited guests from European businesses with interests in Australia. Our Ambassador to Switzerland, Pierre Hutton, who had guided me with an expert hand through the Swiss environment, made a short speech. I made a speech. There was a speech day atmosphere. Everyone had enjoyed the meeting and some had learnt a few new things. In the car driving down the icy road from Davos to Zurich, an Australian industrialist did some simple sums on the back of his chequebook to show me how his business worked. He seemed to have the business right. He made good profits. Somehow that made me feel good too.

It was nearly dark when we arrived in the Swiss capital, Bern. There was just time to see the famous bears in the bearpit at the bottom of the city's main street. It was cold and they were sleepy. They were not interested in strangers.

A meeting and dinner had been arranged with Dr Kurt Furgler and other representatives of the Swiss Government. Furgler was a Federal Councillor and Vice-President of the Swiss Confederation—the equivalent of Deputy Prime Minister. The Council consisted of seven members who rotated positions. The country did not seem overgoverned. Furgler, who was Economics Minister, enjoyed a popular image as a man of action. He had personally supervised the firefighting and rescue operation when a Swiss tourist hotel caught fire. He was said to be a man who got things done.

We met in a medieval building called *Von Wattenwylhaus*.

We sat at a long refectory table, the Swiss group of six or seven people on one side, and my small party on the other. Dr Furgler was precise, charming and formal. He was in command of the situation. You could imagine him leading people down a fire escape. He said that before dinner he would like to raise five issues. Firstly he wanted to explain Switzerland's position on agriculture in international negotiations. Switzerland, he said, prided itself on its independence. This required independence in agricultural production. Agricultural policy was related to defence policy. It was necessary to keep Swiss farmers in the mountains even if they were inefficient producers. They provided the eyes and ears of Swiss defence.

He kept calling me 'Your Excellency'. He said Swiss pharmaceutical companies were disadvantaged in Australia because of the Australian Government's pricing policies. I said we would look at the pricing policies, but we would like the Swiss companies to do more in Australia than packaging and distribution. 'There should, Your Excellency, be a debate in Australia about uranium enrichment.' When would it start? There was a question about tariff concessions. He wanted landing rights in Australia for Swissair. Could that be attended to? I said it was a complex issue but we would examine it in due course. Dr Furgler beamed and clapped his hands. 'Right,' he said, 'all finished. Now we will have dinner.'

At dinner Dr Furgler relaxed. Everybody relaxed. He talked about the Swiss watch industry. Switzerland for a long time had been the world's leading country in watchmaking. The industry, however, had overlooked the potential of digital watches. It had let the technology go to the Japanese and the Swiss industry had gone into decline. They had done a lot of research, however, and were about to bounce back. 'See—' he said, throwing a rubber-cased 'Swatch' down on the table. 'It bounces. This is the basis of our country's new watch industry.' Kurt Furgler began to be merry. He rubbed his hands together and started to call me 'Minister' rather than 'Your Excellency'.

At the end of the main course he rose to his feet and said, 'Now we will make speeches.' In his speech he said that I had come thousands of miles across land and sea from the most distant continent because Switzerland and Australia had 'shared walues'. There were minor differences between our two countries, like Swissair landing rights, but these things were not important. What was important in everything was 'shared walues'. It seemed too statesman-like. I tried to respond in similar vein. As the evening wore on it became more informal. As I was about to leave he leaned across the table and said, 'My dear John, I understand it will take time to get landing rights for Swissair.'

In Zurich the following day I had lunch with a group of Swiss bankers and investors. They were well-informed about their investments in Australia. They worried that the taxation rules for foreign investments should not be changed. I talked about changing attitudes and economic recovery in Australia. The following day a journalist at the lunch reported in the newspaper, *Schweizerische Handelszeitung*, under the headline 'Change in Australia: Islanders with brains' as follows:

> Over the past years, Australia, spoiled by the only partly explored mineral and energy resources, has barely managed a rather sad wallflower existence amidst a rapidly expanding Asian Pacific economy. However the new Labor Government, under Prime Minister Bob Hawke, awoke the giant from its eternal sleep: the success of the past nine months seems amazing. In order to attract the attention of Europeans to the comeback of Australia—and that of desirable investors to the fifth continent—Hawke's Minister for Industry and Commerce John Button is travelling at present in Europe . . .
>
> Amazing things are happening on the fifth continent. A year ago comments on Australia's economic situation were immersed

in silent pessimism. Galloping inflation rates with record levels of close to seventeen percent in the seventies, an unemployment rate of nearly ten percent, wild and endless strikes as well as disastrous droughts were eating away at the self-confidence of the Oceanians. But in March 1983 came Bob Hawke, and with him, the rains.

I read the article a couple of days later. I thought, 'It's never like this at home. Perhaps I should stay here; or rub my eyes and hurry back.'

We were picked up in Zurich in a new Mercedes Benz driven by one of Daimler Benz's test drivers, who was to take us to Stuttgart in Germany. We were to visit the company's headquarters and meet with some senior executives. They had an interest in the future of the car industry in Australia. I'm still surprised we made it. The roads were covered in ice. Thick snow had been scooped by snowploughs onto the roadsides. We had to be there by five o'clock. The driver had no intention of being late and at times we got up to one hundred and eighty kilometres an hour. He seemed totally in control, and I didn't feel nervous. One more trip, two more cold countries, and I would be heading back to an Australian summer.

Vikings: 1984

I read somewhere, probably on a date pad, that 'the use of travelling is to regulate imagination by reality, and instead of thinking things may be, to see them as they are'. I had good imaginings about Sweden and I was keen to see it in reality. I knew they produced good tennis players and beautiful blondes. I had some knowledge of their big international companies like Volvo, Saab, Bofors and Ericsson.

I'd read with fascination about one of their kings, Charles XII, a soldier who took on all-comers. In successive battles he beat the French, the German States and Peter the Great of Russia. Defeated in a battle near the Black Sea, he disguised himself as a monk and rode on horseback home to Sweden to recruit a new army. Then he went back for another scrap. He died in 1718 at the age of thirty-six, killed in a minor skirmish with the Norwegians. He seemed a goer: a descendant of Vikings. Like most military adventurers he sent his country broke, but by the twentieth century it had fully recovered. It seemed a civilised country—productive, well organised, with good social welfare systems. The English philosopher Kathleen Nott called her book about Sweden *A Clean Well-Lighted Place* and this was what I expected.

As the plane from Paris burst out of the clouds near Stockholm all I could see beneath us was snow. It looked, as I had imagined, clean and white. The Australian Ambassador and the Swedish Minister for State Owned Enterprises, Roine

Carlsson, met us at the airport. A former blacksmith, Carlsson was broad and stocky. He'd made his way into politics and the government through the Swedish trade union movement. He spoke English with a quaint, lilting accent and was friendly and easygoing. Driving into Stockholm, I noticed some men with fur coats and guns on their shoulders trudging through the thick snow. 'What are those men hunting?' I asked. Carlsson looked perplexed. 'I don't know 'ow you say it in Engleesh,' he said. 'But it is an animal which is 'igher at the back than the front.' I imagined some strange Nordic animal; something like a buffalo. In bed that night, I kept turning it over in my mind. What sort of animal could it be? The following morning when I met Carlsson again, he said, 'I was thinking about that animal during the night. I got up and looked it up in a dictionary. It is Wabbit.'

Stockholm seemed cold and dark in the wintry late afternoon. Carlsson and the Ambassador delivered us to the Strand Hotel near the water's edge and close to the centre of the city. The hotel was light and airy, with functional attractive furniture, pastel-coloured·fabrics, good spaces and friendly staff. In my room I turned on the television—one channel—wholesome Swedish programs about craft industries, problems of Third World countries, the importance of design in industry. It all seemed as I imagined.

That evening my private secretary Philip Clark and I dined with the Swedish Industry Minister, Thage Petersson, and his wife at their home in a suburb of Stockholm. From the living room we looked out at a moonlit lake frozen over with ice. Petersson pointed out two or three fishermen sitting patiently on small stools at holes in the ice. He told us stories, with a folklore quality about them, of fishermen and skaters who fell through the ice cover into the water below, and how they then got themselves out. Mrs Petersson took me into her study to show me her Australian-made Microbee computer, a small PC, which somehow became a focal point for discussion about the trading relationship between two distant countries. It was a relaxed and informal evening. In the winter cold I began to warm to Sweden. As we left, Petersson handed me a letter from the Swedish Prime Minister, Olaf Palme, apologising for his absence, in the United States, and wishing me a happy and informative visit to his country.

Petersson had arranged a day's presentation by officials of the Swedish Industry Department; an overview of policies and performance of particular industries. Sweden had been through a difficult period of restructuring its basic industries. Between 1970 and 1982 successive governments had spent a lot of money on companies in difficulty. The Social Democratic Government, which returned to power in 1982, had cancelled all government handouts to ailing industries. An agreement had been reached with the trade unions on wage increases for the next two years. The unions had been consulted on industrial development issues. Government industry funding had been diverted into research and development, manpower training, regional support and venture capital in new or emerging industries. At any one time, two percent of the workforce were engaged in retraining. The steel, shipbuilding, and mining industries had been restructured and major Swedish companies were trading successfully in the international marketplace. With a population of seven million, Sweden had eighteen companies in the 'Fortune 500' list outside the USA.

The Swedes believed in a free market and an open economy. The government collaborated with industry in determining what part of the international market Sweden should be involved in. Government resources, in the provision of 'soft' infrastructure, were then directed into these priority areas. The active participation of Swedish universities had been enlisted for industrial research, development training and industry data collation. I was told that there were one thousand PhD students pursuing studies in relation to aspects of Swedish industry. We were shown slides illustrating the position in world markets of major Swedish industries in the 1970s compared with the beginning of the 1980s and where they intended to be in the 1990s. As an Australian Industry Minister used to polarised armchair debates about industry policy, it seemed practical, straightforward and well thought through. And the idea of looking a decade ahead to try to estimate the future requirements of industry for infrastructure, manpower and skills was something unheard of in Australia.

A day or two later we had a meeting with the Federation of Swedish Industry, the representative body of the interests of Swedish industry as a whole. Founded in 1910 it had become, by 1984, an organisation which dealt with the Swedish Government, and overseas governments and organisations. As distinct from the various organisations seeking to represent industry in Australia, it had the advantage for Swedish businesses and enterprises of speaking with one voice. Executives of the federation gave us a briefing and then a lunch. At the briefing we were told of the federation's differences with the Swedish Government, particularly over the high growth in public sector employment. At lunch I found myself sitting next to Mr Roger Sprimont, a former naval officer and a director of the shipbuilding company, Kockums. It was not, I think, an accident. Roger Sprimont gave me a quiet but informative talk about Swedish shipbuilding techniques and the design features of Swedish submarines. It was not the last time I was to meet him. He came to Australia for six months in the period leading up to the Australian Government's decision to choose the Swedish-designed submarine for the Australian Navy. At lunch I was the first Australian ministerial recipient of low-key Swedish lobbying.

The industry federation also raised the issue of Swedish companies in Australia. At that time there were fifty-five Swedish companies, employing ten thousand people, engaged in manufacturing and service industries in Australia and four hundred and fifty other companies had representatives there. I needed only the fingers of one hand to count the Australian companies in Sweden. The industry federation had mentioned its concerns at the rapid increase in Sweden's public sector employment. From time to time others mentioned similar concerns about government policies. In its written publications the federation referred to 'falling capital investment', 'high costs', 'high public sector wages' and 'laws, impositions and regulations which means that industry hesitates to invest'. There was, it seemed, a downside to the Swedish 'miracle'.

I recalled Kathleen Nott's book *A Clean Well-Lighted Place*. She had referred to the Soviet Union as 'a worker oriented society'. 'Sweden,' she wrote, 'was a social worker oriented society.' Sweden had the most advanced social security system in the world. Swedes also paid the highest taxes. From 1969 to 1976 the Social Democratic Government of Olaf Palme had presided over *Folkhemmet*—the People's Home—a nation dedicated to social justice, security and solidarity. Sweden had the biggest public sector in the Western world. In the 1930s the novelist Ludvig Nordstrom had written; 'Why, one might ask, could Sweden not become the model country for the world?' The basis for being such a model seemed to exist. As a publication of the industry federation put it: 'Sweden possesses long and successful industrial traditions. The country is rich in natural resources, has a highly skilled labour force, considerable technological expertise and well-equipped pro-duction facilities.'

The commitment to *Folkhemmet* came, however, at a great price. Swedish taxes as a proportion of GDP were eighteen percent higher than the OECD average. These paid for a smorgasbord of welfare services from free school meals to twelve months paid maternity leave for men as well as women, generous sick leave and social security benefits which allegedly made it more profitable not to work. Wealthier Swedes from tennis players to industrialists sought out tax havens round the world. Discouraged from extensive investments abroad, corporations channelled profits into real estate. At the end of the 1980s real estate halved in value, producing a financial crisis and a total re-examination of Sweden's economic priorities. In 1984 people were muttering about too much welfare, too much state intervention and too much of the good life. Cracks were just beginning to show in the model society. The costly military adventuring of Charles XII in the eighteenth century was reappearing as a burden to the Swedish economy in the form of costly welfare adventurism in the twentieth century.

The Swedes made sure the appointment diary was full. We visited the Academy of Engineering Sciences, an influential body on industrial technology; the aircraft division of Saab–Scania, where the Grypen multipurpose fighter aircraft was being developed; the Swedish Space Agency; the Minister for Finance; the Minister for Foreign Trade; the Ministry of Environment and the Ministry of Foreign Affairs. At the weekend we slithered round the icy streets of Stockholm, visiting the Museum of Nordic History and pausing for an hour or two at the painstakingly restored wreck of the ship the *Vasa*. Built in 1628 and destined for a short life cycle, the *Vasa* was launched amidst much fanfare, sailed a thousand yards or so out on the waters of the harbour, capsized in a gusty wind and sank with the loss of fifty lives. The ship was top-heavy; and overloaded with guns.

After years of searching, the wreck was located in 1956 and raised and brought to shore in an operation which took a number of years. The cold, salty waters of the deep harbour had preserved the ship's timbers and most of its contents. These included guns and other weapons, coins, clothing and bottles of rum. The *Vasa* and its contents now occupy a museum and a place in Swedish maritime history. The Swedes joked about it. 'We seafaring Vikings,' they would say, 'have always led the way in technology.' Undeterred by the fate of the *Vasa*, we took a ferry ride down the harbour and waterways leading to the Baltic Sea; the icebreaking bow of the ferry crushing and shuddering its way through the floating ice which covered the water.

The Australian Ambassador had arranged a dinner for about forty invited Swedish guests and Australians resident in Stockholm. There were six tables with six or seven people at each table and we were invited to change tables between courses. At the start of the meal I was seated between a Swedish industry official and a handsome blonde woman in her early forties. Her accent intrigued me—traces of Adelaide with an English County overlay. Life in Sweden, she explained, was comfortable and quite interesting. It was not, however, without problems. Her children were all at boarding school in England. This was costly, but in the long run it would be worthwhile. Her name was Bradstock and her husband was an Australian government trade representative in Sweden. How were things in Australia? She had not lived there for a long time; just an occasional quick visit. There was a lull in the conversation—a silence which needed to be broken.

'Minister,' she said, 'I've been studying the itinerary for the remainder of your trip. I notice you're going to Singapore on the way back to Australia ... staying at the Shangri La Hotel. We stay there ourselves. I'd like to give you a tip. Go to the Terrace Restaurant and order the prawns, lightly curried. Absolutely delicious.' We finished our first course. I rose to change tables. We shook hands and she gave me an ingratiating smile. 'Don't forget now,' she whispered, 'at the Terrace, lightly curried.'

Two tables later I found myself sitting next to Mr Bradstock. I'd barely swallowed the first mouthful of food when he said, 'Minister, I've been studying the itinerary for the remainder of your trip. I see you're staying in Singapore at the Shangri La Hotel. We stay there ourselves. May I give you a suggestion? Go to the Terrace Restaurant near the pool and have the prawns, lightly curried. Delicious. But make sure you get the right ones: lightly curried.'

The next day we flew in a light aircraft to Gothenburg on the west coast of Sweden. We had been invited to visit the Volvo plant and headquarters. We'd hardly left the ground when Bradstock began rummaging in an Esky at the back of the plane. He produced a bottle of beer which he proceeded to drink. It was 9.30 a.m. A short time later I asked him what his job involved. 'Minister, I'm responsible for Scandinavia and the whole of Eastern Europe,' he said, with a sweep of his hand to indicate the scope of his fiefdom. 'If I had a map I'd show you . . . ' Someone handed him a map in a plastic case marked *Carte*. 'This is not a map,' he declared, 'This is a carte.' Someone took the map out of the folder.

Bradstock showed us the countries in which he represented Australia. 'It's hard to get round all that territory,' he sighed. 'I've been concentrating on Sweden.' He explained his intimate knowledge of Eastern Europe which made it almost unnecessary for him to visit these countries. He'd been in Europe a long time: 'In fact I haven't been in Australia for quite a few years. It's difficult with the kids in school in England.' Bradstock went back to the Esky and poured himself another beer. Half an hour later when we landed at Gothenburg airport, the Esky was nearly empty.

At Volvo we were shown round the factory. We looked at designer models of cars for the next decade; lighter with less steel and more plastic and composite fibre. We had a meeting with Per Gillenhamer, the Chief Executive of the company. A lean, handsome man with twinkling blue eyes, he exuded urbanity and charm. He described the ramifications of the Volvo empire which embraced cars, trucks, pharmaceuticals and processed food. He described the Volvo system of work teams on the factory floor. I asked about the level of labour turnover. He said it was high amongst young people. 'I walk round the factory and I stop and ask them if they enjoy working for Volvo. They say "yes" so I say, "Well you'll be staying with us?" and they say, all too often, "I'm sorry, Mr Gillenhamer, but I'm leaving at Christmas to go backpacking in Australia!" I think it's great for them but a hell of a way to run a business. So I have mixed feelings about your country.'

He told us about a Russian invitation for Volvo to establish a transport and distribution business in the Soviet Union. Volvo had tried, but decided it was hopeless. He'd told the Russians he didn't see why Volvo should invest in the Soviet Union while Russian submarines were spying on Swedish seaports. It was a remark which had earned him a rebuke from the Swedish Foreign Minister. He seemed amused by this. He noted I'd been to the European Management Forum in Davos. Had I found it worthwhile? I said I had some qualifications. He smiled. 'I think,' he said, 'Davos is a very good conference for ex-politicians.' We got up to leave. Bradstock, who had said nothing but seemed excited in the presence of the chief of Volvo, rushed forward with a business card which he handed to Gillenhamer. 'I'm from the embassy,' he said. 'I'll be in touch.' Gillenhamer's blue eyes frosted over. 'Of course,' he said, 'of course.'

I met with Mr Werthen, the Chairman of the Ericsson Telecommunications Group and Chief Executive of Electrolux. Werthen's grasp of technology and imaginative contribution to Swedish innovation had made him something of a folk hero in Swedish industry circles. He talked about the need for innovation to be responsive to the marketplace. Many fascinating inventions had failed as products because too few people had wanted them. 'You must think all the time about what people need.' A year or so before he'd been fiddling with an Electrolux sewing machine one evening at his home. 'I couldn't thread the needle,' he recalled.

'I thought to myself there must be thousands of people in the world with eyesight like mine. The next day I went into the laboratory at work and told them I wanted an automatic, electronic needle-threading device developed. I gave them six months to do it, and they did. Now that sewing machine sells as you say in English "like 'ot cakes".' He smiled. 'That is what technology is all about.' Australia at that time was a land of imaginative innovators and lamentably inadequate marketers. I remembered the story because in 1984 I'd never heard an Australian industrialist speak with the same understanding of consumer needs. When I returned to Australia, I often related the story as an illustration of the importance of market awareness amongst manufacturers.

On our last day in Sweden the sun peeped through the clouds, casting a pale Nordic light on the city and the countryside. We ate a farewell lunch at a summerhouse in a garden on the outskirts of Stockholm. It was attended by a number of the people we'd met in Sweden, including the Swedish Ambassador to Australia, Lars Hedstrom, and the Australian Ambassador to Sweden, who'd collaborated in arranging the program. They seemed pleased with it all; and so they should have been. Bradstock did not attend. We talked about future collaboration and a planned Swedish mission to Australia for the following year. They assured me Sweden was not always dark and cold, and they suggested I should come back in a northern summer.

Three years later in the spring, I went back to Sweden on a brief visit; unfortunately too brief to visit the Arctic North or to sail on the lakes and fiords. In the meantime Roine Carlsson, who had become Swedish Minister for Defence, and Finance Minister Feldt visited Australia for talks and time out on the Barrier Reef. The Swedish mission, led by the Industry Minister Thage Petersson, visited Canberra and State capital cities. The Australian Council of Trade Unions sent a delegation to look at developments in Swedish industry and the wage fixation system. The Business Council of Australia sent a small group of members to look at the same issues. For a while, at least, the two countries grew closer together.

I left pondering the similarities and differences between Australia and Sweden. Sweden, with half our population, had turned itself into a significant trading nation. Parked, as it were, offshore from the continent of Europe it was nonetheless close to it. Close enough for Swedes to skate across the sea to Copenhagen in a cold winter. Sweden conducted most of its export business to the three hundred million people in the European Community. Australia sat like an aircraft carrier, offshore from the world's most populous and fastest growing region. We lacked Sweden's export culture; its technological sophistication and its commitment to open trade. We had a bit to learn from them. On the other hand, we were probably fortunate in not having a novelist who had suggested that we might be a model country for the world. And Australians were, in any event, too sceptical for that.

A country with a king who rode his bike around Stockholm seemed to have a lot going for it. The people were friendly and informal; characteristics I liked to associate with Australians. Proud of their Viking ancestry, they had become a peace-loving nation with a highly developed sense of tolerance. Some Europeans regard them as strange and different. They are. I think that's a compliment. We flew out of Stockholm airport late in the afternoon for London, and Singapore and then home. In Singapore I forgot about the 'prawns on the Terrace'. Instead I spent half a day writing a long letter to the Australian Prime Minister about industry and what we might learn from Sweden and other countries overseas.

A new Soviet
man: 1985

It was 4 a.m. and very cold. We were standing on the tarmac outside the operations room of a United States airforce base on the south island of Japan. The Commander of the base was a lean steely-eyed man with crew-cut hair—a Clint Eastwood sort of man. He was dressed in a battle jacket, well-pressed trousers, leggings and brightly polished boots. 'What do you do here?' I asked, pointing to a long line of F14 Tom Cat fighter aircraft on the edge of the tarmac. 'From here,' he said, 'we keep an eye on the "Ruskies". But I have to say it's fairly quiet on the base these days. Not so much activity. In fact I'm doing a correspondence degree in international trade law,' a topic which he spoke of with some enthusiasm. 'But I still get a buzz out of those babies over there. I stand out here and watch them take off at night. With their afterburners glowing in the night sky they look really great. I remember the night the Korean airliner was shot down by the Ruskies. I stood here as the guys walked to their aircraft and I shouted at them "get up there and bring one back".' He grinned. 'It sounds funny now, but that's what I said. Bring one back.'

He invited us into the operations room for a cup of coffee. The Australian Ambassador, Sir Neil Currie, was in there clutching a huge wreath. He had travelled down from Tokyo during the night to deliver it to us. The wreath was about six feet high with a card attached: 'In memory of Konstantin

Chernenko, from the people of Australia.' Three US airforce men took it from the Ambassador and loaded it into the hold of our RAAF 707 aircraft. The Commander showed us the operations room. Three or four men sat watching the screens of radar monitors. The Cold War was alive and well.

We said goodbye and boarded the aircraft. We flew north in the dark over the main island of Japan. Dawn broke as we crossed the northern island of Hokkaido. Below us the snow-covered mountains shimmered in the early morning light. A short time later the Captain announced on the intercom: 'We're about to make a bit of airforce history, gentlemen. In a couple of minutes we'll be the first RAAF plane to penetrate Soviet airspace.' There was an air of excitement. The Korean airliner had been shot down nearby. The Captain came down to the cabin. 'Keep an eye down there on those mountains,' he said. 'If you see anything that looks like a telegraph pole with a lighted wick on the end, sing out.' I looked down at a moon landscape: stark, slate-grey, rocky mountains which looked colder than the snow-covered peaks of Hokkaido. I couldn't see any telegraph poles. A few minutes later the pilot made contact with the Soviet air traffic control. Up on the flight deck we could hear a Russian voice on the radio saying 'Come in Aussie. Come in Aussie One'. Everyone relaxed. We flew on across Siberia. It was a calm, clear day. We landed at Moscow's Sheremetyevo Airport at 11 a.m.

I had last been in the Soviet Union in the late 1950s as a student masquerading as a member of the Italian Communist Party. On that occasion I went by train from Italy to attend the 'World Youth and Student Festival for Peace and Friendship' in Moscow. The festival had been widely advertised in the Italian left-wing press. The Communist Party acted as a sort of ticket agency, like Bass. I went to the Communist Party headquarters in Perugia, where I was studying, and arranged a ticket. It cost thirty pounds sterling for the return train fare and three weeks in Moscow.

The train set off from Venice packed with two thousand young Italians, mostly members of the Communist Party, and me. At the Russian border I was hauled off the train by the soldiers and taken to a guard for interrogation. Why did I have a different passport from everyone else? What was an Australian doing on this train from Italy? 'Siberia, Siberia, they'll take you to Siberia,' I could hear my Italian comrades shouting from the doorways of the carriage. For twenty minutes or so I feared they may be right. Then I was released; relieved and slightly shocked. The train set off through the Russian countryside. 'The Russian language is very similar to Italian,' I informed my travelling companions, 'I could understand most of what that officer who took me off the train and interrogated me said.' 'He was speaking Italian,' said the man sitting next to me.

It was a very hot summer and the train was not airconditioned. Instead it was heated at a temperature appropriate for the depths of the Russian winter. Every time the train stopped at a station the passengers struggled to get out and stand on the railway tracks to get some fresh air. We were five days on the train. It remains in my memory as the most uncomfortable journey I have ever made. For most of the young Italian communists it was their first journey to the promised land and they endured the crowded carriages and the heat with stoical good humour.

In Moscow we slept in dormitories in 'tourist hotels'. The thirty-two thousand delegates from one hundred and twenty-six countries were greeted warmly, like welcome pilgrims. We were the first large group of foreigners to visit Moscow since the Revolution. The festival slogan *Mir Droozbá*, meaning peace and friendship, was on everyone's lips—the best, and sometimes only, means of communication at a multilingual event.

The festival was an extravaganza of some proportion, designed to win over or consolidate the hearts and minds of the young delegates. In the three weeks in Moscow we were offered a choice of sixty-two concerts; seventeen festival films; six circuses, including the national circuses of China, Poland and the USSR; twenty theatre performances and four international sporting competitions. The opening ceremony in the Lenin Stadium was a spectacle which rivalled an opening of the Olympic Games. The procession through the streets of Moscow went for nineteen kilometres and lasted four hours.

I suspect most of the delegations were enormously impressed, although some were sceptical. The British delegation, which for some reason comprised a few communists, some bank clerks on annual leave, and groups from the Young Conservatives and the League of Empire Loyalists, remained unconvinced. A young Englishwoman who stood on the steps of the Lenin Mausoleum and announced to the crowd below 'I am a capitalist' was treated with grave suspicion by the authorities and tolerant good humour by members of the crowd.

I went to the Bolshoi Ballet, the Lenin Museum and Mausoleum, rode in an open jeep in the procession through the streets of Moscow, and attended a spectacular ball in the Kremlin. I claimed proudly to have been the first Australian to have attended an audience with the Pope, and a ball in the Kremlin in the one year. I became lost on the circle line of the Moscow Underground, going round and round for three hours not knowing where to get off. I was finally rescued by a French-speaking Russian girl. Out of relief and gratitude I fell instantly in love. We went boating on a lake and explored the centre of Moscow together. She visited me in a hospital where I spent two days with bronchitis in the care of a hearty woman doctor who 'cured' me with vigorous thumps on the back. *Mir Droozba.*

In spite of these freedoms, Moscow in the late 1950s was heavy with the atmosphere of a totalitarian system. Stalin was dead but the 'ism' lingered on. His mantle was passed on to a series of lesser lights: less brutal, less paranoid, less feared; but administrators of the same system. Only Krushchev stood out from this dull lot as a man with a sharp tongue, Thespian flair and the courage to reveal and denounce the worst excesses of Stalin's reign.

Twenty-five years later Konstantin Ustinovich Chernenko assumed the roles of Chairman of the Supreme Soviet of the USSR, General Secretary of the Soviet Communist Party and Chairman of the Soviet Defence Council. Chernenko had followed a career which seemed to have few highlights. A man of bureaucratic bent, he had progressed slowly upwards through the hierarchical structure of the Russian Communist Party. History and experience suggest that he would have had little appreciation of the need for the cataclysmic reforms about to be introduced by his successor. His place in history is as the last of the Soviet *ancien regime*: a dull caretaker figure with few particularly memorable qualities. Chernenko died in Moscow on 10 March 1985.

On that evening in Canberra, government ministers were having an informal dinner at the Nineteenth Hole restaurant. It was a quiet low-key affair, celebrating the second anniversary of the Hawke Government. The news of Chernenko's death was brought to the Prime Minister halfway through the meal. 'Chernenko's dead,' he announced in a matter of fact tone. 'That will make things interesting.' He resumed eating. There was a brief discussion about possible successors. Nobody had a firm view, or an accurate one. Bob Hawke said, 'Someone will have to represent Australia at the funeral.' He looked up and down the table. There was not much enthusiasm for a trip to Moscow. I thought about it for a few minutes. It was more than twenty years since I'd been there. I said that I would go.

The arrangements were made quickly the following morning. There were no international commercial flights which would get to Moscow in time for the funeral. It was decided that I should travel in the Prime Minister's RAAF plane. Hurried arrangements were made about travel documents. A small party of officials was assembled. I phoned my wife in Melbourne and raced into Canberra's Civic Centre to buy some warm socks and singlets. Bob Hawke lent me his fur hat. A curfew at Narita and other commercial airports in Japan meant that the plane could not land to refuel during the night. We waited for permission to land at a United States military base in Japan. When this arrived, we set off from Sydney in the early evening. There were five passengers and a RAAF crew of nineteen. The small group of passengers comprised an officer from the Foreign Affairs Department; an officer from the Prime Minister's Department; the Commonwealth Protocol Officer, John Chessels; my private secretary, Philip Clark, and myself.

Chessels, an abrasive and flamboyant character with a strong sense of the ridiculous, was to be the life and near death of the party. 'Minister,' he said as I sat down in the plane, 'on this trip I would like you to call me "Wingco"—short for Wing-Commander. I will call you "Excellency". It will be a long flight. I suggest you begin with a drink.' At Moscow Airport the tarmac was lined with the jets of many national leaders. The Australian Ambassador and the Soviet Deputy Trade Minister, Mr Smelyakov, were there to meet us. I was bundled hastily into a black limousine. Chernenko was lying in state and it was expected that I should visit him before the body was removed for the funeral. The rest of the party and the wreath were left at the aircraft to follow later on.

We slithered at high speed along the snow-covered road into Moscow. I was taken into a palatial old building. Inside the door the interpreter whispered 'Where are you from?' 'Australia,' I said. 'Do you have a wreath?' 'No wreath,' I replied. He said something to a couple of men in military uniform, who quickly disappeared down a corridor. Within a minute or so they re-emerged with a huge wreath. It had a black-edged card with 'Australia' written on it. The wreath was given to two military guards dressed in leather greatcoats, high boots and large fur hats. They looked about seven feet tall. The interpreter hissed 'Follow'. The two giants carrying the wreath set off on a slow Russian goose step down a passageway. I followed.

The small procession entered the hall where the body was lying in state. 'Stand here,' said the interpreter. The two guards moved forward and placed the wreath at the foot of the bier. I looked up. Chernenko was lying on a sloping, raised platform with his head at a level higher than his feet. His feet pointed at the place where I was standing. The arrangement of the body made him look very big. I was conscious of a grey head and a broad, flat face with wide, flared nostrils. I stood for a minute or so. Then I heard the sound of more goosestepping soldiers. I turned my head. President Mitterrand of France entered the room in a similar little procession. The soldiers stopped. Mitterrand bowed gravely at the corpse and then at me. He did not smile. I bowed back. 'Come,' said the interpreter. Our procession marched slowly back to the entrance of the building. The interpreter whispered, 'You have come a long way. You have an excuse. He has no excuse. The French, they are always late. It is a disgrace.'

At the Australian Ambassador's residence we had a quick sandwich and coffee before heading off for the funeral. Red Square was crowded with people behind barriers and in temporary stands. Soldiers, with arms linked, surrounded an empty space in the centre of the Square. It was four degrees centigrade—a warm day in Russian terms. I was ushered into a standing-room enclave directly in front of the Lenin Mausoleum. I looked around. There were many familiar faces from international television news. I recognised amongst others: Imelda Marcos; Yasser Arafat; Brian Mulroney, the

Prime Minister of Canada; Neil Kinnock; Margaret Thatcher; Willi Brandt and Gandhi—all jammed in a small enclosure. Behind us on the top of the mausoleum there was a group of men in the uniforms of high-ranking officers of the Soviet Army and Navy. They looked old. Flanked by the military brass there were a handful of men in civilian clothes: grey fur coats and felt hats.

In the VIP enclosure everyone seemed to be gossiping. I found myself standing next to the United States Secretary of State, George Shultz. Someone tapped me on the shoulder. I turned round and confronted a man who looked like a genial licensed grocer from an Australian country town. 'Excuse me,' he said in the lilting accent of the Indian subcontinent, 'I believe you are from Australia. I am General Zia. We are very pleased and surprised with the success of our Pakistan cricket team in Melbourne.' 'We were surprised too,' I said. 'Ah,' he said, 'It is very good. Tell me, how is Bob Hawke?' 'Do you know Bob Hawke?' I asked. 'No, as a matter of fact I have never met him, but I have seen him on television.' He seemed affable and friendly. I pinched myself. Is this the man, I wondered, who keeps his political opponents in gaol and sometimes has them executed. I supposed that answer was 'Yes' and that he was a follower of a time-honoured tradition in the politics of that country.

The crowd suddenly became still and silent. The funeral ceremony was about to begin. Then, at the far end of Red Square, there was a movement in the crowd and a murmur of sound. I craned forward to see what was happening. I saw three Australian officials pushing their way through the crowd with the wreath we had picked up in Japan. There was an eerie silence as they shuffled round the edge of the square and handed the wreath over to Soviet officials. The silence was broken by the sound of brass bands and the rumble of heavy-armoured vehicles. The procession had begun. There were regiments of slow marching, goosestepping Russian soldiers, armoured vehicles and trucks loaded with big rockets. 'I think,' George Shultz whispered, 'I've seen this stuff on television.'

My concentration on the procession was interrupted by the arrival next to us of another man. A tall Svengali-like figure, he was introduced as Shahabzada Yakub Khan, the Foreign Minister of Pakistan. A survivor in Pakistani politics, he seemed very excited. 'I've met this new man Gorbachev; their new leader,' he said breathlessly. 'What's he like,' asked Shultz. 'I tell you,' said Yakub Khan, 'he's a tough baby. He told me to tell you, that if you don't lay off in Nicaragua he's going to put the heat on us in Pakistan.' General Zia grimaced. George Shultz nodded his head. 'Sounds tough,' he said.

The procession wound its way out of the square. There was a brief and pregnant silence. People turned to look at the podium on the top of the mausoleum. A man stepped forward to the microphone and began to speak. 'That's Gorbachev,' whispered Shultz. 'I wish I understood what he was talking about.' To me it didn't seem to matter so much. I listened carefully without understanding any of the words. This, I thought, is a good speech, fluent, relaxed, authoritative. The crowd listened in total silence. One sensed a significant new presence on the international stage.

Gorbachev finished his speech. Someone else spoke briefly. People began to shuffle and talk, the funeral was over. We filed past the gap in the Kremlin wall where Chernenko's body was to be entombed. Already he seemed irrelevant. 'Quick,' said the Australian Ambassador, 'we have to go and meet the new leadership.' It was a few minutes walk to the Grand Kremlin Palace. At the entrance to the palace an armed guard said in English, 'Only two representatives from each country.' 'We're from Australia,' said Chessels. 'We have five.' The group pushed through the door past the dumbfounded guards. We joined a long queue on a stone staircase heading up to a large reception room. We filed round the perimeter of the room to the point where Members of the Soviet Politburo were standing. We shook hands with Prime Minister Litvinov and with Gorbachev. 'You've come a long way,' Gorbachev said with a smile. 'Is that why you have five representatives instead of two?' 'We have come a long way,' I said. He smiled again. 'Good luck,' he said in English.

In the evening we went to a restaurant in the centre of Moscow. It was a jolly place with lively music, a boisterous crowd and a number of women who seemed to specialise in caressing the customers. For a while we felt out of it all until we got the message that all the patrons were drunk. I remember a large and comprehensive menu of which only one item was actually available: roast chicken.

I had a meeting with Mr Smelyakov, the Deputy Minister for Foreign Trade. He received me in a boardroom in a large ubiquitous civil service building. I presented him with a letter from the Australian Trade Minister, John Dawkins, addressed to his boss, the Soviet Trade Minister, Mr Potolichev. I expressed regrets at the death of Comrade Chernenko. Mr Smelyakov had been Deputy Minister for Foreign Trade for many years. He put the letter in his pocket and dismissed my regrets with a wave of his hand. 'These things happen,' he said. He'd seen it all before. He seemed a weary man. He asked what did Australians think of Russian tractors. I mentioned some technical and maintenance problems. 'Perhaps,' he said, 'these could be fixed, and Australia would buy more.' I said Australia would like to help to reduce the trade imbalance between the two countries. He gave a wan smile: 'It's getting better. It used to be three hundred to one in your favour; now it's only thirty to one. Perhaps in twenty years time . . . '

There was no more official business to be conducted. In the afternoon the Australian Ambassador took us to visit the old Kolomenshoz Monastery and Church in a wooded park on the outskirts of Moscow. The church was richly furnished with the trappings, candles and gold-coated icons of the Russian Orthodox Church. A few old people sat quietly in the pews. Later we walked in Red Square looking at the Kremlin walls, the tower allegedly used by Peter the Great as a viewing point from which to watch executions in the square below, and the sixteenth century onion-domed cathedral of St Basil the Blessed standing at the end of the square. In a *beriozka*, a 'hard currency' shop exclusive to foreigners, we thumbed through the racks of classical LP records and browsed among the shelves of art books: all well produced and extraordinarily cheap.

The following day we flew to Leningrad. We arrived early at Moscow Airport for the Aeroflot flight and there was a crowd of milling passengers in the departure lounge. Our group of six people was instructed to wait while the other passengers boarded the aircraft. Then we walked out to the plane. It was full and we were told to wait on the tarmac. Two Russian officials went on board and a couple of minutes later six Russian passengers were bundled down the steps of the plane. We were taken on board and seated in their places. As the plane taxied to the runway we could see them standing in an unhappy huddle on the edge of the tarmac.

In October 1941 German General Jodl issued a directive on behalf of the German Supreme Command: 'We must not accept the capitulation of Leningrad. It must be turned into ruins by artillery fire and air raids.' Fortunately for Leningrad, and mankind, that didn't quite happen. For months on end the city withstood a siege in which the defending troops and the population suffered constant bombardment, freezing cold and starvation. As our plane began to descend into Leningrad the captain announced on the intercom, 'You are now approaching the city of heroes'. The announcement was followed by the playing of martial music. Within half an hour of leaving the airport, we stopped at a huge monument and underground museum displaying relics of the siege of Leningrad.

The monument marked the spot where the German infantry was stopped in hand-to-hand fighting by the Russian defenders. It was about ten minutes away from the centre of the city.

We were provided with an Intourist guide and interpreter. Her name was Ludmilla. A stout, strongly built woman, she was one of those people who induces an apprehension of physical threat. Her stern gaze transformed a disparate group of six Australians into a well-disciplined platoon. Stragglers were rounded up, sceptical questions were brushed aside, her frosty glare reduced inattentive chatterers to silence. Even Chessels seemed subdued. Ludmilla had plenty to show us and plenty to talk about. She knew her stuff. Many of the historic buildings and old streets of St Petersburg had survived the siege. She pointed out the street which had provided the setting for Dostoevsky's novel *Crime and Punishment*. She took us to the Smolney Institute; a handsome building which had once been a girls academy for young ladies of the nineteenth century upper class. Now it was a museum of the Revolution. She showed us the famous buildings of old St Petersburg: the Winter Palace, the Smolney Convent Church and the Hermitage.

At the Hermitage we peered through the gloomy light at the magnificent collection of paintings. Someone queried the poor lighting. Ludmilla said we were lucky to see the paintings at all, they could have been destroyed by the Germans. Young Russians who stopped us in the street to talk, or try to purchase our jeans, were sent packing by our guide. We stood and admired the great Neva River and the distant port. Sheets of broken ice floated downstream. In the distance we could see the battlements of the Fortress of St Peter and St Paul: a view almost unchanged since the time of Peter the Great. 'They're Finns,' said Ludmilla dismissively, pointing at a group of inebriated tourists nearby. 'They come across on the ferries at the weekends to get drunk. The liquor is much cheaper in the Soviet Union.'

In the middle of the day we left Ludmilla for an hour while we had lunch in a restaurant recommended by the Australian Ambassador. The restaurant was situated in a high, vaulted hall with a spectacular and colourful leadlight roof. It could have been a church. At each side of the hall there were sections with an ordinary low roof from which the glassed roof was not visible. The tables in the central atrium of the restaurant were all occupied. The Ambassador insisted that the head waiter give us a table in the centre of the hall. The head waiter pointed out that there were no free tables. The Ambassador suggested that some people be asked to move so that 'the Minister from Australia' could see the glassed roof. Chessels, temporarily liberated from the supervision of Ludmilla, intervened. 'I think, the Minister would be content to sit at a side table. He hasn't come all this way to be stuffed around with bureaucratic arguments.' There was a chilly silence. I said, 'I don't want to make a fuss.' Chessels beamed triumphantly. 'See,' he said. 'I told you so. He doesn't want to be stuffed around.' We sat at a side table.

We said goodbye to Ludmilla at the Intourist office. She shook hands vigorously with each of us. She smiled happily. 'See,' she said. 'I give you very good day. I show you many things. You understand Russia better now.' We talked about her on the plane back to Moscow. Strangely, everyone agreed that she was 'a good sort': tough, efficient, no nonsense. We even decided she had a sense of humour, and the joke was on us.

The day we left Russia we went with staff from the embassy and trade commission for lunch at the Rosskaya restaurant in a little village in the woods outside of Moscow. Snow was falling, and thick on the ground. The poplar trees stood still and leafless. The houses in the village and the restaurant were made of logs. We pulled up at the restaurant in a cavalcade of five cars. The restaurant was warmed by a log fire. There was plenty to eat: sausages and roast chicken, potatoes, cabbage, thick soup. We drank vodka and wine: sobriety rapidly eluded us all: a group of Australians relaxing in the heart of Russia.

We left the restaurant in dribs and drabs. I climbed into the car. One of the officials travelling with us was the last to leave, he staggered out of the restaurant and started to get into my car. Chessels emerged from the snow with his greatcoat, fur hat and beard bristling with snow. He looked like Ivan the Terrible. 'Get out of there you fucking idiot,' he shouted. 'That's the Minister's car. You're in car five. Why don't you wake up to yourself, you dopey bureaucratic bastard?' The official closed the door and skulked off to car five. We drove out of the village, and through the snow-covered countryside. 'After all,' I thought to myself, 'Chessels is the Protocol Officer. I suppose that's what they do.'

At the airport Mr Smelyakov, the Deputy Foreign Trade Minister, was waiting with a group of Russian officials to say goodbye. As we walked into the lounge he clicked his fingers and a waiter appeared with a tray of drinks. There was no choice: it was brandy in large tumblers. Smelyakov handed the drinks around. *Skol*, he said as we drank. Through an interpreter Smelyakov explained that now he would like to propose a toast. The glasses were refilled. He raised his glass: 'To peace and friendship between Australia and the Soviet Union. *Mir Droozba.*' We drank to that.

We staggered out to the plane and took our seats. The steward came up to us with a tray of drinks. 'I've prepared some Bloody Marys for you,' he said. 'The Russians gave us a couple of cases of vodka for the trip home.' I protested. He looked disappointed. 'Just one for the road,' he suggested. Damn Russians, I thought. It's all Lenin's fault. Why can't they keep their system, their hospitality and their vodka in Russia?

On the plane I tried to think it all through, but my brain wasn't working very well; maybe not at all. Warm but moody people in a cold grey country. Tough people: people whose glimpses of the good life had been few and far between. They'd been celebrating the fortieth anniversary of the victory over fascism. Chernenko had made his last speech about it. Nobody seemed in a celebratory mood. From Peter the Great through to Chernenko one suspected that life for the average Russian had been much the same. I remember the crowd listening intently to Gorbachev's speech at the funeral. Perhaps this time it would be different.

Reagan's
America: 1987

Dave Packard took his hearing aid out and planted it on the tablecloth in the middle of the lunch table. It seemed a strange thing to do, but he said it sometimes worked better that way. I was his guest for lunch. I thought that the man who was co-founder of Hewlett-Packard, one of America's great high-tech companies, probably knew what he was doing. In a way, however, it made me slightly ill at ease. He was very deaf. I didn't know whether to shout at the object in the centre of the table or at Packard.

Packard was a tall and fit-looking man. I guessed he must have been in his early seventies. We were at the headquarters of Hewlett-Packard in Cuportino, close to Silicon Valley on the outskirts of San Francisco. He and his partner, Hewlett, had begun the business in the late 1930s in the garage at the rear of a house not far from where we were having lunch. It had begun as a company producing high quality electrical measuring equipment. By the time it moved into the computer business in 1965, it was a business with a good culture; a commitment to quality and doing things well. So it started in computing with a big advantage. The garage in Palo Alto where it all began is classified as an historic monument. Americans have a strong sense of the history of technology and innovation. They've been good at it.

Packard told us some stories about the history of the business. Now in 1987 it was having difficult times in some of its divisions. In Japan there had been some problems in manufacturing. These things were related to management and the overall issue of competitiveness. They were not insurmountable problems, but it became pretty clear, that management didn't have their act together. Richard Newton, a Professor of Electrical Engineering and Computer Studies, and an Australian, told us that in the early 80s their best students had been Japanese. More recently their best students tended to be Korean. The Koreans, and to a lesser extent the Japanese, were more interested in the research being done at the university than American industry. 'Nowadays,' he said, 'they come here and recruit our best students the moment they graduate.' American industry had lost its appreciation of the importance of being at the cutting edge of technology. He thought it didn't augur well for the future.

At Stanford we negotiated successfully about bringing home one of their best 'artificial intelligence' researchers, an Australian, Dr Michael Georgeff. At the evening investment presentation for West Coast venture capitalists there was a fair degree of goodwill about investing in Australia. The problem, people kept telling me, was that small Australian firms wanted the money, but didn't want to give away any share in controlling the business. That was the experience of a number of those present. If I could solve this problem, things would be much better. Another Australian who introduced himself to me was also from the University of California and ran an organisation called 'The Centre for the Study of Silicon Valley'. He said Silicon Valley had lost a lot of its glamour, but it was still a Mecca for politicians and business-tourists from underdeveloped countries. They visited in busloads. It seemed many of them thought it could be copied in their own countries.

After a day in San Francisco we left at 7.00 a.m. the following day and flew to Los Angeles. I was still jet-lagged from the Sydney to San Francisco trip. From Los Angeles

Airport we flew by helicopter to the headquarters of Rockwell on the other side of the city. We landed on the roof of the building and went down some stairs to an executive room for a briefing. The helicopter trip woke me up and I felt capable of a ten-minute discussion without dozing off. Rockwell was a large company with diverse interests in electronics, aerospace and high-tech gadgetry. In Australia they had several businesses, but their main interest was weapons systems for submarines. A lot of their business was defence related. There was talk in the United States about cuts in the huge defence budget and the Rockwell people sensed that a share of their business might be slipping away from them. They also worked as a subcontractor on civil aircraft with Boeing and we were told this was also a demanding business to be in. A black guy called Earl Washington, who dealt a lot with Boeing, said you had to deal carefully with a company that size. 'When you walk into a room with a six-hundred-pound gorilla, you let him sit down first,' Washington said. Ken Black, the Chief Executive of Rockwell who I'd met in Australia, was in Dallas. They said he wanted to talk to me and they'd arranged a video conference in a small theatrette. I sat in the theatrette and talked to Ken Black in Dallas. It was new technology at the time and they were pleased with the demonstration.

We flew to Washington the same afternoon and checked into a stylish hotel called the Madison. Our rooms were on the fourth floor and the whole of the second and third floors were occupied by a South American dictator and his staff. The United States Government was propping up his regime and he was in Washington for talks with the State Department and presidential advisers. Ronald Reagan was one of the few people in the world who seemed to approve of him. There were security agents in the hotel passages, the foyer and the elevators; and sometimes guard dogs. Every now and then a cavalcade of black limousines swept up to the front of the hotel with sirens wailing. We had no idea what was going on, so my wife approached a well-dressed man standing in the foyer and asked him what was happening. It was Caspar Weinberger, the Secretary of State for Defence, who explained it all to her while his bodyguards hovered nearby.

After a briefing at the Australian Embassy, I went to see Dr Bruce Merryfield, the Assistant Secretary for Productivity, Technology and Innovation in the United States Department of Commerce. Dr Merryfield had a longstanding concern about America slipping behind Japan, and to a lesser extent Europe, in technological leadership. It seemed that the Reagan administration showed little concern about this issue. They believed that in a 'free market' these problems would take care of themselves. Merryfield had been trying to get a handful of American companies to collaborate in research and development of semiconductor technology. He'd put together the elements of a consortium called 'Semitech' to enable the companies to work together, but his efforts were inhibited by US Anti-Trust legislation. He wanted an anti-trust law exemption for 'Semitech', but received little support from the administration. He was depressed about this but persistent. Some time after our visit he succeeded and slowly the American industry began to compete with Japan again. But at the time we left him, he was far from sanguine about a successful outcome from his efforts.

Mr Robert Ortner, the Under Secretary for Commerce, gave us a rundown on the economic situation in the United States. He then came with us to meet the new Secretary for Commerce, William Verity. It was Mr Verity's first day in office and his first appointment was with me. We introduced ourselves. He pointed at Mr Ortner and asked who he was, so I had the pleasure of introducing the Under Secretary to his new boss. Mr Verity had been appointed by the President, who was a personal friend. Verity made no pretence of understanding much of what his job as Secretary of State for Commerce involved. He thought his first task would be to get the new Trade Bill accepted by the President. A former Chairman of Armco Steel Corporation, he told us he'd been to Australia in the 1970s to investigate the possibility of establishing a steel mill at Jervis Bay. He'd met Prime Minister Whitlam and 'Mr Hawks', who was then President of the ACTU, and talked to them about industrial relations in Australia—an issue which preoccupied potential foreign investors at the time. He showed us his new office. The previous Secretary of State for Commerce, Malcolm Baldridge, had been killed in a horseriding accident at a rodeo. Baldridge, Verity told us, had kept a wooden horse in his office for recreation and used to lasso the furniture for practice. He had been known to lasso visitors in their chairs. Verity disclaimed the possibilities of any eccentricities in the office under his administration. He wanted to improve trade relations with Russia, and expressed concern about the level of imports into the United States.

I wished him luck with his new job and headed off to the Stanford Research Institute for a presentation on 'Comparative assessments of strategies for competitiveness', which embraced a critique of the contribution of business schools to American competitiveness. It was said that the better companies in the United States were ignoring the business schools and concentrating more and more on training their own people. Business schools had produced too many paper shufflers and not enough managers. Only in some parts of the United States where there were progressive State governments were attempts being made to address the real issues. Massachusetts had been such an example, Colorado another. In 1987 North Carolina seemed to be the most innovative in its policies and, as a result, firms were moving to that State, which was developing a critical mass of advanced industries.

We made the rounds of Congress, meeting with a senator and three congressmen. They were members of the Congressional Committee on Competitiveness. They talked about the new Trade Bill which would enable the United States to introduce sanctions against Japan, if that became necessary. We were told that a senior official of MITI in Japan had said that the United States didn't produce anything the Japanese wanted to buy. This upset the Americans. The senator thought that there was a need for a new business tax package which could perhaps be financed by a new tax on imported oil. Others thought there was just a need to breathe fire into United States business and harden the administration of laws to encourage competition. The main thing was to put pressure on Japan and 'to compete' with its industrial might. The contrast between the politicians' attitudes and practitioners', like Dr Merryfield, was quite stark. The politicians thought there was a need for a bit of bluster at home and abroad. Dr Merryfield thought the challenge was about being at the forefront of technology.

At Washington's Georgetown University, Professor Bill Niskanin, an economic adviser to the President, thought Ronald Reagan and Margaret Thatcher had the right ideas. He was a ventriloquist type who fed the President lines and the author of a book on the burden of government regulations. These regulations, he suggested, were probably the main problem. I wondered if that was why Japan and Germany were so successful. Didn't they have any regulations? Georgetown University is financially well endowed and the students looked as if they came from privileged socioeconomic backgrounds. As we left the campus and walked through the car park, we ran into an Australian film crew which was travelling with me and making a film called *Australia, Overseas and Undersold*. 'Spike' the cameraman had been looking around the university. 'What do they learn here?' he asked. 'How to drive a BMW?'

Every day was crammed with appointments. Cars rushed us from one place to the next: America seemed like the inside of a limousine. In the evenings there were always compulsory dinners and sometimes obligatory cocktail parties. At one in the Library of Congress, a man went 'psst' at me from behind a stack. He was from the French space company, Arianne, and he wanted to tell me about Australia's European legacy and the dangers of having rockets launched by interloping Chinese. Sentiment, he suggested, was more important than price. At a dinner at the Australian Ambassador's residence, the Ambassador had skilfully rounded up some of the usual Washington suspects: a man from the National Association of Manufacturers, the President of the National Academy of Engineering, an economist, two people from the International Trade Commission, and a couple who had knowledge of American research and development.

At another dinner, the most notable guest was Mr John Mars of Mars Bar fame.

The dinner was held in a private house and I guessed Mr Mars was there because he had substantial business operations in Australia making confectionery, processed food and dog tucker. Mars was reported to be one of the richest men in America. The evening began coolly because my wife and Mrs Mars were wearing exactly the same dresses made by the Canberra fashion designer Maggie Shepherd, who had a number of shops in America. I felt good about it: the sight of a can of Fosters or a pie or an Australian-made dress in America gives you a buzz. I tried to figure out how many dresses and cans of Fosters would have to be sold to fix up the trade balance which was two to one in America's favour.

Mr Mars told us he liked coming to Australia to fly his plane in the open skies near Albury–Wodonga. He had few complaints about business and it seemed that he ran a tight global operation. He was interested, however, in expanding his company's exports out of Australia. He liked round-the-clock operations and the best technology in his factories because the equipment wore out faster and you replaced it with the latest available. He was a tough and quiet achiever, with the Midas touch of business success. He talked bluntly about the qualities he expected in management which made me recall a previous meeting in Australia when he'd given a 'motivational' talk to a management seminar of company executives. It was a sort of good news–bad news address. He'd begun by saying: 'The first point I want to make is that one-third of you shouldn't be here.' His brother, Spencer Mars, was considered to be much more eccentric. It was said that he'd dedicated himself to producing the perfect chocolate and that he lived in a penthouse on the roof of a chocolate factory. From time to time he descended into the factory to do random quality checks. As the evening wore on we exhausted the topic of the pastimes of the mega-rich and moved on to speculation about the fate of a lost poodle belonging to the wife of the owner of the house.

When we checked out of the Madison Hotel the following day, the man from Arianne Space was loitering in the lobby. Just in case I'd forgotten, he wanted to tell me about Australia's ties with Europe and the strategic dangers of Australia dealing with the Chinese. Australia, he insisted, would be making a mistake if it allowed its satellites to be launched by Chinese rockets.

Boston in 1987 was gaining a reputation as a bit of a high-tech centre, with a number of small innovative companies establishing along Route 128. The Massachusetts State Government had helped with this, encouraging R and D and synergistic business clusters. Boston had prestigious universities and a number of the larger computer companies were in the region. On our first morning in Boston we drove for an hour or two into the countryside to the headquarters of Digital Equipment Corporation, situated in an area of beautiful woodlands. It was 'fall' and the trees looked proud and handsome with their brightly coloured leaves glowing in the pale sunlight. Frank Wroe, the Australian Chief Executive of DEC, was there together with a number of senior managers.

They told us about the company. I said to the Vice-President, Mr Dick Poulsen, that I was there to try to persuade the company to expand its operations in Australia: more R and D and more exports. Poulsen grinned: 'I know that,' he said. 'The only thing that surprises me is that it's taken you so long to get here.' We talked for two hours and later Poulsen made an announcement of increased commitment to Australian R and D and exports. Leaving the place, I felt good about the visit. It seemed promising and the DEC headquarters a place where the action was, because on the way out we passed Rajiv Gandhi on the way in. Going back to Boston, we drove past a large and beautiful stone factory complete with clock tower and a waterwheel resting in a stream which ran under the building. It had been there for nearly 200 years. I was told it used to be a textile mill but was now being used by DEC for assembly of computers.

In the afternoon Dr David Charles, the Secretary of the Industry Department, and I made a sweep into Harvard University. We walked through the grounds enjoying their gracefully ageing charm on our way to separate appointments with three university professors. One wanted to talk about the possibility of a company in which he had shares building an electronics plant in Australia. The others gave us a thoughtful analysis of Reagan Government trade and industry policies. They felt America hadn't got it right; that there was a need for new directions and a new level of intellectual input. There was more talk about the Japanese model. In the evening we were given a dinner at a seafood restaurant by the Massachusetts High-Tech Council. They were mainly boffins and creative people, who looked more like musicians at the Newport Jazz Festival than businessmen, although businessmen they were. My wife kept passing me disconcerting notes: 'Stop making so much fuss about the water spraying on your shirt from the lobster' and 'Oysters make you love longer, claws make you last longer'.

The following morning I sat in a penthouse office in one of the famous Wang towers at Lowell talking to Mr Fred Wang, the Chairman of Wang Corporation. He talked about future directions for the company. In fact, like a number of the other giants of American computing, Wang was to fall on hard times. Mr Wang had been briefed about the corporation's Australian operations and asked about a voice-recognition project developed by a woman at Canberra College, who was working with Wang in Australia. Later he announced three major projects which the corporation would undertake in Australia. At lunchtime I gave an address to the New England–Australia Business Council, a mixture of American high-tech people and Australians working in Boston. Then there were press interviews; a meeting with a senior official of Massachusetts Administration, who told me about strong employment growth in the State; and a final dinner with leaders of some of Boston's new and rapidly growing computer and electronics companies.

From Boston via New York we flew by jet and helicopter to the headquarters of UNISYS at Blue Bell, New Jersey. Again, it was a friendly and positive meeting. At lunch, I told Mr Blumenthal, the Chairman of the company, about the old stone textile mill, which was now a computer factory. Blumenthal had served as a Secretary for Commerce and at the United States Treasury during the Kennedy and Carter Administrations. He said it all brought back memories. In the early 1960s Jack Kennedy had been under pressure in Massachusetts from the textile lobby, and Blumenthal had put together the so-called 'multi-fibre agreement' which provided high protection for the United States and European textile industries. Essentially it was about saving Jack Kennedy from constituency pressures. 'It was supposed to last four years,' he said ruefully. 'And the damn thing is still going.'

From New York we made separate trips by helicopter to General Electric at Fairfield, Connecticut, to IBM's Watson

Laboratories and to Sikorsky Helicopters. At General Electric the Vice-President gave me a taste of the company's perceptions of Australia, which seemed about ten years out of date. Even in the charitable light of retrospect, it couldn't be described as a profitable visit. At IBM we were given a highly professional and fascinating presentation of their view of future developments in computing. It was all lateral think-tank stuff, projecting possible technical outcomes and examining the implications for work, leisure, education and human skills.

At lunch with the Chairman, John Akers, there were no indications that the company was about to run into serious trouble. Big was still beautiful. I thought of all these little companies beavering away in Boston and wondered who would be proved most successful as the future unfolded. At Sikorsky I looked at the Blackhawk helicopters being built for the Australian Forces and took a ride in a flight simulator, enjoying boyish fantasies of modern desert warfare. After a dinner with executives from Sikorsky and United Technologies we flew back to New York in a helicopter, arriving about 10.30 p.m. It was cold and clear, and from the air the 'Big Apple' was a magical fairyland of skyscrapers, bustling canyons and glistening waterways.

In retrospect it was a strange experience to arrive in New York the day of the great 1987 share market crash, with only a vague idea of what had happened and little idea of its implications. New York is a place where issues and people are easily lost. At a breakfast the following morning I spoke at the Asia Society on the topic of 'Australia and the World Economy'. Most of the audience were wondering where the world economy was going and it was a fairly difficult task to persuade them that Australia was part of it. Wall Street was besieged by rumours and panic. Outside the New York Stock Exchange a group of miraculously assembled 1960s hippies had assembled chanting 'jump, jump, jump' to the unhappy inmates of the building.

At lunch the Australian Consul-General in New York had assembled a group of New York businesspeople and bankers. Jim Wolfensohn, a successful Australian merchant banker and financier living in New York, was there, and so was Rupert Murdoch. Murdoch told me his office was besieged by angry lesbians objecting to something published in one of his papers. Not surprisingly, he was more concerned about the stock market crash. He said he was worried about the effects on little people: owners of small parcels of shares. For him it would be difficult, although not disastrous, but Holmes à Court would be in great trouble. But it was early days: everyone was speculating about what it would mean. Nobody was quite sure.

In New York, Harry our driver tried to educate us with a running commentary delivered in a classic New York accent. He liked Madison Avenue. It was 'very elegant' and full of celebrities. Fifth Avenue, well, that was alright, but you saw more celebrities on Madison. Harry came from 'Noo Jersey'. My wife asked him if he'd been born in New Jersey. Harry said 'I wasn't goin to tell you but see'n' you've asked, I was born in Poland and my Dad and Mum came through Ellis Island.' At the weekend Harry recommended a cruise round Manhattan on the 'coicle line'. 'It's very interesting,' he said. And so it turned out, on a sunny Saturday afternoon with an expert and entertaining commentary on the sights of Manhattan. The man with the microphone spiced his commentary with bits of New York gossip about celebrities including Donald Trump and Rupert Murdoch. 'We now,' he said, 'have one of our newspapers owned by a guy called Murdoch. He comes, if you please, from Australia and believe me he makes Vlad the Impaler look like a child's nanny.'

My final appointment in New York was at the hotel with the President of a specialist food company. I was not in America in relation to the food industry but I agreed to talk to him. He brought samples of his products and talked about the food of the future, which would be light in weight and easy to carry or transport by air. He thought he might manufacture in Australia and export to Asia. My head was already cluttered with information about likely developments in the computing industry and possible scenarios about the way people might live in the future. The idea of different sorts of foods seemed too much on top of all that. He gave me a can of dehydrated apples and I said I'd think about it. I kept the can of apples and sampled them in my office on a Saturday afternoon two or three years later. They tasted like blotting paper.

A newspaper article on my visit to America reported that I'd told a number of American companies that their 'obligations to Australia were no longer satisfied by an annual donation to the Seeing-Eye Dogs Home'. Thinking about it some years later I found it hard to believe that I'd said that: but I might have. I think I might have said it because I believed it. The same article said that, 'Corporate leaders were concerned US multinationals may have acquired a somewhat odious reputation in Australia as greedy exploiters who repatriated every dollar the system would allow. They realised times had changed—Australia now had a more assertive government with a balance of trade problem more serious than their own.'

It required a little assertiveness. The Australian Government of the 80s had a big task in restructuring the Australian economy, and trying to shift it from one predominantly dependent on raw materials, to one in which other industries would play a significant role in export earnings. It was a story of 'woodchips and microchips'. Paul Keating had illustrated the problem with a rhetorical question—'How many bags of wheat do you have to export to pay for an imported computer?' Australia also needed to improve the technical sophistication of its manufacturing and services sectors. This required the development of 'critical mass' in computing and telecommunications skills, investment in research and development, and increased capacity to export.

In trying to deal with these problems Australia was stuck with its history as a raw material producer with a manufacturing culture content to rely on technical 'goodies' imported from the United States, Europe and Japan. Some people thought it could be done by the government spending massive sums on subsidies and incentives to Australian companies. But computing and telecommunications were already global industries, Australia had to find its niche in the international arena. Enlisting the collaboration of the multinationals seemed a good place to start, particularly in America where we had a large trade deficit.

Before I went to America a friend who'd spent a lifetime in the computing industry gave me a warning. 'They don't know much about Australia and they think we're technologically primitive. If you tell them you're from Australia they look at you to see if you've got a bone through your nose.' In fact, with one or two exceptions, all the corporations we visited gave serious presentations about their industry, and were prepared for thoughtful discussions about the role of their Australian subsidiaries in Australia and the Asia–Pacific. Americans, on these visits, turned out to be an hospitable and friendly bunch. The art is to engage their attention. With these global corporations it was less difficult: the legendary insularity of Americans was hardly in evidence.

Christopher Columbus is said to have discovered America, and remains one of the most famous explorers in the history books. In the late 1980s—the era of Ronald Reagan—discovering and understanding America had become harder than ever. The country seemed like a giant teenager, all legs and arms and aspirations, and no coordination. It was too big, too rich, too diverse to get any sense of focus. Perhaps, I thought, it's just a huge magic pudding from which you could only take a small slice at a time.

In 1987 America seemed to have lost some of the confidence which so impressed me on my first visit nearly a decade before. A number of its manufacturing giants seemed to be in trouble, the culture of quick money through paper shuffling had reached its heights and the things which had made America great didn't seem to be working. The President was a treasured icon, trotted out to articulate jumbled but reassuring platitudes, rather than giving leadership on issues which Americans worried about, but didn't quite know how to deal with. In Washington it was hard to get any sense of who was responsible for what. All the competencies were there, with nobody to bring them together.

Americans had become used to the idea of being the world's most powerful nation, the place where everybody wanted to live and where wealth and individual freedom were regarded as the theoretical birthright of every citizen. In fact this birthright was seriously flawed by a growing discrepancy between conspicuous wealth and poverty. Notions of individual freedom and citizens' rights had produced a highly litigious society, and a tendency to ignore the rules of convenience which help make day-to-day life work smoothly. It's a trivial example, but travelling on American airlines I watched with fascination when the senior flight attendant asked passengers to fasten their seat belts. Not infrequently passengers took this as an invitation to stand up and get something out of a luggage rack or talk to another passenger. It was as if to say 'this is my right as an American. If anything happens I'll sue the airline.'

It was the idea that suddenly they were not the best at everything which bothered Americans most and produced Japan as a convenient scapegoat. Industrialists, businesspeople, politicians and taxidrivers talked about Japan; about Japanese buying cherished American institutions, building cars in America, producing better technology. Somehow it had to be the fault of the Japanese, because American patriotism uncritically embraced the idea that everything Americans did was the best.

The extent to which Americans were bothered about Japan was all the more evident because Americans are not naturally interested in the success or shortcomings of other countries. Australians perhaps notice the legendary insularity of Americans more than most because we happen to come from the Asia–Pacific region. In 1987 insularity and worldly indifference were understandable in a country of the size and diversity of the United States. It was a world in itself without any compelling need for its citizens to worry about other countries. Japan was a worry because its success reflected on America's view of itself, and upset American self-esteem. But hardly anywhere in America did you have a sense that Americans had any view about Asia. In spite of spectacular growth and developments in various Asian countries, Americans didn't seem to regard it as significant or as a place they ought to think about. If they talked about it at all, it was as a homogeneous continent in which the subtleties, the differences and the excitement were matters of indifference to the future of the United States. To have an 'Asia Society' was sufficient recognition, an acknowledgment adequate enough in the peculiar isolationism of Reagan's America in the aftermath of the Vietnam War.

Perhaps it would all change with one of those paradigm shifts which occurs from time to time in the political history of the United States: the sort of change represented by a Marshall Plan, 'A New Deal' or a more subtle and sophisticated bout of international diplomacy. America's idea of itself, and its destiny, was still blinking away like a navigation light on a distant hill. The talents, the energy and the creativeness were still there in abundance. In 1987 the light seemed a bit obscured by a mist of uncertainty. It would, no doubt, take time to go away.

To the Shunchang Station: 1988

It was a Sunday, 11 December 1988, and I had to catch a plane to Fuzhou on the South Central coast of China. My wife phoned me at my Hong Kong hotel shortly before I left for the airport. She said that she hoped I missed her and not to get AIDS. Of course I missed her, although circumstances made it difficult: I didn't get AIDS, but I fell in love with the interpreter. It's something which can easily happen. In a place like China you can become totally reliant on an interpreter. So the relationship involves power and dependence which is hard to adjust to.

Not surprisingly, the plane to Fuzhou was full of Chinese. Most of them had special travel documents different from mine. They were Taiwanese businessmen visiting the mainland where they had investments and trading operations. Australia at the time was under constant pressure from the Chinese Government to limit its relationship with Taiwan. The possibility of Qantas flying directly to Taipei was a source of constant and protracted negotiations. We were asked to pretend that we didn't have a strong commercial relationship with Taiwan. Australia was supposed to implement a 'One China Policy', while trade and commerce bubbled along between the 'two Chinas'. Such were the mysteries of the Orient.

At Fuzhou Airport the Secretary General of the Province of Fujian was waiting on the tarmac to greet us. We were ushered into an airport lounge for a short briefing and a cup of tea. I shook hands with dozens of people: 'Nin hao, Nin hao' I kept saying in a dazzling display of Chinese language skills. We sat down in the familiar Chinese formation—chairs arranged around three sides of the room with two chairs on the fourth side for the most important people. On this occasion they happened to be the Secretary General and myself. He and I exchanged friendly banalities through an interpreter. The audience in the other chairs listened politely. I wished that someone else would say something. Out of politeness or laziness they refrained. We kept talking, which is hard work sometimes.

From the airport we drove for half an hour to a modern glasshouse hotel, built and operated by a Hong Kong investment company. There was a red carpet along the path leading to the entrance of the hotel and the hotel staff were lined up on either side of the carpet. The manager, who came from Hong Kong, stood at the end of the carpet. He was dressed in tails and spoke English with an accent you'd expect from the manager of the London Savoy. He told me the hotel was very comfortable, but that there were some teething problems in training the staff. As we entered the foyer, as if to illustrate his point, a passing waiter dropped a tray of drinks on the marble floor.

We sat round in a large reception room in the hotel. The Vice-Governor of the Province of Fujian was there to meet us. I did not know a lot about Fujian Province. My briefing notes told me that a 'sister State' relationship between Tasmania and Fujian had been agreed in 1980, but that it had since become inoperative. It seemed lacking in promise as conversational material. I decided to let the Vice-Governor do most of the talking. Waiters flitted in and out with cups of tea and glasses of 7 Up while the Vice-Governor spoke of the warm relations between Australia and China. He said that the cement plant, to be opened the following morning, was a symbol of the good relations between the two countries. The Australian company, BHP Engineering, had built it well and it would produce six hundred and seventy thousand tonnes of cement a year for the Chinese construction industry. Unfortunately we would have to travel for six and a half hours by train to Shunchang, in the mountains, where the cement plant was situated. There would, of course, be a special carriage for the Australian guests. In the meantime I would be welcome to have a quick look around Fuzhou. In turn, I expressed appreciation for the arrangements which had been made and I said that the cement plant would undoubtedly strengthen the relationship between China and Australia.

Fujian Province had, over the years, been a big source of Chinese migration, particularly to South Asia. Historically, the economy of Fujian has been based on maritime industries and along the coast there were some fine natural harbours. The interior of the province was rugged, mountainous and inaccessible. The theory was that as the ports grew into prosperous trading centres, large numbers of the population migrated outwards to other countries. It was the only way to go. More recently the railways, built by the government, had begun to change the nature of the provincial economy. The resources of the interior could now be exploited, industries could be established and people could travel to other parts of China by rail. Fuzhou, a pleasant port city with a population of half a million, sits on the banks of a large river. From 1861 on it had been another Chinese port with a European settlement of French, Dutch and British traders. The railway was now providing it with access to the interior.

China must be a trainspotters' paradise. Some of the old-style carriages and engines reflect the history of European influence. The special carriage in which we travelled to Shunchang evoked the exotic flavour of the Orient Express. My compartment had rich wooden panelling, a large double bed, a heavy wooden desk with a hard upright chair, an early model electric fan and a desk lamp with a bright-pink shade in the shape of a tropical flower. It was uncomfortable, hideous and luxurious in the worst Victorian manner. A Chinese official indicated to me that I should sit in the chair. I did so while the train pulled slowly out of the Fuzhou Railway Station. Then I stood on the chair to see out of the window, the lower half of which was frosted glass. It seemed a silly way to travel.

The official came back ten minutes later to tell me I was required for a briefing in the meeting room at the back of the second reserved carriage. The meeting room had drawn curtains on all the windows. It was furnished with couches, one at the narrow end and two along each side. There was a long, low table in the middle laden with bottles of 7 Up, pots of tea and bowls of oranges. The official party for Fuzhou was sitting round the tables. It included a number of Chinese officials, the Australian Ambassador to China and three representatives of BHP. There was a pretty Chinese woman who interpreted the briefing given by the senior Chinese official. It was eye-glazing stuff, reflecting the Chinese obsession with production figures—so many tonnes of cement, so many kilometres of steel, so many years of man hours and People's Republic effort had gone into the plant. He knew it all backwards. It sounded like a tape-recording of the official journal 'China Reconstructs'. I began to think that if I could remember it all backwards it might be a useful thing to do. Our interpreter reeled off the figures as if in a trance.

Later, when the briefing lapsed into a desultory conversation, she permitted herself a smile. She told me her name was Twee, which is not a Chinese name but it is what I came to call her. She seemed warm, charming, civilised and attractive amongst all the grey-suited cement men. I had a sneaking suspicion she was not turned on by production figures, but she was on duty and kept to her script. There was no frivolity. The train chugged on through the growing gloom of the late afternoon of a Chinese winter. I looked forward to our arrival: somewhere.

Then a nice thing happened, which broke the tedium of the journey. Russ Finemore, the senior BHP man on the train, rummaged in a case and produced a tie. In fact he produced ties for everyone: all the same, green and red stripes on a blue background; the sort of tie you'd buy at a military outfitters in the West End of London. The word 'Shunchang' was embroidered in Chinese characters and English at the bottom right-hand corner of each tie. 'This,' Russ Finemore explained in a formal presentation speech, 'is to celebrate the opening of the Shunchang Cement Plant.' The Big Australian, I decided, had taken leave of its senses; presenting ties on an ancient train in the remote mountains of China. I thought of mad dogs and Englishmen. But I kept the tie: maybe, I thought, we'll have a reunion some day.

It was about 9.30 p.m. when the train pulled into the station at Shunchang. The place is high in the mountains. It was dark and very cold. Shunchang was in an area closed to foreign tourists. There was a large crowd on the platform and outside the station on the roadway. I thought for a moment that the entire population had turned out to meet us, but on second thoughts I decided they'd turned out to look at us. It was as if we were the first 'round-eyes' they had ever seen. They stood in the cold, staring and pointing. Policemen pushed a way through the crowd to a fleet of old limousines. We were driven to the Foreign Engineers Quarters. The building where we were to spend the night looked like a military barracks.

Zou Jiahu, a State Councillor and Minister for Machine Building and Electronic Industry, was waiting to meet us. He was accompanied by eleven Chinese officials from various ministries in Beijing. Nine months before, I had met Zou Jiahu in Beijing. We had signed a memorandum of understanding providing for the establishment of a joint Australian–

Chinese working group on machinery manufacture. Zou had impeccable credentials. The son of a 'Communist Martyr' executed in the late 1930s, Zou had studied in Russia for six years then worked his way up through the Party and bureaucracy. We went into another reception room and sat down in the Chinese formation. Zou beamed into the empty space in the middle of the surrounding chairs and made a speech of welcome. It was cold and I was tired. Twee interpreted his speech as he reeled off an impressive array of production figures. She translated the figures like a racing commentator at the end of a long and tiring day. I listened and tried to remember some of the figures without much success. I wondered how Twee coped with all the detail: the figures and the technical information.

I thanked Mr Zou and suggested it was time to go to bed. He said there was a reception first and clapped his hands. The doors at the end of the room opened and about twenty young Chinese women entered carrying pots of tea, bottles of 7 Up and trays of cakes. They began to serve the guests. I thought they must have been hand-picked: perhaps by the editor of *Playboy* magazine. They were all exceptionally good looking. I heard a voice behind me say, 'See the one with the yellow shoes. She's got a beautiful arse.' I didn't dare look round. It was a tired and emotional Australian voice. I think it was the voice of the Australian Ambassador.

The following morning we were up at 7.00 a.m. It was a cold, grey day with a pale sun. From the 'Foreign Engineers Quarters' I looked down on the wide swift flowing river, Min Jiang, on which rafts of logs floated down with the current. On the other side of the Foreign Engineers Quarters there were administrative buildings and the silos and glistening steel girders of the cement plant. I was directed over to the plant. Walking past a building I heard a terrible squealing noise which sounded almost human. I was startled by it and looked round anxiously for Twee. Nobody near me seemed to speak English. Then a man said 'Killing pig for cocktail party. It's all OK.' Partly relieved by the explanation, I walked on. A huge red banner on the main building said 'Presence of honoured Australian guests is warmly welcomed'. The plant workers wore grey trousers, fatigue jackets and caps, and were lined up in military formation. The cement plant band played in front of the main building. The music was military in flavour, scratchy in sound but played with enthusiasm.

The opening ceremony took place in the open air, in front of the plant. It was cold and I wore a thick coat and thought of Charles I before his execution. The official party sat on chairs on a raised dais covered with a red carpet. Mr Zou and I each made a speech; the plant was declared open and the crowd, lined up in front of the dais, cheered. Four little girls in traditional colours marched up and presented each member of the official party with a bunch of flowers. Then we had a 'photo opportunity' session. Pictures were taken of the official party, the senior engineers, the construction team, and a massed group of the plant workers.

Twee said: 'I have been instructed to take you on a guided tour of the plant.' We set off on foot across the rough ground, pausing from time to time in front of huge vats or pipes or conveyors or towers. Each time we stopped Twee would say something like, 'This conveyor will carry fifty cubic metres of sand per day which will be discharged into hopper number eight and from there dropped into Vat twelve.' Maybe I was tired and I was certainly cold. I think we'd reached Vat Number fourteen when I asked Twee: 'Do you know the English word "bullshit".' She gave me a curious look. 'Bullsheet,' she said, 'what is "bullsheet"?' I told her that it was a word in English much used in Australia. It meant many things like 'exaggeration' or 'lies' or 'half-truths'. She looked slightly angry. 'It is all true,' she said. 'I know it is true, Twee,' I replied, 'but there is another meaning. It can mean "too much information". I don't want any more production figures, and I won't remember them anyway. To me it doesn't matter.' She smiled. 'Ah this,' she said, 'is the meaning of your bullsheet.' 'Not my bullshit,' I replied, 'your bullshit.' She began to laugh and we started to talk about other things—where she learnt English, her family, her work, Australia.

We headed off to a reception in the administration building. A large red banner at the end of the room said 'Cocktail Party'. I shook hands with many officials and the managers of the plant. No-one seemed to speak English and without Twee interpreting at my side I would have been reduced to sign language. I asked people questions about the weather and the river and the mountains: anything but cement. Some of them told me about the weather and the river and the mountains, and one or two talked about cement. There were to be more speeches. The pig which I had heard squealing in the morning was brought in on a trolley and placed in front of the dais at the end of the room. It had been glazed and its protruding eyes seemed to be studying the reception guests. It seemed to be listening attentively as I made a speech about the cement plant representing a symbol of goodwill between China and Australia. Not only, I said, was it a symbol of goodwill, but it was clearly a very good cement plant. I had seen it all, the figures had been explained to me in detail and I understood how it worked.

I walked back to the Foreign Engineers Headquarters. On the way I met a couple of young Australian engineers who had supervised the building of the plant. They'd been up there in the mountains for months, part of a small Australian team. They were proud of what they'd done and confident of their abilities. The Yanks or the Japanese would have 'thrown a heap of money' at the project and couldn't have built it any better. They made me feel the whole thing was worthwhile. I thought they were Australian pioneers in China.

From Shunchang Station we caught the train back to Fuzhou.

In the crowd on the platform at Shunchang I lost sight of Twee. I wanted to say goodbye, but she was nowhere to be seen. In the train I sat in my little compartment. For a while I put the hard-backed wooden chair on the desk and sat gazing out of the top half of the window. The train line hung precariously to the sides of the mountains. Below the train I could see the Min Jiang River flowing down to the sea and burdened with barges and huge timber rafts. It was all busy: beaver-like. There were quarries gouged out of the sides of the mountains and dams being built on small tributaries of the river. Soon, I thought, there will be huge barges carrying cement down the river to the port. China was building, reconstructing and all those things. I wanted to ask Twee what she thought the point of it all was, as she seemed like the only person who could tell me. But somehow the system had taken her away. I imagined her guiding some more visitors round the cement plant: 'This conveyor will carry . . . '

At Fuzhou there was another reception. It was not particularly different from the others, but there was a surprise. I was just about to leave, when Twee pushed through the crowd of dignitaries full of apologies and explanations. She'd been told to travel in another carriage of the train and that I would like to rest in my compartment. Nothing, I explained, could have been further from the truth. I felt pretty sad as it was time for me to leave to attend a dinner hosted by the Fujian Government. Twee said, 'I came to see you just to say that it has been an honour and a great pleasure to interpret for you.' I said something silly like 'Maybe we'll meet again some time.' I told her I was leaving by car early in the morning for Xiamen in the south of Fujian Province. From there I would be going to Zhangzhou, where I had to visit an Australian–Chinese joint venture textile plant. Perhaps she could come along and explain it all to me. She laughed and said that she knew nothing about textile production. I squeezed her elbow, 'Perhaps then you could come with me and interpret the meaning of life.' 'I'd like to do that,' she said, 'but you understand it is not possible.'

Deep down I understood it was not possible. I had a brief to read on China's 'Coastal Development Strategy', announced earlier in the year by General Secretary Zhou Ziyang. It would be impossible to arrive in Xiamen without at least a rudimentary knowledge of this new strategy, regarded by some as a divergence from traditional socialist principles. Leaders in those Provinces which were not part of the coastal strategy thought that it was a very substantial departure from the ideas of Chairman Mao. It needed to be understood and before I embarked on reading the documents I had to go to a dinner hosted by the Fujian authorities at the plush Lakeside Hotel.

At the dinner there were more speeches. The guests were all government officials and cement men in grey suits. One speaker gave us some anticipated production figures for the cement plant; just in case we hadn't understood. The plant, it was emphasised, was a symbol of the good relationship between China and Australia. I said something of the same kind in my own speech.

BHP hosted a breakfast at 7.00 a.m. It was informal: no figures, just farewells. Then Bing Chen, a Commercial Counsellor at the Australian Embassy in Beijing; Ross Maddock, a consultant on my staff; and I piled into a large, black and rather old car for the trip to Xiamen. I was glad Ross and Bing both spoke Chinese. The driver didn't speak any English at all. In 1988 the road between Fuzhou and Xiamen wasn't very wide and it had a lot of very large potholes. The driver was keen to cover the distance in ten hours and started off at breakneck speed.

I tried to look at the scenery, which somehow reminded me of Italy: wispy pastel-green trees; distant lines of poplars running across the fields and a backdrop of misty-blue mountains. The road, however, distracted me. I spent half the time with my head in my hands as the driver steered headlong towards oncoming trucks; slowing miraculously at the last moment. There was much blaring of the horn as groups of pedestrians, geese and cyclists loomed up in front of the car and parted to let us through. I tried closing my eyes, even sleeping, but was jolted back to consciousness as the car crashed into another pothole and shuddered on its way again. When the car pulled up at the Lu Jiang Hotel in Xiamen I felt as if I'd spent the day in a huge cocktail shaker. I was glad to get out.

'What,' I asked the Mayor of Xiamen at dinner that night, 'is a typical day in the life of a mayor? What, for example, did you do today?' 'At present,' he said, 'there is quite a regular pattern about it all. This morning I began by having breakfast with a group of Taiwanese investors. Later I dealt with some correspondence and routine office matters. Then I had lunch with another group of Taiwanese businessmen. This afternoon I took a party of Taiwanese on an inspection of the housing estate they are building on the far side of the city. Now, I'm having dinner with you.' He smiled and continued, 'Things may get more complex with the new coastal development strategy. But right now the Taiwanese are the big investors here. I have to look after them.'

The Mayor gave me a glossy brochure about Xiamen. It contained many coloured photographs of factories, housing estates and universities. In the text it said: 'Most compatriots from Taiwan, Hong Kong, Macau and abroad love their hometown and their motherland. Inspired by China's open policies, they are all enthusiastically concerned with hometown construction; cordially give their economic cooperation and make investments in their hometown.' Reading it later, I thought it wouldn't be too bad to have the Mayor's problem. There was still, however, room to encourage more investment. Only a month before, officials from the Mayor's office had been in Melbourne and Sydney taking part in 'China Investment Seminars'.

In the morning we were taken on a small ferry to the island of Gulangyu, which lies five to ten minutes offshore from the mainland Xiamen. Gulangyu is a fascinating place. It is an island with meandering cobbled streets, handsome colonial buildings and splendid views. Its fascination lies, however, in its history: reflected in the opulent villas built by Europeans in the nineteenth century. First settled by Europeans in the 1840s, it became within fifty years another example of the country's interface between Chinese and Europeans. There are churches, hospitals, former consulates; the well-provided remnants of a complete European settlement in the Orient. We met with Xiamen 'Special Economic Zone' officials to discuss commercial relations between China and Australia in a charming Italianate mansion, which exuded an atmosphere of high-life diplomacy.

Later we climbed the rock steps to the highest point of the island, from where we could look back to the Chinese mainland or across the straits to the Taiwanese-occupied islands of Matsu and Quemoy. This, I thought to myself as we walked down the hill towards the ferry landing, is a place one could spend a holiday in; uncluttered, elegant, a free environment and plenty of fascinating places to explore. My thoughts were interrupted by a clunking noise as a group of men came towards us along the narrow roadway. As they passed I saw that they were chained together, hands and feet. 'Who are they?' I asked. 'Prisoners' someone said. There was no further explanation.

The textile plant in Zhangzhou was a joint venture between an Australian company, Macquarie Textiles, and the Zhangzhou Textile Industry Corporation. Prime Minister Bob Hawke and the Secretary General of the Chinese Communist Party, Hu Quili, opened it in 1986. The Managing Director of the Australian partner had come to China to meet us. We had lunch in the factory and were shown around the plant. It was another Australian outpost in China.

That night the Mayor of Xiamen and some other officials from the Special Economic Zone came to our hotel for dinner. We were served with a dish called 'drunken prawns'. A large bowl of live prawns were placed in the centre of the table. Brandy was poured over them and then set alight. 'If you listen,' said the Mayor, 'you can hear them screaming.' He'd been very kind during our visit: but that was the remark I remember best.

The following day at lunchtime I found myself speaking at the Australian Chamber of Commerce in the Hong Kong Jockey Club. The purpose of the function was to tell the Hong Kong business community about the Shunchang plant and the visit to Xiamen, and discuss globalisation issues. I couldn't remember all the production figures. I spent most of the time telling them about Australia's new outposts in China: a cement plant and a textile mill—tentative steps into the global economy. They seemed most interested in China. It was December 1988 and at that time they didn't know a great deal about it.

Tradition and reality in the Philippines

The plane from Tokyo landed at Manila Airport at 10.00 p.m. At the end of the aerobridge a smiling Filipino girl hung a lei round the neck of each of the small group of passengers, as we disembarked. Arrows painted on the floor directed us down a long and empty concourse. At the customs barrier nobody seemed to be on duty. We walked straight through into the huge dome-shaped passenger hall.

A cleaner, leaning on a broom, grinned at us and said, 'Welcome to Manila.' There was no-one else around. It seemed strange. After all I was there as a guest of the Philippine Government and the keynote speaker at the ASEAN Science and Technology Conference—the first Australian Minister to be invited. I probably expected a red carpet; at the least, a pink one.

I dropped my bags in the centre of the empty passenger hall, lit a cigarette and sat down to wait. Something had to happen. The cleaner went silently on with his sweeping. Then from a distant part of the concourse I heard a hubbub of voices. I looked up in the direction of the noise. A gaggle of people were running towards me like a crowd in a Jacques Tati film. I recognised the tall, gangling figure and balding head of the Australian Ambassador, the plump, squat figure of the Philippine Secretary of State for Science, and the ubiquitous collection of officials and journalists. Within a minute I was surrounded by a group of excited, breathless people all talking at once; full of warmth, excitement and profuse apologies. They had, it seemed, all been waiting in the VIP lounge, and had somehow managed to lock themselves inside. They had escaped by breaking the lock. This, it was explained, was not a normal occurrence. Would I oblige with a brief press conference to talk about Australia's relations with the Philippines?

The journalists asked me a few desultory questions about Australia, our immigration policy, and the prospects for investment and technology exchange. I recognised the signs. They had their story already: an embarrassing little incident involving politicians. The Philippine Minister hovered nervously in the background. The next morning my photo was to appear on the front page of the Manila newspapers with stories about the 'embarrassing international incident' at Manila Airport. 'Welcome arrangements for Senator Button and his party were fouled up,' one newspaper reported, 'after the welcoming party was inexplicably locked inside the dignitaries' lounge ... Airport police could not explain how the welcoming party got locked inside the lounge.'

The purpose of my visit to Manila was to participate in the Science and Technology Conference and for discussions with other ministers from the countries of the region. But I also wanted to gain a better understanding of the politics and the people of one of Australia's nearest Asian neighbours. I wanted to check out some superficial impressions shared, I suspect, by most Australians. Impressions gained over the years from media reports of typhoons, insurrections, Filipino brides, poverty, corruption, girlie bars, the Marcos regime and its dramatic overthrow, and Cory Aquino and her place in the country's history.

The morning after my arrival I opened the door of my hotel room and discovered two dishevelled looking men asleep on the floor of the outside passage with hand guns lying on the carpet beside them. Still half asleep myself, I hesitated between a retreat into my room or stepping over them and escaping down the passage. Finally I decided on a discreet cough and an overly loud and cheery 'Good morning'. It seemed to work. 'Good morning, Excellency. Security—we security. Keep you safe.' It was the one moment in my time in Manila when I had any real feeling of apprehension and disquiet.

Manila had all the characteristics of a stereotyped Asian city. The climate, traffic snarls, the racial mix, tropical smells, the contrasts of obvious wealth and obvious poverty—collectively and separately these things reminded me of other places. Watching a white-uniformed policeman blowing his whistle and trying to sort out an unruly traffic jam, I began to invent composite names for urban conglomerates in Asia: 'Banmontok' or 'Shangbay'—there were many possible combinations in trying to imagine the quintessential Asian city.

Perhaps it is the limitations of a European culture and tradition which enable the Australian traveller to identify and remember the particular character of cities like Paris, London and New York; but not recall the same sharp impressions of Asian cities. Australians converse about experiences of theatres in London, galleries in Paris, buildings in Rome and Greenwich Village in New York. But discussion on the physical characteristics of Asian cities is usually conducted in superficial generalisations: Singapore is 'clean', Bombay 'dirty', Tokyo 'congested'. Impressions and memories of Asian cities are most influenced by personal experiences: meeting an interesting man or woman in Kuala Lumpur, a taxi ride in Bangkok, a floating restaurant in Hong Kong.

If anything makes Manila different from most other cities in Asia, it is probably the legacy of its long and repressive colonial history. More than three centuries of Spanish colonisation of the Philippines was followed by nearly fifty years of rule by the United States. In the Second World War the Japanese occupied the country. Manila was almost totally destroyed in successive bombardments by the Japanese Navy and then the American Navy. Postwar independence produced a semblance of democracy and in the 1960s a period of strong economic growth. The Philippines was one of the 'Asian Tigers'. Independence also brought a 'special relationship' with the United States and the huge and frequently controversial naval base at Subic Bay. By the 1970s the fledgling democracy had given way to the Marcos regime, sometimes described as a 'kleptocracy' in which the political system was almost entirely based on patronage. The Marcos period impoverished the country and struck a further blow to national morale.

In spite of superficial changes in the public face of Philippine governments, significant power has traditionally been exercised by a system of political bosses and warlord families. Accommodating to the whim of successive regimes, they have advanced family interests ahead of public interest and perpetuated the divisions of very rich and very poor. The present system of congressional government, derived from the United States model, has been manipulated and exploited by the traditional rulers.

During my stay in Manila I was invited to visit a parliamentary session of the Senate. We entered the building through a line of heavily-armed soldiers, and listened to a debate about the shipment of illegal arms seized by the navy near one of the outer islands. The speeches were entertaining and full of innuendo. It was apparent, even to an outside observer, that one of the senators was thought to have financed the arms shipment. The 'in-joke' was that he had been caught out and was embarrassed by the incident. After half an hour or so, the President adjourned the debate and I was invited on to the floor of the Senate to meet the senators. I was received with great courtesy and charm. One senator I met had one leg missing and walked with crutches. Later I was told that he had lost his leg in a car bombing believed to have been instigated by another senator from a rival faction.

The Philippines is a 'victim society': a victim of its past, of other countries, and of its own political and social values. And while the poor are the principal victims, there is a feeling that the whole society is demeaned by the absence of unity and political will to tackle its problems.

As hosts of an international conference, the officials of the Philippine Government could not have been more hospitable. The plenary session of some three hundred delegates and observers from various countries in the region began with a fanfare of trumpets. The Chairman announced that Father Fernandez would pronounce a blessing on the delegates and the conference deliberations, then President Aquino would open the conference. There was a hushed silence while the audience waited for Father Fernandez to appear. But Father Fernandez did not appear. President Aquino studied her shoes, the silence turned into a buzz of conversation. The Chairman obviously wished he was somewhere else. Then a priest, identifying himself as Father Dominic, stood up in the audience and offered his services as a substitute for Father Fernandez. There was a ripple of applause from the audience as he made his way to the platform. He pronounced the blessing and the conference was underway.

Half an hour later, the Ministers from various countries met with President Aquino. The meeting was relaxed and informal. The President talked about the importance of broad-mindedness and the understanding of different points of view. She had recently addressed graduates from the Military College and told them that they should think beyond the narrow confines of a military education. The country had to abandon its habits of allegiances to sectional interests. She cast a spell of courage and philosophic charm. I wondered if it was enough and recalled a remark of Alan Bond, 'The trouble with Aquino is she has no balls.' Not like Marcos who got things done: for a price.

The Chairman of the plenary session at the conference

introduced me to the audience. He announced that Mr John Elliott had kindly agreed to lead the discussion on my paper. I knew only one John Elliott. I had a moment of confused speculation as to why he would come to Manila for this purpose. Then Mr Elliott walked up to the platform. He was from the Caribbean; large and black, and a representative of the United Nations Industrial Development Organisation. I gave my speech. I talked about cooperation in research between Australia and ASEAN. I warned of 'the intense competition and suspicion which exists in some areas between the larger science and technology powers'.

The next day I had an arranged meeting with Dr William Graham, the Science Adviser to President Bush. We talked about the possibility of United States collaboration with the Japanese 'Human Frontiers in Science' program. The words from my speech came back to haunt me. Dr Graham didn't think that would be possible. For him the prospect of collaboration in science with the Japanese did not appeal.

As on every visit of this kind there was an obligatory schedule of commitments: I had lunch with the ASEAN ministers; I visited the impressive Australian Science and Technology display at the exhibition located in the conference centre; I signed a government-to-government agreement on cooperation in Science with the Philippine minister; and I presented him with a package of microchips designed and manufactured by AWA as part of the Australian–Asian cooperation program founded by Australia.

I had dinner with the same ASEAN ministers with whom I had lunched a few hours before. I attended a meeting with the Philippine Board of Investment. The President of the Board and her two advisers were women. They sat on a raised platform like a bench in a Magistrate's Court and seemed equally authoritative. They were a reminder of the extent to which senior executive positions are occupied by women in this most Catholic of countries. The Philippines desperately needs foreign investment, but for the foreign investors, community enthusiasm for it waxes and wanes with changing political and economic circumstances. One suspected that life for the Board of Investment was not easy, but their virtuous performance assured me they were not overcome by adversity.

My 'minder' for the ASEAN conference was a charming woman who handled the arrangements with great efficiency. A public relations consultant, she suffered from the disability of her profession that made it difficult to decide when she was working and when she was just being nice. On one or two occasions, however, my uncertainty was resolved. She took me to hear a band in a hotel restaurant. They were very good and she spoke enthusiastically about the quality of Filipino music. 'They are very poor,' she said, 'and want to play in Australia, but the Unions will not let them.' She also spoke to me at length and with great passion about the overthrow of the Marcos regime. She had been one of 'Cory's crusaders', the group of women who linked arms in the streets, gave flowers to the soldiers and stopped the Marcos regime tanks. She described these incidents as things which had transformed her life. It was as if in those few weeks she had discovered a great cause which would open a new chapter in her country's history; ending corruption, cronyism and disunity which had always been part of her life.

On my second day in Manila I visited the Church of San Augustin, the only major building in the city to survive the bombardments of World War II. Built by the Spaniards in the sixteenth century, the church is situated *intra muros*, within the walls, of the old city of Manila. Near the altar is the Tomb of Legazpi, the so-called founder of Manila. The words inscribed on the tomb in sixteenth century 'doublespeak' inform the visitor that: 'Here lie the remains of Adelantudo Miguel Lopez di Legazpi, a Basque Captain and a Mariner who by the force of his destiny became a Conquistador when in his heart he was a man of peace.'

Legazpi's orders from Philip II of Spain to establish Spanish hegemony and the Catholic faith in the Philippines overcame any peaceful instincts in his heart. These instructions were carried out with ruthless dedication, establishing a Spanish Colonial rule which was to last more than three centuries. In the museum of the same church of San Augustin is the *Sala de la capitulation*, where in 1898 a successor of Legazpi, Governor General Fermin Judenes, prepared the draft documents for the Spanish surrender of the Philippines to the United States of America. A kilometre or two away, in the ruins of a Spanish fort, is the cell where in the same year, 1898, the popular Philippine patriot, Dr Jose Rizal was incarcerated by the Spanish prior to his execution. The museum, containing some of his personal possessions, is a reminder that he remains something of a popular cult figure in the story of the Philippines' struggle for independence.

The day after my visit to San Augustin, I was taken to the Macapagal Palace, a more contemporary monument to the historic plunder of the Philippines. The Marcos' treasures had been well displayed on Australian television. The actual sight of room after room of expensive antiques from around the world, racks of clothing, shoes encrusted with precious stones, paintings and jewellery was nonetheless impressive. The guide explained it all in hushed tones. It was as if Imelda Marcos was listening: a wicked fairy with extrasensory powers.

The arrival and eventual demise of the Marcos regime is vivid in the memory. In Manila's Ayala Museum, the visitor soon realises that it was just another chapter in a long history of brutality and suppression. The names of some of the exhibits speak for themselves: 1475, the arrival of Islam; 1521, arrival of the Spanish Catholics; 1567, the arrival of Legazpi; 1575, the Limalhong Chinese riots and so on.

Curiosity persuaded me to visit the Manila bar district one evening. In one of the more up-market 'girlie bars' the establishment proprietor was cultivating the art of conversation. Each customer was given a card decorated with a drawing of a scantily clad female lounging beside a tray of drinks. The card was headed 'Talking', and provided a native translation of the following essential phrases:

A very cold beer, no ice please.
What's your name?
Where do you come from?
How old are you?
Too much.
Would you like a drink?
I'm feeling horny.
You are very beautiful.
I love you.

I doubted my capacity to quickly run through the gamut of emotions from 'cold beer to falling in love'. One bar, complete with loud disco music, flashing lights, girls in G-strings, huge mirrors and drunk male tourists, reminded me of Dante's *Inferno*. In another quieter bar we got down to some serious drinking and conversation in primitive English with Sibelle, Nicole, Fleur and Vivienne. The obvious questions are all answered in the same way—an apparently rehearsed 'bar-girl speak'.

They all said they were 23, although it was hard to believe that any were older than sixteen. They had all been working in the bars for two months, they all liked pouring cold beer with no ice. They were all skilled at beating tourists at a simple puzzle game. The conversation struggled on with my answers to questions worse than theirs. 'Where do you come from?' 'France,' I said, 'Paris, France. My name is Jean. I am thirty-four years old. Yes, I would like a cold beer. No, you cannot come to my hotel tonight. My English girlfriend is waiting for me at the hotel. She gets so jealous that I am taking her back to England tomorrow. But, yes, Sibelle, you are very beautiful. When I have parted from my English girlfriend I will come back to see you.' I felt warmed by the cold beer. The conversation was conducted with much laughter. No-one believed me, other than me.

Prostitution of women and children is the obvious public and urban face of poverty in the Philippines. In some small towns near Manila the strength of the local economy is described in terms of tourism and trade in boys. Young girls drift into the city, knowing that their only employment prospects lie in the bars. The Church turns a blind eye on the issue. Birth control is condemned in an already overpopulated country. The government remains silent. Foreign 'entrepreneurs', predominantly Australians, conduct much of the business.

What other business does Australia conduct with our near neighbour? There is some Australian investment attracted by tax incentives and cheap labour, a trade balance which runs about two to one in Australia's favour, and an aid budget which amounts to less than three per cent of Australia's total overseas aid. The aid vote includes assistance provided by voluntary agencies, emergency food and humanitarian aid in response to national disasters, training and aid directed to specific infrastructure projects.

Of course, aid is a palliative and not much help in solving longer-term problems. And problems there are indeed. The history of the country has seen tragic disasters, exploitation by colonial powers and multinationals, the savage consequences of war and the deprivations resulting from nepotistic and misguided leaders. The San Augustin Church is 'the lone survivor of World War II'. And visitors are told that 'this historic landmark is still contributing to the strengthening of tradition and to the cultural awareness of the modern Philippines'. Maybe. Certainly the walls of San Augustin's have witnessed much over four centuries. Its tradition has been one of ministering to the needs of an oppressed people. Perhaps in the future they will have a bit of luck as well. The people are charming and the country has a well-educated and hardworking population. Alongside the sectional interests there is a strong national will. Perhaps the 'cultural awareness' will mean a rejection of the past and new hope for the future.

Leaving Manila seemed as bizarre as our arrival. We drove to the airport through peak hour traffic with a police escort on motor scooters. At the airport entrance for VIP visitors the gate was closed. Heavily-armed police lounged in front of the gate. We sat in the car in front of the entrance. The driver tooted, but the gate remained closed. The escorting police cyclists sat on their scooters. The police on the gate didn't move. Finally, through the help of an interpreter, it was explained to us that there was an intense feud between the Manila police and the airport police. If we could persuade the motor scooter police escort to leave then the airport police would open the gate.

We accepted this advice and the gate was opened. The driver took us to some stairs leading up to the airport concourse. The stairs were locked so we climbed up a fire escape. Finally we found the VIP lounge where we had been told to wait. The door was locked. An announcement on the loudspeaker system informed us that our flight had been cancelled. For two hours we tried to change to another airline. Then it was announced that our flight would be leaving, but three hours late. When we boarded the plane and sat down, the Captain informed us there was a bomb scare. They would have to unload the luggage and search the aircraft. Would we kindly remain in our seats while this was done. I wondered if we should keep our seat belts on.

We flew to Hawaii. On the plane I reflected that this sort of thing could happen anywhere. In fact it happened again on an American airline in Hawaii. It was just that it occurred twice in Manila; on arrival and departure. I discussed it all with the Philippine Airlines flight attendant. She had Cory Aquino's philosophic charm. The problem had all been caused by a truck backing into the plane at Manila Airport. She apologised for the delay. 'We don't,' she said, 'have any spare aeroplanes. We are, I'm afraid, a poor country.'

India: an elusive magic: 1989

The only time I'd been to India was during a short stopover in Bombay. I remember the man at the Air India desk, where we queued up to have our tickets endorsed for the flight to London. 'Are you veg?' he asked, as I reached the front of the queue. 'I beg your pardon,' I replied. 'Are you veg?' he repeated. 'I'm sorry, I don't know what you mean?' He glared at me and raised his voice: 'For the last time, are you or are you not veg?' I turned to my wife. 'I think,' she whispered, 'he wants to know whether you're a vegetarian.' 'Oh,' I said, 'I am not a vegetarian.' The man behind the desk sighed theatrically for the benefit of the other passengers and exclaimed 'At last!' in a loud voice, banging a large blue stamp on my boarding pass. It was my first encounter with an Indian bureaucrat.

My second visit to India was an official one, as a guest of the Indian Government. My hosts were kindly and hospitable: always helpful in facilitating progress through the crowds and the bureaucracy.

India has, of course, a huge population. It also has a large and ubiquitous bureaucracy. On my second day in India, lunching with Nan Palkhivala, a distinguished lawyer, businessman and economic commentator, I asked him if Hindus were just naturally bureaucratic. 'In many ways, yes,' he replied, 'but it has been greatly exacerbated by British colonialism.' He went on to explain that historians usually attributed the size and significance of India's bureaucracy to the moguls: the maharajahs who during the period of British paramountcy acted as administrative agents for the British. In the process they effectively ruled two-thirds of India and developed their own bureaucracies and vested interests. 'India,' Mr Palkhivala emphasised, 'is a land of large bureaucracies.'

Mr Palkhivala had a high opinion of the virtues of the successful entrepreneurial class of India. 'I have always said that an Indian entrepreneur can buy from a Jew and sell to a Scotsman and still make a good profit. That is an achievement. It takes an awful lot of bureaucratic effort to keep a country like that poor.' He despaired of Indian politicians and the standard of government. There was, he suggested, a need for a Margaret Thatcher-style politician of superhuman proportions to sort it all out. Superhuman such a person would need to be. Sixty-five percent of the population was illiterate. He thought the voters could always be relied on to support opportunistic and short-sighted policies. In India communalism always rears its head at election time.

The theme of 'despair' runs strongly in much of the literature about modern India. It is pervasive in the writing of the Bengali writer Nirad Chaudhuri and lurks beneath the surface of the astringent prose of V.S. Naipaul in *India: A Wounded Civilisation*. In *The Nehru Dynasty*, the Marxist writer Tariq Ali developed the theme in descriptions of political corruption, vacillation and nepotism. Quality Indian newspapers provided for us during our visit referred constantly to corruption, bureaucratic heavy-handedness and communal violence. None of these topics emerged in dialogue with our hosts, they represented 'official' India. A query about a reported incident of corruption was more likely to produce a shrug and a smile than an explanation.

The population of India increases each year by about the same number as the total population of Australia. It is a population increment which would be regarded as awesome by governments of the richest countries in the world. Talking with Indian politicians, I detected no coherent view about the priority accorded this issue. People have children out of ignorance or as an insurance against high infant mortality. It is an accepted fact in most of the country. No-one mentioned the State of Kerala. There, population growth is constrained as a result of successful education programs implemented by the government of that State. Kerala, however, has for most of the years since independence been governed by the Communist Party of India.

The Government of Kerala is anathema to the dominant Congress Party. Its success is envied but not emulated. When I raised the population growth issue with Prime Minister Rajiv Gandhi, he told me that India's population was close to being the largest in the world. 'Have we,' he said turning to an official, 'the largest population yet?' 'Not yet, Prime Minister. But it won't be long now.' One sensed another Prime Minister guiding his country into the Guinness Book of Records.

'The racial sense is alien to Indians,' wrote V.S. Naipaul. 'Race is something they detect about others, but among themselves they know only the subcaste or caste, the clan, the gens, the language group. Beyond that they cannot go: they do not see themselves as belonging to an Indian race: the words have no meaning.' The absence of a sense of race is compounded by the absence of a sense of continuity in the culture and in social and political institutions. The great traditions of Indian art and architecture were interrupted and partially destroyed during the period of British dominance. And the political institutions established at the time of Independence have always had a fragile quality about them—the government of a state can be overthrown by force, the national parliament suspended and the press constantly threatened by political and bureaucratic interferences.

In the sense of political independence, India is, of course, a

young country. Australians, in much more favoured circum-
stances, understand the search for a sense of national identity
in a post-colonial era. It is a slow and difficult process. In
India it is often manifest in feelings of despair and frustration.
'We hate the British and yet ape them in everything we do,'
I was told by an Indian journalist.

In the *Times of India* on 10 October 1989, the 'Thought for
Today' on the editorial page was from Swami Virekananda:
'You are part of the infinite. This is your nature. Hence you
are your brother's keeper.' At dinner the night before I had
sat next to a wealthy and somewhat overweight Parsee woman.
When I declined her invitation to a further helping of food
she remarked, 'You must be dieting. That is admirable. The
problem with us Indians is that we don't diet. We eat too
much.'

There were beggars outside in the street. In the Indian
newspapers the same week there were pictures of a group of
film personalities indulging in an orgy of eating and drinking.
This, it was said, was to counteract the influence of the film
star, T. Rajander, who had embarked on a protest fast against
spiralling food prices. Perhaps these are extreme examples of
insensitivity and cultivated oblivion to the realities of life in
India. They occur, however, again and again. They illustrate
the absence of any sense of national identity, social cohesion
or concern.

There is another India in the minds, the trinket boxes and
snapshot albums of the thousands of tourists who visit the
country each year. Back in Australia I looked at the photographs
taken during our visit. They illustrated what a one-dimensional
instrument the camera can be. There are pictures of handsome
smiling children, handsome Sikhs and handsome palaces.
Beautiful women in colourful saris glide through the lush
landscape balancing ornate jars on their heads. Sacred cows
garlanded in flowers for a Hindu festival look as if they are
enjoying themselves. There are pictures of the ubiquitous

bodyguards provided for foreign guests—sleek detectives from the CID, a young conscript soldier outside our hotel room with an ancient rifle chained to his arm. There is a picture of the obsequious valet in our hotel suite who insisted that his name was 'Sir Roger George'.

Pictures mirror the adjectives of the satisfied tourist. India is a land of colour, rich diversity, contrast, spirituality and warmth; where East meets West in a jewel box of history and mankind displays its unique capacity to cope with real adversity.

In mid-1988 Mr Krishnamurthy, the Chairman of the Steel Authority of India, called on me in Canberra. He wanted to talk about the restructuring of the steel industry in Australia and to invite me to visit India. He said that historically the Indian steel industry had enjoyed a good relationship with BHP. Unfortunately, some 15 years ago the relationship had lapsed. There had been no further contact. I phoned BHP and arranged for him to meet them. Subsequently BHP and Kinhill Engineering entered into an agreement to provide technical assistance to the steel industry of India. I wondered what had happened in the interregnum. What happened in Australia? What happened in India? It was not that we had simply failed to move closer to each other. In fact the two countries had drifted further apart. The steel industries were merely an example of what had happened.

Krishnamurthy's visit to Australia was followed by visits from K.R. Narayanan, the Indian Minister for Science; Dinesh Singh, the Minister for Commerce; and Dr Abid Hussain, a member of the Indian Planning Commission. Each visit was a tentative response to a 1988 agreement between Prime Ministers Gandhi and Hawke. They agreed that efforts should be made to improve political relations and trade between the two countries.

Minister Narayaran was one of the few untouchables to make his way to the top of the Congress Party. At our meeting in Canberra he talked about his hopes of establishing scientific exchanges between Australia and India. Dinesh Singh, an aristocratic man with thirty-one years as a Congress Party parliamentarian, discussed his ambitions for increasing trade and Australian investment in coalmining projects in India. Would I go to India to discuss these possibilities?

I read the official brief on the plane between Singapore and Bombay: production figures; trade volumes; potential for Australian involvement in resource projects in India; a 'defensive briefing' on sensitive issues and 'talking points', prepared by some artful conversationalist in the Canberra public service. The links between the two countries, I discovered, go back a long way. The first shipment of Australian coal was sent to India in 1801. Our commercial relationship has not changed significantly. Our largest exports to India were still coal and wool. The briefing provided the chilling information that 'we share a common administrative heritage'; but warned that an impediment to trade is 'the vastness, structural rigidity and dogmatic approach of the Indian bureaucracy'.

I supplemented the information in the official brief with a copy of the *London Economist* picked up in Singapore. It contained a fortuitous article about India's new 'booming' middle class, estimated at two hundred million people, with a hunger for consumer goods from the West. I wondered if Australia might be eligible for a small share. What linkages might be created to improve the exchange of business and trade between India and Australia?

My first official engagement in India was with a group of about twenty-five Bombay businessmen. They were sleek, elegantly dressed and polite. They represented large companies, consortia of business interests and traditional trading families. I talked about the visit of Prime Minister Gandhi to Australia, the changes taking place in the Australian economy and the need to establish better trading and business links between the two countries. I asked about the possibility of business cooperation in other countries. What prospect did they see for dismantling some of the bureaucratic impediments to business activity? There were hardly any questions about Australia and few attempts at answering some of the questions which I had asked. There seemed an unbridgeable gulf of time, distance and culture. A wool textile merchant invited me to visit his mills. He said his enterprise employed seventy thousand people, because 'in India we have never addressed the question of overmanning'.

At a further meeting the same day with the Governor of the Reserve Bank of India, the sense of engagement and interest was not much greater. A charming man, he gave an impression of permanent tiredness as he talked about the difficulty of his job. There were so many banks, so many financial institutions. A governor's lot was not a happy one. I had been warned in advance that he may raise the question of applications by Indian banks to operate in Australia, but he did not do so. It might have been from politeness or perhaps indifference. As I left, he presented me with a bunch of roses for my wife. With a warm smile he expressed the hope that we should both have a very happy time in India.

On the waterfront opposite Bombay's Taj Mahal Hotel there is a grey stucco monument built in the proportions of the Arc de Triomphe. Completed in 1911, it is known as the 'Gateway to India' and is prominently engraved with the names of George V and Queen Mary. Through the open windows of the hotel room, I was attracted by the sound of a brass band playing in a small park in front of the monument. Making my first excursion onto the streets of Bombay, I was accompanied by two detectives pushing away the outstretched hands of the ubiquitous beggars.

The music was being played by the Bombay Police Band, standing in full uniform of black trousers, white jackets and white pith helmets in the hot sun. I listened from a position on a set of concrete steps in front of the bandstand. There were stirring if scratchy renditions of 'Soldiers of the Queen', 'The Blue Danube' and 'The Road to Mandalay'. On the opposite side of the band a few people were sitting in rows of neatly arranged chairs. In the front row there was a handsome old man with thick white hair, a military moustache and medals on his immaculate white jacket. He sat on his own. I had the feeling that he sat there every day in the same seat listening to the music, his mind wandering and remembering the past.

I had to leave the music for an appointment with the Chief Minister of the State of Maharashtra. I was told the appointment had been confirmed by phone just before we left the hotel. At 3 p.m. we arrived at the State Civil Service Building and were directed to a long queue of people waiting to use the lift.

Twenty minutes later we were ushered into a small and uncomfortable reception room outside the Chief Minister's office on the sixth floor. A young man introduced himself as the Protocol Officer. He asked us if we would like some tea. We said that we would wait until we saw the Chief Minister. 'That would be unwise,' said the Protocol Officer. 'You will not be seeing the Chief Minister. He is not here.' 'But,' protested the Australian Consul, 'we had an appointment at 3.30 p.m.' 'Yes,' replied the Protocol Officer, 'but the Chief Minister is not here. He has gone to Delhi. He is definitely not here. I can assure Your Excellency that he is not here.' There was no queue for the lift going down. The Australian Consul in Bombay speculated for the whole six floors as to why the appointment had been cancelled.

Mr Rao, the Minister for Business Enterprises, received me in a room at the top of two flights of stairs, in a building which reeked of bureaucracy. We had to push and jostle our way up through a throng of civil servants passing up and down. Mr Rao sat in a chair facing me with a group of officials sitting on stools behind him. A large and unsmiling man, he was dressed in the flowing white robes of the Congress Party. He waited patiently, fanning himself in silence for several minutes until the tea was served. An official then handed him a sheaf of papers and he began to intone a prepared speech—statistics on the number of business enterprises under his control, growth rates, bankruptcies, hopes and apprehensions, the parameters of the eighth Five Year Plan.

Trying to digest this avalanche of information, I found myself concentrating on his pudgy sandalled feet poking out from under his robes. I kept thinking this man reminds me of someone, but couldn't quite work out who. As he read on I realised that it was the actor Sydney Greenstreet playing the Indian Minister for Business Enterprises. The appearance, the style, the hint of ruthlessness, the calculated boredom were almost identical. I began to worry about my reply. Should it be in the obsequious style of Peter Lorre or direct and aggressive like Humphrey Bogart? I decided my reply should be somewhere in between. It would be unwise to call him 'Your Excellency' or 'Fatso'. I should be pleasant but firm. However, by the time he finished there was hardly any time to reply. I offered some tentative suggestions about possible collaboration between Australian and Indian businesses. But the Minister had no more sheets of paper and his mind was on other things.

Rajiv Gandhi was not just a Prime Minister with a pretty face. He was also Minister of Communications and Minister of Science and Technology, Atomic Energy, Space, Electronics, Ocean Development and Personnel Administrative Reforms. He was the third Prime Minister of the Nehru–Gandhi dynasty. Following the assassination of his mother in 1984, he was elected by the largest majority in India's history. He came to office as a reluctant politician: perhaps this contributed to his electoral success.

We met in his simply furnished office at Parliament House in New Delhi. The office was dominated by a bare, highly polished white marble desk. Dressed in a white Nehru jacket and white trousers he exuded the persona of a mythological prince charming. He spoke in a soft, beautifully modulated voice and set the informal tone of the discussion with the question, 'Tell me, how is Bob?', a reference to his close rapport with R.J. Hawke.

His enthusiasm for the modernisation of India had an infectious quality about it. One suspected that he believed or hoped that out there, somewhere, there were some wonderful technological breakthroughs which would provide a solution to the awesome problems of contemporary India. Questions crowded into my mind. Were all these ministries he held serious or were they merely symbols of his dreams? Or were they personal indulgences which he tinkered with like a child in a toy shop? 'How effective,' I would have liked to have asked, 'are your policies on personnel administrative reforms.' 'Might I rest my cup of tea on this splendid marble desk?'

The fascinating thing about Rajiv Gandhi was that his passions and intellectual curiosity were real. He asked about the multifunction polis in Australia with genuine interest and thoughtful questions. I undertook to deliver him a copy of the concept documents. 'See,' he said to an official, 'that they come to me personally. I want to read them myself.'

He was about to announce an election which he assured me he would win. I had been told that a CIA document, circulating in diplomatic circles in Delhi, suggested that he would lose for all sorts of reasons which we could not discuss. As I left he told me he had assured 'Bob' that India would vote for Malcolm Fraser as Secretary General of the Commonwealth. 'It has been worrying me,' he said, 'I think such an appointment might be somewhat divisive.' But with an election coming, perhaps his dilemma would be resolved.

The appointment with Rajiv Gandhi had been tucked into a busy schedule, which included a meeting with the officers of the Confederation of Engineering Industry. The meeting took the form of a luncheon engagement. It was friendly and informal. We helped ourselves to excellent curry and sat down round a large U-shaped table. There were twenty-five people present. Mr Krishnamurthy from the Steel Authority of India was in the Chair. He introduced me and I made a short speech, followed by questions and a lively discussion.

These engineers from successful Indian companies were practical and well informed. They had a high regard for Australian engineering and a low regard for Australian tariffs. They talked enthusiastically about the possibility of collaboration with Australian engineering companies, combining Australian technology with low-cost production in India. Some of them had been to Australia and were keen to pursue ventures with Australian companies. At the conclusion of the lunch everyone seemed reluctant to leave. The conversation could have gone on. But it was hard to see what steps could be taken to follow it up.

The Senior Trade Commissioner hosted a cocktail party so I could meet some of the Australian expatriates in New Delhi. This party was held in the garden of the Australian High Commission compound. Apart from the venue, it had a familiar quality about it. I had been to similar functions in Singapore, Hong Kong, Malaysia, Bangkok and Manila, all held under the auspices of a Sundowner Club or a Chamber of Commerce. The theme drink is always cold Australian beer, the theme conversation usually about Australia and the expat concern that Australia should be well regarded internationally and perform better. The guests were mainly consulting engineers. There was also a banker, a Qantas manager, and a couple of representatives from mining companies—the typical lonely shock troops of Australia's trade and commercial relations in Asia.

The official objective of a meeting with Sri Sam Pitroda, the Chairman of the Indian Telecommunications Commission, was 'to emphasise Australian technological and industrial

147

capabilities relevant to India's telecommunications needs'. An experienced engineer from Telecom came along to help. Pitroda saw us on his own.

He had enjoyed a successful business career in the United States and had returned to India at the request of Rajiv Gandhi to head up the Telecommunications Commission. He was charming, a smooth talker articulating a huge challenge with a mixture of passion and awe. He spoke of a waiting list of eight hundred thousand people seeking telephone connections: by the end of the century it would be eighteen million. His Commission employed eight hundred thousand people and he was not sure why. There were many bureaucratic obstructions to what he and a small coterie of technical experts wanted to do. He admired the engineering excellence of Telecom Australia and would like to keep in touch. For the moment, he had bigger problems to deal with. I thought he was telling us politely to come back in a few years time. An intelligent man, he seemed trapped in an Indian spider web.

Indian officials like the form of the colloquium. My visit to the Confederation of Engineering Industry was a sort of colloquium. We discussed improvements which might be made to the world in a more liberal and intelligent trading environment. At the Technology Development Board we talked about methods of supporting research and development, and innovation and technology transfer around the world. People argued, listened and made lengthy notes. It was a learning experience. At a seminar organised by the National Planning Commission I gave a speech about the multifunction polis. There was an enthusiastic discussion about what it might do for Australia, for India, for the region and the world. It was a case of distance lending enchantment to the view; a fascinated belief that somewhere there was a planning or technological solution capable of ameliorating the tragedy of the human condition in India.

'I am pleased both governments have recognised that our trading relationship can be improved and that we have gone about it by identifying specific opportunities and setting realistic targets.' This was my first talking point in the official brief for the meeting with my Indian host, the Minister for Commerce, Dinesh Singh. Confronted with his gentleness and hospitality, I found it difficult to say anything quite so formal. Instead I told him that I knew a young Indian in Australia called Dinesh Singh, who was at school with my sons and who was not too bad at cricket.

We talked about cricket until the conversation slowly wandered back to trade and the impediments to it, which existed in both countries. I expressed my pleasure at the fact that an Australian company would develop the Pipiwar coalmining project in North India. He too was pleased, and hoped we would be successful in winning other projects. I asked him about India's controls over investment and their high tariffs. He reminded me gently that things take time to resolve in India. There were no reciprocal questions about Australia and no need to resort to 'defensive briefing'. It was as if Australia was too far away, too small, and quite irrelevant to his daily preoccupations.

At the end of the week I was exhausted by meetings. On the Sunday we went to Agra by train from Delhi. Contrary to our prior perceptions it was a comfortable and smooth-running train. A platoon of soldiers met us at Agra Station and we were marched like prisoners of war to two large and ancient Mercedes which took us, accompanied by a noisy police escort, to the Taj Mahal.

Our guide, a sparkling man who darted from one point to the next, might have been a role model for Peter Sellers' Indian imitations. Captivated by the splendour of the building, my mind wandered temporarily away from his description of the detailed history of its creation. 'I think,' he chided, 'that Your Excellency may have missed the last point. I will run through it again.' He specialised, it seemed, in trick questions. 'Here is a trick question for Madame. Is the tower on the left higher than the column on the right? Very good, Madame, very good. Now another special trick question for His Excellency.' I hesitated and guessed. 'No, no, Your Excellency, you are quite wrong. For the second time you are wrong. Madame is better at trick questions.' Uncomfortable in the blazing sun, I found his verdict depressing. It seemed a long way to come to be denounced as a failure.

We drove from the Taj Mahal to the magnificent Red Fort. Approaching the fort the car slowed to a walking pace. We had to cross a narrow bridge, crowded with pedestrians, and pass through the stone archway into the courtyard. In the middle of the congested bridge the Mercedes drew to a halt. Almost immediately we were surrounded by another different crowd of people. They were instantly recognisable; two busloads of Australian tourists from the Gold Coast attracted by the Australian flag on the front of the car. 'Our taxes at work,' shouted a jovial fatty through the car window. 'Good on ya mate,' said another.

Escaping from this ordeal, I was dismayed to see our guide from the Taj Mahal waiting to show us around. This time he gave a virtuoso performance demonstrating the acoustics in the various parts of the building. Mercifully there were no trick questions.

On our second last night in India, the Australian High Commissioner hosted a dinner for us at the Residence in Delhi. It was held in a large marquee on a lush and expansive lawn lit by flares. Colourfully dressed and turbaned valets hovered between the tables. Although the British departed from India forty years before, the legacy of their influence and lifestyle lingered on in the compounds of the various embassies in Delhi. The High Commissioner, Graeme Feakes, and his wife Nicki had spent some time in India at various points of their lives. They both had a deep knowledge and understanding of Indian life and culture, and their enthusiasm as representatives of Australian interests in India was refreshing. It was a sharp contrast with the sometimes scarcely concealed resentment of some Australian diplomats who feel themselves exiled from the Melbourne Cricket Club and the Members Stand at the Sydney Cricket Ground. At the dinner they had arranged a group of guests ranging from the essential politicians to businessmen, academics and the actor/manager of a street theatre for the children of Delhi. If we departed from India with narrow perceptions it was not the fault of the High Commissioner and his wife.

I left India with mixed feelings—gratitude for the warmth of our hosts, some slight sense of a larger understanding, gastroenteritis and a dose of despondency. So many people, so many problems, so much manageable despair and illusory hopes. Had I done much to improve the contacts and understanding between our ancient continent and their ancient civilisation? Perhaps, I thought, one needed to be in India for four hundred years, like the British, to make a lasting impression.

As I checked out of the hotel, I could not help overhearing the conversation between a middle-aged American woman and the clerk at the cashier's desk. 'I've had a very happy time in India,' she said. 'You know, my mother died in 1974 and ever since then I've been travelling round the world trying to forget it. On this trip I've felt better about it.' 'Thank you, Madame,' said the clerk. 'I am very pleased.'

Maybe, I decided, the real magic of India had eluded me.

Peeling an onion: Japan

In late November 1983 Mr Koji Kobayashi, the Chairman of the giant Japanese electronics company NEC, called on me in my office in Canberra. He was in Australia to visit the company's subsidiary industrial plants. Kobayashi was the first Japanese industrialist with whom I had a long discussion. He had made an appointment for half an hour, a 'courtesy call' as it is called. He stayed for an hour and a half, and I listened with some fascination to what he had to say.

At the time Mr Kobayashi was seventy-eight years old. It did not prevent him speaking with youthful enthusiasm about his life in business and about likely technological developments in the computing industry. He described his own company as being like Mount Fuji, with a broad base in consumer electronics rising to an advanced technology pinnacle of experimentation in 'artificial intelligence' and fifth generation computers. In the late 1940s he had visited the United States. Wandering round the streets of Los Angeles he had asked himself the question 'What makes this country great?' The answer he decided was communications, and he returned to Japan determined to build NEC into a large communications company. Not only was it to be a huge company: he wanted it to be the best. So in the 1950s he had undertaken, earlier than most industrialists, a continuing search for innovation and excellence.

When Mr Kobayashi left, he presented me with an electronic clock made in the shape of a tennis racquet. He told me that he had brought this gift because he knew that Australians were very good at tennis. I thought at the time that the unstated implication was that Australians were not much good at anything else and that Mr Kobayashi was too polite to mention it. But why shouldn't he have thought that this was so? Cricket was something the Japanese did not understand. Shipping raw materials to Japan was something which he would have understood, but it was not in his line of business and it was not an area in which the necessity for excellence was entirely obvious. There he was, the Chairman of an electronics company which had grown in three decades into a large and successful multinational company, visiting the Australian subsidiary where in 1983 Australian workers screwed together imported components for consumer goods to be sold on the Australian domestic market. It was all a microcosm of the Japanese 'miracle'. Australia had no miracles to compare with it.

In the 1960s and early 1970s Australian ambivalence towards Japan was based on two emotionally satisfying assumptions: a residual resentment from the Second War War and the belief, not without validity in the 1960s, that Japan's success was based on the export of cheap goods made by cheap labour. By the 1980s the wartime resentments were slowly fading as one generation replaced another. The perception of the 1960s, that Japanese success was based on exploitation of cheap labour, had gradually transmuted into a suspicion that Japan was the custodian of arcane Oriental business practices with which no self-respecting Western country could possibly compete. Military imperialiam of the 1940s had been replaced by a new industrial imperialism. It was alternatively described as 'a miracle' or a 'conspiracy'. In November 1983 I was planning a trip to Europe and Scandinavia. The visit of Mr Kobayashi encouraged me to consider a visit to Japan. I had fantasies of walking round Tokyo and asking myself 'What makes this country great?' I wanted to try to understand the Japanese miracle.

Japan in 1983 was Australia's largest trading partner. Australia exported the raw materials for Japanese industry, predominantly coal and iron ore, and Japan exported to Australia a range of manufactured goods from ships and cars to sophisticated electronics. Australia had few investments in Japan. Japanese companies invested heavily in Australian real estate, resource companies and some areas of manufacturing. Big Japanese trading houses like Mitsui handled a large proportion of Australian trade. Japan not only seemed and was rich: it also appeared immensely sophisticated in economic management and trade. Australia seemed unsophisticated and unprofessional. Increasingly, the Japanese tended to see the relationship in this way. Unconsciously they were encouraged to do so by the attitudes of Australian industrialists, politicians and bureaucrats, who often carried domestic arguments to their hosts in Japan, a practice not understood in Japanese culture. Australians were still struggling to shrug off a longstanding culture of dependency, which had slowly moved from the United Kingdom to the United States and now towards Japan. In the 1950s 'threat experts' had warned of British economic imperialism in Australia. In the 1960s the 'Yankee dollar' symbolised a new menace. In the late 1970s and early 1980s a new cloud emerged on the horizon; the industrial might of Japan.

Australia's long trading relationship with Japan, in commodities such as wool, was interrupted by the War. So were Japanese manufactured exports to Australia; a market which Japanese companies had started to use as a test bed for product acceptance by a predominantly European population. The first motor cars ever exported from Japan were Datsuns exported to Australia in 1935. In the early 1950s Prime Minister Menzies invited a small delegation of Japanese industrialists to Australia. It was, in the postwar political climate, a courageous and prescient invitation. The delegation included Eishiro Saito of Nippon Steel, who subsequently became one of the icons of Japanese industry. In 1991 Saito told me about this visit. He regarded it a seminal point in the relationship between Australia and Japan. And indeed it was. It was the starting point from which Australian exports to Japan of coal, iron ore and other mineral resources began a steady climb to the point where Japan became our largest trading partner. In Japan heavy industry grew on the back of these exports. Mr Saito became a success. In Australia the new corporate heroes were the chairmen and chief executives of resource-producing companies. Australia became richer, as the quarry joined and overtook the farm as the basis of Australian wealth and standard of living. There were always allegations that the Japanese were tough negotiators, but generally Australian companies had the benefit of a seller's market. It was a useful and productive relationship on both sides. How deep the relationship became was a different matter.

Australian businesspeople, politicians and bureaucrats made frequent visits to Japan. They learnt to bow, eat at low tables waited on by geishas, and drink saki; but not to speak Japanese. They employed Japanese translators and interpreters because there were few Australians able to do it. The language was translated but the nuances and subtleties were seldom understood. Merchant princes at home, some of them became recipients of high Japanese honours awarded by the Emperor; but not for sophistication or deep understanding.

In Australia, Japan was increasingly seen as important, but not important enough to warrant profound study. There were few Japanese linguists and few students of the Japanese economy and way of life. Amongst economists the Japanese economic powerhouse was regarded as aberrant. It might be working in practice, but it didn't work in theory. As a new

Minister I was warned about the mythology of MITI (the Japanese Ministry for International Trade and Industry). In some circles, particularly in the United States, MITI was seen as the invisible coordinating hand of Japanese success. In Australia I was told by people who'd never coordinated anything, that MITI had made mistakes: like advising Honda not to go into motor vehicle manufacture.

The successes were reluctantly acknowledged and attributed to hard work and a variety of mysterious 'externalities'. I wondered about Australia's successes and failures. Were the failures all due to the trade unions, as industrialists and politicians so often told the Japanese at the time? On balance it seemed unlikely. But people who spoke for Australia in Japan had little or no sense of corporate Australian identity. Industrial relations in Australia were usually the excuse for price increases or failure to deliver. It was as if it were a problem for Japan, but not a problem for Australians to solve.

By the 1980s apprehension about Japan was constantly fortified by an increasing outpour of sensationalist books from the United States, denouncing Japanese business culture and alleging unfair practices in international trade. These books were a reflection of the declining relative competitiveness of traditional sectors of American industry. It was difficult for Americans to believe that they were not the best at everything. Corporate giants of the American and world industrial landscape, like General Motors, Chrysler and later IBM, were beginning to feel the winds of Japanese competitiveness.

Japan assumed the technological lead in semiconductors and chip technology. In defensive mode, Americans were enjoined to buy American: governments to protect and subsidise American industry. Later, the anxiety affected some European industries in a similar way. In the late 1980s I was told by a vice-president of Italian manufacturing conglomerate Fiat that the Japanese were unfair traders. It seemed a strange complaint at a time when Italian governments, at the instigation of Fiat and others, would only allow two thousand Japanese cars to be imported into Italy in any one year. The particulars of this allegation were even stranger than the allegation itself. I found myself in a vigorous argument on the side of Japan.

So much has been written about the Japanese economic miracle that it requires close and patient study to sort the wheat from the chaff. It is a complex story of an island people with strong traditions, culture and commitment to national goals. Japan is a country of one language, culture and race, which for two centuries, ending with the arrival of Commander Perry's 'black ships' in 1853, was sealed off from the rest of the world. These factors were the basis of strong motivations to succeed and the Japanese capacity to work together. But success was also based on a number of facts and circumstances which were largely ignored in the Western world and particularly in Anglo-Saxon countries such as Australia and the United States. When Dr Edward Deming, the American industrialist psychologist, went to Japan in 1951 with a message about work organisation, productivity and quality, the Japanese listened and adopted many of his methods. In the United States he was ignored until the 1980s when ideas about quality circles and workforce participation began to filter back from Japan to America and to other manufacturing economies.

This commitment to efficiency and quality was underpinned by a culture which attached great importance to making things and adding value to products. While Japan concentrated on the production of goods and services, the glamour boys of the Anglo-Saxon business world in the United States and Australia were the paper shufflers, creating what has been called a 'Ten minute profit-cycle economy'. As Mr Akio Morita, the former Chairman of Sony, put it in a speech in America: 'Japan is focussing on business ten years in advance, while you seem to be concerned only with profits ten minutes from now. At that rate, you may never be able to compete with us.'

The importance of this longer-term business outlook, in a world of rapidly changing technology, was perhaps Japan's greatest strength in establishing itself as a powerhouse of manufacturing production. And, as with other elements of Japanese business culture, it was copied exclusively in the fast-growing economies of North Asia and the Asian Tigers. The West, instead of examining how and why it worked, produced a spate of allegations of unfairness and a range of conspiracy theories. More thoughtful American analysts of Japanese success were largely ignored. As one of them, Professor Chalmers Johnson, concluded in a 1985 speech at the Centre of Technology and Policy at Boston University, 'Firms or nations that want to compete with the Japanese must become at least as serious.'

I made my first visit to Japan in May 1984. On the way to Japan, I spent a day in Kuala Lumpur to speak at an international symposium on the theme of 'ASEAN, Australia and Japan— breaking down the barriers'. It was a timely event. The Australian Government was committing considerable time and thought to these issues. It turned out to be a friendly occasion, made memorable for me by an amusing speech given by a senior civil servant from Thailand. It was, he told his audience, important to get the relationship in proper perspective, a point which he illustrated with a remark made to him by a Japanese industrialist. ASEAN, the Japanese had said, was like men's underpants: an important part of a man's clothing, which you never think about. If you didn't have them they would be missed, but, in the scheme of things, they are taken totally for granted. Australia, it seemed reasonable to conclude, fell into the same category. I caught the plane to Tokyo with a new sense of perspective and some apprehension.

The main purpose of my Japan visit was to meet with the senior management of the Japanese car manufacturers Toyota, Mitsubishi and Nissan, prior to the forthcoming announcement in June of a new plan for the Australian industry. I was aware of the sensitivity of the Japanese to any change in government policy which might affect the value of their investments in Australia. The point had been made explicitly in a memorable discussion with the Chief Executive of Toyota Australia, Mr Tamura, in my Canberra office. After a brief exchange of pleasantries I had asked Mr Tamura what he wanted to tell me. He leaned forward in his chair and said, 'I have only one message. Don't change plan.' 'Anything else?' I asked. 'Nothing else,' he said. 'I know you are busy, I will go now.' And he did.

I was accompanied on the Japan visit by two officials from the Industry Department and two members of my own staff. We had limited time and a heavy program. It included discussions with the MITI Minister, Mr Okonogi; other Japanese politicians; the car manufacturers; some of the companies importing cars into Australia and officials of the Japanese Business Council, the *Keidanren*.

We met with the President of Nissan, Mr Ishihara, and other senior executives of the company in the boardroom of the Nissan headquarters. The meeting was followed by lunch. My explanation of our proposals for the car industry in Australia was received with polite but stony silence, interpolated with loud grunts from the president, which reminded me of Japanese Samurai films. The idea that Australia could have a car industry without high levels of protection was received with a degree of incredulity. Later in 1984 following the announcement of the 'Car Plan', Mr Ishihara attacked the plan and threatened to withdraw Nissan's investment in Australia unless it was changed. At Mitsubishi, the President, Mr Toyoo Tate, seemed less outraged. A quiet, charming man, he seemed mainly concerned to establish the details of the proposed changes and how they would work in practice. Mitsubishi, he indicated, would prefer fewer changes; but if they had to take place, the company would try to work with them.

For the meeting with Toyota we travelled by bullet train to Nagoya. Mr Tamura, the chief executive of the Australian operations, was there to meet us. As we waited to go into the meeting he whispered to me, 'I have told Chairman Toyoda, that Minister is very blunt man'. It was, I suspect, a way of telling me that the Japanese negotiating style was different from ours: his implication was cool it, don't thump the table, take your time. Chairman Toyoda deserved and commanded considerable respect. He was a man in his early 70s, but astute and very fit. In his lifetime he had built Toyota into the world's largest car manufacturing company. Eight years after this first meeting he was still travelling the world with a schedule which would have horrified most businessmen twenty years younger. In Nagoya he was something of a legend. When he swam a kilometre in the city's swimming pool on Saturday mornings people went to watch him do it.

We outlined our proposals to the Chairman. He listened patiently with a steady smile on his face. Occasionally he rolled his eyes in seeming disbelief. From time to time he asked questions or addressed comments in Japanese to his managerial colleagues, designed I suspected to elucidate particular issues. At the end of the discussion I had little idea what he thought. I decided from his questions that he was sceptical but capable of being persuaded. In the afternoon we visited a Toyota manufacturing plant. It was the first time I had seen Japanese workers doing aerobic exercises in a group between shifts. Nor had I seen a motor vehicle assembly line with robotics and comparatively few workers. Our guide pointed to a large letter box on the wall. 'That is the suggestion box. We get eight thousand suggestions a year from workers on how to improve the production process.' My private secretary, Geoff Evans, whispered, 'We could do that in Australia. But all the suggestions would be the same: "get stuffed".'

From Kyoto, the ancient capital of Japan, we drove to the

factory of Kyocera Corporation, a company which was raising eyebrows around the world with its development and marketing of a new range of industrial products made from ceramics. Kyocera was a high-growth company seen as a trailblazer in high technology. It was producing a range of industrial products made from new materials. We watched workers pouring a muddy liquid into huge vats, then looked at a mass of stainless steel piping. We were shown nothing else of the process until we reached a display of the products, ranging from small motor vehicle components to imitation jewellery. The art of the technology seemed to be a close secret. I was presented with a pair of ceramic scissors, symbolising the cutting edge of new technology. Some of the raw materials, it was explained to me, came from Australia.

Back in Kyoto, a company hosted a dinner for us in a famous geisha restaurant. We were entertained with traditional music and dancing. It was a banquet of a number of courses, exquisitely presented. Later we were told that a feast of this kind, at this particular restaurant, would have cost about six hundred dollars a head. Geoff Evans, a devotee of Australian country cooking and tired of an exclusive diet of Japanese banquets over several days, asked for a toasted egg sandwich and a cup of tea. It was duly produced: the most expensive snack in my experience. On the bullet train back to Tokyo we talked about how we would present the proposed car industry changes to the companies in Australia. We allocated the task of speaking to the chief executives. I would speak to Ford and General Motors. My adviser Nick Gruen said, 'Tamura belongs to me.'

In Tokyo we had a number of appointments including a dinner with the MITI Minister, Mr Okonogi. Mr Okonogi was a ponderous man who, like many Japanese ministers, had been promoted as a reward for factional loyalty in the Liberal Democratic Party. He enjoyed a short reign as Minister. The conversation was fairly heavy going. A geisha sat beside me to help me with the food. She spoke very little English and I spoke very little Japanese. I leaned across the table to an Australian official sitting opposite me. He had spent a lot of time in Japan. 'What should I talk to her about?' I whispered. He looked at me with a deadpan face. 'Minister,' he said, 'ask her if she "goes off".'

The Australian Ambassador, Sir Neil Currie, gave a dinner at the embassy, which produced more thoughtful and lively discussion. He had chosen the Japanese guests carefully. They included several politicians, the deputy editor and foreign editor of *Nition Keizhl Shimbun* (the Japan Economic Journal), some senior executives from the major Japanese trading houses and several academics. They all spoke English. The discussion was an interesting introduction into Japanese views about their own country and its relationship with other countries. I sat next to the Dr Chikara Higashi, President of Temple University. He was a youngish man who had spent some time as a research scholar at the Brookings Institute in New York. Higashi had just published a book on Japanese trade policy, a copy of which he delivered to my hotel the following day.

A foreword by the Japanese Prime Minister, Yasuhiro Nakasone, described the book as a contribution to 'better understanding' between Japan and the United States at a time when 'we are faced with sizeable discrepancies in industrial and trade structures, international competitiveness and people's sentiments in the two countries'. The book is a frank and illuminating account of Japanese trade and industry policy. It will, I suspect, remain a classic for its explanation of Japanese style and behaviour in negotiations, and the tortuous consensual method of decision-making by a corporation or group.

I left Japan with a slightly better understanding of the Japanese, as if I'd peeled the outer skin from a large onion. In a five-day visit we'd met many people, been introduced to Japanese food and had opportunities for superficial observations of Japanese customs. Like most Westerners visiting Japan for the first time, I'd experienced the shock of a powerful and different culture. It took a lot more trips to Japan before I began to absorb it.

During Bob Hawke's visit to Japan as Prime Minister in 1984, he had a meeting with Mr Naohiro Amaya, a former Vice-Minister of MITI. In earlier days Amaya had been the Japanese Consul General in Sydney. His son had studied at the Australian National University and he himself had visited Australia regularly. Amaya had spent a number of years with MITI and was a highly regarded 'thinker' within the department. In the late 80s he was to chair a committee charged with reforming higher education in Japan. Amaya talked to Hawke at length about the history of Japanese industry policy, the methods used in developing major industries with 'infant industry' protection and the process of consensus building to achieve better performance.

The two men talked about the problems of industry restructuring. Japan's goal, Amaya said, was 'to develop new technological frontiers', a process which required government leadership and coordination. The free market alone would not achieve it. The 'visible hand' of the government must perform supplementary work. It was on this basis, of government coordination of private sector effort, that Japan had taken the lead in the semiconductor industry. Policy on industrial development, according to Amaya, had to be subject to constant adaptation. He used a metaphor. Policy was like a five-storey building by the sea, with energy-intensive industries on the ground floor, labour-intensive industries on the first floor, and a series of gradations with each floor to the top, which housed 'human' labour-intensive industries like research and development. 'High tides and floods' were liable to sweep away the industries on the bottom floors. Industry had to make vertical shifts upwards assisted by a sophisticated education system and government assistance to facilitate social change. Hawke was impressed. He invited Amaya to visit

Australia and Amaya came later in the same year.

In Australia Amaya talked to industry and Union groups about the importance of consensus in manufacturing industries and outlined the history and objectives of Japanese industrial policy. He and I had lengthy discussions. I remember his use of rich metaphors. Australians, he told me, swam strongly in the hotel swimming pool. Now they would have to learn to swim in the ocean, where the currents were strong; but the rewards much greater. In Japan a year later, he referred to the same theme. Australian companies needed vigorous competition. They needed to exploit Australia's innovative capacities and concentrate on export markets with higher technology products. Korea and Singapore and perhaps Taiwan had created 'the appropriate climate and good soil' to make this transition. He was not sure that Australia could do it. We were a country 'too much blessed by God'.

In January 1985 Japan's new Minister for International Trade and Industry, Keijiro Murata, made a short visit to Australia. Murata was an ebullient, outgoing personality who told offbeat jokes, wrote poetry on the back of menus and boarding passes and sang with passion in karioke bars. He was an idealist who remained a Minister for a short period. On his arrival he handed me a poem entitled 'Thoughts in Flight', which presented an Arcadian view of the Australian–Japan relationship in which Australians graze sheep, grow fruit, and fish while Japanese sweat and produce goods:

> At night—mid-winter Narita recedes
> To morning—approaching Sydney's summer sun
> Over mountains and rivers, and seas like plains
> To what was once an enemy land
> but now as envoy of our mutual benefit.
>
> The cobalt seas so infinitely broad
> A vast new continent bathed in softest light

Enormous flocks of golden sheep, on pasture land
The kangaroos are loping on the plains
The koalas snoozing in their trees.

For fruit grown in their mountains and their seas
We trade the produce of our people's sweat
A gentle people, theirs, so kind and pure of heart
A brilliant rainbow is forming in our skies.

The poem was dated 16 January 1985, the day of his arrival.
In Canberra the Trade Minister, John Dawkins, hosted a
lunch for Mr Murata, attended by several Australian ministers
and a number of Australian officials. The conversation
wandered along a well-trodden path strewn with banalities.
Dawkins proposed an appropriate toast for the occasion.
Murata responded and embarked on an effusive tribute to the
quality of the Australian wine. When he sat down the
conversation became quite animated, with everyone talking
about Australian wine. It remained the principal topic for
the rest of the lunch. It reminded me of the clock in the
shape of a tennis racquet given to me by Mr Kobayashi. It
provided a focal point for conversation; avoiding the growing
horror of nothing to talk about. The combination of Japanese
reserve and Australian reticence in dealing with the unfamiliar
inhibited discussion. In fact there was plenty to talk about.
Nobody quite knew how to do it.

In June 1985 I went back to Japan to attend the joint
ministerial meeting which takes place every second year
between ministers and officials of the two governments. My
wife and I had been in China; at the time, a shambling giant
of friendly inefficiency. She had enjoyed it. As the Japan
Airlines plane approached Narita, the airline hostess
announced in that mincing accent which young girls in
American soapies reserve for their fathers, 'Welcome to Tokyo:
Have a nice day.' My wife said, 'I don't think I'm going to

like this place.' For the next couple of days she complained about the efficiency with which everything worked. Culture shock manifests itself in various ways. Five days later, at six in the morning eating raw fish and drinking beer for breakfast at the Tokyo fish market, she told me she thought Japan was not a bad place after all.

The Australian delegation for the ministerial meeting comprised six ministers and a large group of officials. The ministers represented areas in which Australia's interests seemed to coincide with our trading relationship with Japan: foreign affairs, trade, resources and energy, primary industry, tourism and industry. The Japanese delegation, led by Foreign Minister Abe, comprised ministers and officials representing similar interests. It was the first Japan ministerial meeting for ministers in the Hawke Government. We met as a delegation the day before to discuss how to handle the negotiations. Nobody had much idea. There was a feeling that in the bilateral relationship with Japan, we somehow had hold of the wrong end of the stick. John Dawkins suggested that we should try to redress the balance by raising, as a threshold issue, the provisions of the Treaty of Nara.

Nobody had much idea what the Treaty of Nara was. Officials were asked to look it up. It was a a treaty signed in 1974 between Australia and Japan, which provided for non-discrimination in trade. Maybe we were being discriminated against: or perhaps we were about to be. The following morning at the hotel an hour before the meeting, the Treaty of Nara negotiating initiative was still being developed. 'What,' I asked an Australian diplomatic official, 'do you think we should do?' He looked at me blankly. 'I think,' he said, 'we should assemble at the lifts on this floor and go down together.' Which is what we did.

At the meeting two ministers on the Australian side made early references to the principles inherent in the Treaty of Nara. The Japanese looked nonplussed. No direct response was made. Mr Abe, a consummate chairman, genial and relaxed, guided the discussion on to other issues. The Treaty of Nara went back into its pigeon-hole. The meeting went on to discuss developments in international trade, Japan's changing relationships with the United States, the mutual dependence of the Australian and Japanese economies, and the strengthening of the relationship in new areas such as tourism and Australian manufacturing exports. Later in the day old hands of the Japan–Australian connection said it had been a good meeting, businesslike but informal and friendly.

The friendliness continued at an elegant dinner hosted by the Foreign Minister, Mr Abe. My wife sat next to Mr Murata. She asked him about his family. Mr Murata said he had three children and made a complicated and tasteless joke about the number of shots you could get with two balls. The following night Mr Murata hosted an informal dinner at a karioke restaurant. It was a night of sushi, song and saki. Gareth Evans and Mr Murata sang 'Waltzing Matilda', which made everyone drink more saki.

The Australian ministerial delegation was received by Prime Minister Nakasone. An experienced politician, Nakasone was outward looking and keen to hold constructive relationships with the United States and Europe. He was a smooth operator. He exuded the sophisticated urbanity of the polished inter-national statesman. He talked for a few minutes about a major preoccupation of Japanese prime ministers: the relationship between Japan and the United States. He moved on to the longstanding relationship between Australia and Japan. As Japanese industry changed and moved away from energy-intensive industries, so would the relationship. It was important to explore ways of strengthening ties between the two countries in a changing world. Japan was the largest economic power in the Western Pacific, Australia was the second largest and the second most sophisticated economy. It was logical that the two countries should work together constructively. It was an issue to which he seemed to have given some thought.

From Tokyo we went to the huge International Technology Expo at Tskuba, Japan's much vaunted high-tech precinct. It was Australia's National Day at the exhibition and I had to participate in the opening ceremony, and make a presentation to the one millionth visitor to the Australian Pavilion. Support was on hand. A group of Aboriginal dancers performed and James Morrison played some golden notes on the trumpet. The Australian Pavilion had a strong theme relating to tourism. There were few products, but together with the director of the Tuma Zoo I performed an official task of wading into a pool to collect coins thrown in there by visitors to the Expo. The money was to support research into contagious diseases affecting koalas. We visited the Japanese Pavilion, symbolically high-tech. I remember a robot playing a piano. Why, I wondered, do we want robots playing pianos? High-tech sometimes carries people away, and Japanese are particularly susceptible to high-tech gimmickry.

The following day we left Tokyo to go to Hiroshima. At Haneda Airport we waited in the departure lounge to board the plane for Hiroshima. A conspicuously dressed group of men occupied a block of seats in the lounge. They were powerfully built; like a rugby team. One was more flamboyantly dressed than the others. He was wearing a loud checked sportscoat and sat in the middle of the group. Two others from the same group stood at either end of the lounge watching the other passengers. No other passengers sat near them. On the plane they sat across the aisle from us, and behind us.

'Who are these men?' my wife whispered nervously to an official from the Australian Embassy sitting in a nearby seat. 'They're *Yakuza*,' he said, 'gangsters. In fact, if you look closely you'll see that most of them have the first joint of their little finger missing. They cut if off as a sign of loyalty to the boss; he's the one in the loud sportscoat.' A minute or two later several of the group stood up. They each took a wooden box from the overhead rack. For a second or two my imagination ran riot. In fact they were lunch boxes identical in size and shape, and packed with the same meal.

At Hiroshima Airport I stood up to get something out of the overhead compartment. A heavy hand pushed me back into the seat. It belonged to one of the *Yakuza*. The boss got off the plane first surrounded by his bodyguard. They swept away from the terminal in a convoy of black cars. It could have been a scene from a movie set in Chicago in the time of Al Capone, except that they were Japanese and we were in Hiroshima.

At Hiroshima we visited the Peace Park, a memorial to the victims of the Atomic Bomb. I laid a wreath on a memorial shrine. We paused at the Children's Tree dedicated to a peaceful world. It was a sad interlude on the way to visit the Mazda car plant at Hofu.

I returned to Japan on a number of occasions. There were more rounds of ministerial talks, visits to various businesses with operations in Australia and, in 1986, a large delegation of Australian businessmen from various industries, as part of an Investment Mission. I made presentations at well-attended seminars in Tokyo and Osaka. Businessmen made supporting presentations of their own. There were discussion groups organised for particular industries. Interpreting and translation services were provided by young Australians fluent in Japanese. There was great esprit de corps amongst the Australian delegation who were positive and enthusiastic, with the exception of one person who was not an official delegate. He came from a company with a near monopoly on a particular product in the Australian market and attended the seminar sessions warning Japanese businessmen not to invest in Australia. He told stories of alleged proposals to increase long service leave and pay in Australia and hinted at likely outbreaks of industrial unrest. Other businesspeople on the mission characterised him as what might be politely prescribed as a self-interested dissident. Some of the Japanese businessmen were nonplussed. Most regarded the mission as a success. One described it as organised 'like an ikebana flower arrangement'.

For the Japanese, however, Australia still had a long way to go as a desirable destination for Japanese manufacturing investment. In the same year as the mission, 1986, the Industrial Bank of Japan published a report on Japanese manufacturing investment in Australia. The report was largely based on a survey of Japanese companies with manufacturing plants in Australia. It was a tale of two cultures. They identified problems such as Australia having a small population in a large landmass. The market was small and distribution was costly and difficult. Japanese companies invested in America to try to reduce trade friction with the United States. In Australia this problem did not exist. Other problems did. The Australian economic structure was inflexible, the Australian dollar was weak and service industries such as transport, telecommunications and maintenance services were unreliable. Demarcation disputes reduced productivity. Whilst strikes had reduced significantly in number and duration, 'harbour and railroad strikes are practically annual occurrences, which last for what in Japan would be considered an inconceivably long period of time'. Perhaps it was best summed up in a comment under the heading 'Differences in corporate culture':

Manufacturing industries in Australia have been developed mainly by British and American capital with the primary objective being the promotion of import substitution. Therefore, the management attitude differs from that of Japanese businesses in several fundamental aspects.

(i)   Management is conservative in viewing corporate operation and gives weight to short-term investment returns.

(ii) Management is passive toward the introduction of new technologies or investment in research and development.

(iii)   Management does not always view business entities as being perpetual or belonging to the public. Rather, they are often regarded as assets and sold as such.

At the time this seemed a harsh assessment. But it was hard to fault. Almost a year before, the *Australian Financial Review* had put a not dissimilar but less empirical view in an editorial:

> For half a decade now we have been hearing the wails of investors who somehow assume that they have been double-crossed by a fast-moving industrial society that refused to stand still. In reality Australians have been let down by their own entrenched institutions and prejudices. This is the true message of recent meetings between Australian and Japanese businessmen and government leaders.

In 1987 the Australian Football League attempted to export Australian football to Japan with a demonstration match between Carlton and Hawthorn. I attended the match at a stadium on the outskirts of Tokyo. A Japanese commentator gave an excited explanation of the game over a loudspeaker. He called it 'Ozzy Ball'. At the end of the match I presented medallions to the players and remember standing on tiptoes to hang one round the neck of a very tall player, Justin Madden. On the way back to Tokyo in the car, I talked to the chairman of a Japanese television station. He had represented Japan in the 1936 Olympic Games and went on and on about the declining moral fibre of Japanese youth. They needed toughening up. Australian football might be the answer. Sadly he was wrong. Football did not export well. I thought of Mr Amaya's suggestions about what Australia ought to be exporting. We'd have to try something else.

In Tokyo in September 1988 the Emperor Hirohito was critically ill and believed to be dying. In fact the reports were premature. But appointments with ministers and officials were delayed or sometimes cancelled. The city had a solemn atmosphere about it; people were anticipating the end of an era. There was time to walk around Tokyo, go to a performance of kabuki theatre and visit a stadium for the sumo wrestling. On the plane back to Australia we talked about the latest political scandals in Japan and the high prices for consumer goods in the shops. There had been another spate of allegations of corruption against Japanese politicians. Japanese consumers paid high prices. We wondered if it was a calculated policy— subsidise Japanese industries with high domestic prices and enable them to export more cheaply. It was easy enough to identify flaws in the system, but it still continued to work.

Each time I returned to Japan I met with the Prime Minister of the day or with senior Japanese ministers. The high ministerial turnover during the long reign of the Liberal Democratic Party usually meant that there were new faces. In my ten years as Industry Minister there were nine different MITI ministers. This included Hadjime Tamura, who had the job for three years and was a friend to Australia, and became a personal friend of mine as well.

In spite of different faces, the theme of Nakasone's remarks— the need for a special and close working relationship between Australia and Japan was always repeated. Each country was important to the other and we should work on our relationship for the future. On the Japanese side it was manifested in various ways. The Japan external trade organisations made attempts to help Australian exporters develop products for the Japanese market. In 1987 Japan came up with the proposal for the multifunction polis. An imaginative if perhaps ill-fated proposal, it involved collaboration in the exploration and development of ideas about technology and urban lifestyles in the twenty-first century.

There were always sound economic and political reasons for Japan and Australia to work together and cultivate their relationship. The Japanese recognised that things would change as their economy restructured and climbed the levels in Mr Amaya's building by the sea. They hoped for complementary changes in Australia. Amaya added a different dimension in the report of a large Japanese business investment mission which he brought to Australia in 1987:

> Among the many nations of the Western Pacific, Japan and Australia have the most nearly attuned standards of values. The two are not only economic allies but are also political companions with common ideals. Japan does not possess many real friends in the international community. Of the few that it does have, Australia is the closest ... in the long term national interest, I believe it is extremely important that Japan prove itself as a true ally of Australia.

The report praised aspects of Australian innovation and criticised work practices and managerial attitudes. It called for greater efforts to build an export culture. Amaya returned again to his swimming metaphor. 'Australia,' he said, '... now has to change its attitude if it is to swim and not sink in the Pacific Ocean.'

Australians have always been puzzled, and sometimes appalled, by aspects of Japanese society. Corruption seemed endemic in Japanese politics. It can be understood only in the context of an almost one-party state. The Liberal Democratic Party, which presided over Japan's rise to economic supremacy, changed its public faces, but remained in office. It was seldom threatened with defeat. Bribing and nepotism increased the power of local members and factions. In a country like Australia, an inheritor of the Westminster tradition, it was hard to understand. Japan kept succeeding whilst prime ministers and Cabinets came and went. A powerful public service kept it going. Japanese society seemed tolerant of the *Yakuza* and intolerant of people from other countries, the place was too homogeneous. Japanese industry seemed rapacious and uncaring of the world's natural resources. Their consensual negotiating style seemed frustrating to people who clinched deals with a nod and handshake. The Japanese had a great sense of fun, but a different sense of humour. Relations between men and women seemed structured and hidebound.

Like every country, however, Japan changed in the 1980s. Japanese insularity began to break down. The older generation became concerned about what this meant for a future Japan. Did it mean a decline in the work ethic, an erosion of tradition, a falling commitment to social and national aspirations? Time alone would tell.

Australian puzzlement about the Japanese economic miracle of the 1970s and 1980s was less understandable and more reprehensible. Like the Americans and some Europeans, we sought to explain it on the basis of ignorance and prejudice. We were 'too blessed by God' to bother much, and insufficiently serious to ask the question 'What makes this country great?'. There were always signposts, however, for those who wanted to read them. Japan did begin to open its economy to quality products from other countries. The Japanese economy did begin to restructure, moving from the ground level of energy-intensive industries up the floors of Amaya's building by the sea. And the relationship with Australia strengthened as Australia began to develop an export culture and show that it could participate in a global economy.

The Japanese economy had its own inefficiencies, including protected agriculture and complex, costly marketing and distribution systems based on historical tribal networks and self-serving loyalties. There is a tradition of looking after your own. While the government has pursued policies designed to liberalise the Japanese market, with much greater effect than most Western countries acknowledge, it is still a tough place to do business. The morass of middle men and officials consciously and sometimes unconsciously doing favours for Japanese companies produces a result which is frustrating for foreign business, particularly Americans. Historically this is understandable in a country with a large population crowded onto a cluster of relatively small islands. And by and large the Japanese have made it all work. As time passes, pressures from within Japan will mean further changes and further liberalisation.

Each time I went back I felt more at ease and increasingly fascinated by the efficiency of Japanese engineering solutions to different problems, the inherent strength of strong traditions and the commitment to quality and design. And Japanese politeness and sense of order were powerful traits of a society where though many things might be wrong, many things were also right as a basis for constructive human relationships. Japan is a place where you need to peel away at the onion if you want to savour the best.

If you catch the eye of a Japanese woman—a stranger across a crowded restaurant or room—her eyelids will drop down like shutters on a closing shop. She may be a very stylish woman, well-educated, travelled, strongly influenced by Western culture and taste. But it will still happen. It is quintessentially Japanese. It represents the shyness, modesty, exclusiveness and diffidence of a strong tradition and culture. It symbolises Japan as it was before the arrival of the Black Ships; cut off from the outside world and preoccupied with its own values and society. If the shutters are raised for a moment, it hints at the changes which are leading Japan to engage the world. It is to be hoped she gets it right. Japan has much to offer and much which is worthwhile to protect.

REFERENCES

Akio Morita, 'What the Japanese power clique really think of the Americans.' *Sunday Herald*, 11 March 1990

Chalmers Johnson, *The Japanese Economy: A different kind of Capitalism*, Centre of Technology & Policy at Boston University

Chikara Higashi, *Japanese Trade Policy Formulation*

Keijiro Murata, 'Thoughts in Flight'

Industrial Bank of Japan, *Direct Investment in Australia by Japanese Manufacturing Industries: Current States and Problem Areas*, September, 1986

Australian Financial Review, Editorial, 18 June, 1985

Naohiro Amaya, *The Australian Investment Environment Survey Mission Report*, May, 1987

Margaret Thatcher's party: 1989

For some Australians Britain is a destination in itself: the centrepiece of an overseas trip. For others it is a stopover on the way to Europe, or Scandinavia or even Africa. One way or another we keep going back there, enjoying the luxury of ambivalent feelings about a place which used to be called the Mother Country.

I spent a couple of days in London in October 1987 on what might be described as a typical ministerial visit. I had three meetings with senior executives of major British firms with substantial operations in Australia; a lengthy discussion with Sir Francis Tombs, the Chairman of the Advisory Council on Science and Technology; and a meeting with Lord Young, the Minister for Trade and Industry. At a lunch I gave a presentation on investment opportunities for British companies in Australia. These sorts of visits are about keeping in touch, finding out what they're up to, trying to establish better relationships, refurbishing common interests.

In 1988 Margaret Thatcher came to Australia for the bicentennial celebrations—a sort of 'happy hour' event, when various heads of state paid us a visit, full of goodwill. It was agreed that there should be a return visit to Britain led by Bob Hawke. It would be a trade and investment mission and an opportunity to improve relations between the two countries: a big bang affair. It all took place in June 1989 with Hawke, four other ministers and a business delegation representing

Australia. The British arranged a program suitable for the occasion. It included a day at the cricket, a business conference, meetings with the British Government, dinners, *The Phantom of the Opera*, visits here and there.

We stayed at the Hyde Park Hotel, a baronial pile cluttered with furniture collected over the last century. A retired Wing-Commander had been assigned by the British Government to look after me. He took the job seriously, thrusting schedules and programs into my hand at every opportunity, standing at my elbow to make sure protocol was observed, making sure I got up at the right time each morning. He became a sort of amicable burden. People kept telling me that he was accident-prone. They alleged he'd shot down more British planes than German ones during the war. This made me nervous. I think he thought I was a casual, ill-disciplined fellow. Halfway through a cocktail reception, which I hosted for British delegates to the conference, he touched me on the elbow and said: 'Come along Minister, time to go now.' 'What do you mean?' I said. 'I can't be the first to leave.' 'I'm afraid Minister,' he said, 'you will have to leave. You're going to No. 10 for dinner tonight. You'll need a *barf* before you go there.' It was not entirely surprising that our relationship remained cool, although I cheered him up from time to time by calling him 'Wingco', a nickname he seemed to rather like.

Our host at *The Phantom of the Opera* was the Right Hon. Kenneth Baker, the Secretary of State for Education and Science. A genial, slightly donnish man with a permanent grin, Baker had assembled a list of guests for *The Phantom* and supper afterwards at the Ritz. At interval I ran into Robert Holmes à Court, who was sitting in a box with his wife. I asked him what you had to do to get a box. He said it was not difficult because he owned the theatre. 'In fact,' he said, 'I own sixteen theatres in London.' I mentioned that I was tired from jet lag. He said the best solution to jet lag was to own your own plane and sleep all the way from

Australia to London. I went back for the second half of the musical with my mind cluttered with this valuable information.

I'd met Kenneth Baker on previous occasions in the United Kingdom and Australia. At a dinner in Canberra a couple of months before the London conference he'd remarked that 'you Australians dine very well'. In response I had uncharitably commented that 'that's more than I can say for your lot'. 'My God, that's a challenge,' said Baker. 'When you're in London I will take you to the Ritz.' I went for supper at the Ritz with limited anticipations. London restaurants are the only ones I know with a capacity to 'stuff up' something as simple as a cheese sandwich. This supper was more complex, more up-market. It was served in an attic-like room several floors above ground level. The lift got stuck with a group of guests and the rest trudged up a number of flights of stairs. It was a hot oppressive London night. The attic had a low ceiling. The service was understandably bad as the waiters had to bring the food up the stairs from a lower floor. There was an interesting group of guests and Kenneth Baker was a charming host, but it was not a great meal.

The following morning Bob Hawke led the official Australian group out of the Hyde Park Hotel to a fleet of waiting cars. There were a few bystanders in the street, including Australian tourists. Hawke strode straight to the car waving his hand and saying 'Gday, Gday, G—day', the last word elongated into a noise like a cockatoo makes flying out of a gum tree. He was in a businesslike mood for a meeting at No. 10 Downing Street. The meeting took place in a Cabinet room at the rear of the house, with several ministers participating on each side. The prime ministers did most of the talking, circling each other like boxers in a friendly charity fight which both wanted to win.

Hawke pursued the issue of Australia's initiative to have the Antarctic declared a protected wilderness area. He sought British support, which Mrs Thatcher was not prepared to give. 'Don't you think, Bob,' she cooed, 'that the question is a larger one, better considered in the light of the whole ecosystem?' Hawke persisted. She dropped her scientific academic credentials into the ring. The discussion ended in a stalemate. The talk moved on to other things—the buzz words of collaboration and the gossip of international politics. At pre-lunch drinks Denis Thatcher hovered like a drink waiter, dispensing smiles and hospitality: an apparently perfect consort and yet his own man. The lunchtime conversation turned again to international affairs with Mrs Thatcher elaborating her views on the Soviet Union and Mikhail Gorbachev, with whom she had developed a considerable rapport. The task of rebuilding the Soviet Union, she thought, was too big for any individual. The country had no entrepreneurs, no-one experienced in business. Each time she met Gorbachev his insights into the problems had deepened, the solutions seemed further away.

Lord McAlpine, the Treasurer of the Conservative Party, hosted a cocktail party at Lancaster House for Australian ministers and officials. McAlpine, a diffident, friendly and unpretentious man, had substantial investments in Australia in hotels, property and the stylish Cable Beach Resort at Broome. He had a large collection of Australian paintings including many Sidney Nolans. He collected antique bush furniture. At Broome he had built a splendid zoo in which he tried to breed endangered species from around the world. With grand visions for the sympathetic development of the north of Western Australia, he was a modern day private-sector Cecil Rhodes, with an ameliorating level of cultivated taste.

Ultimately his Australian empire fell victim to the pilots' strike, the recession and the restraining hand of family business interests in the UK. A totally committed supporter of Margaret Thatcher, I once heard McAlpine describe a British Conservative politician as 'not one of us', meaning someone not totally committed to Thatcher. At the dinner at No. 10 Downing Street which followed McAlpine's party the British guests were all luminaries of Margaret Thatcher's Britain— politicians, officials, cricketer David Gower, the youthful entrepreneur Richard Branson and, of course, McAlpine.

In 1989, Lord Young of Graffham was Secretary of State for Trade and Industry and official host at the Trade and Investment Conference. I'd met him on several occasions. He was a former businessman, a life peer and a Thatcher favourite. He believed strongly in enterprise, competition and entrepreneurship. Each time I met him he gave me a little card printed with the essential principles of private enterprise; a kind of tract encompassing the ten commandments of business competition. He once told me that the British Government was officially against any form of intervention in industry. 'Actually we do it all over the place.' It was an honest acknowledgment of the messy realities of international trade and industry policy.

The Thatcher Government, which adopted a high profile as a protagonist of the free market, was a frequent interventionist on behalf of British firms. It paid four hundred million pounds to attract a major Japanese motor vehicle manufacturer to invest in a large plant in Britain. The government was accused, in Lord Young's time as Secretary of State, rightly or wrongly, of interfering through the Monopolies and Mergers Commission in potential takeovers of British companies by overseas firms. Lord Young himself believed in his tract. The problem was that a lot of British industry didn't and most of the countries in the European Community didn't either. In Britain there was, however, not much debate about these issues. Beneath the public rhetoric many attempts were made by government to encourage a new level of entrepreneurial drive in a persistently sluggish British economy. Only in Australia was the idea of a 'level playing field' consistently cited as the benchmark of industrial and economic virility.

About one hundred Australian businesses were represented at the conference led by the Confederation of Australian Industry. A briefing session was scheduled at Australia House at 4.30 p.m. on the day before the conference. It was designed to explain the program and to consider the benefits which might be derived from it. The delegation needed to be well prepared. It was one of those well-laid plans in which fate intervenes. The police closed and cordoned off Australia House a few minutes before the proposed briefing because of a bomb scare. Australians are nothing if not adaptive to unforeseen circumstances. The briefing turned into a street party in The Strand with beer and glasses being provided by nearby pubs. Everyone enjoyed themselves, and left none the wiser.

The conference took place in the Queen Elizabeth II Conference Centre. The two prime ministers spoke; Thatcher almost without notes but precise and commanding. Ministers from both sides spoke. Then Alan Jackson, the Australian Chief Executive of BTR, dazzled the audience with a series of block graph overheads showing his companies' growth rates in Australia, returns on capital, profits and so on. It all seemed too good to be true. Simon Crean, the retiring President of the Australian Council of Trade Unions, embarked courageously on the obligatory attempt to overcome negative perceptions of Australia's bad industrial record. The business speakers on the British side were Sir Ralph Robbins of Rolls Royce and Richard Branson of Virgin Records and Virgin Airlines fame.

I'd met Robbins several times before in the United Kingdom and Australia. On one occasion over lunch he spent half an hour warning me of the dangers of a re-emergent Germany. It was scary stuff. Two years later, after Rolls Royce had entered into a strategic alliance with a major German company, he seemed to think the problem had gone away. He was the sort of man you'd expect to be a senior executive of Rolls

Royce. Just as people who spend their lives with horses tend to appear horsy, Robbins looked and sounded 'Rolls Roycey': clean lines, handsome, well-turned-out, but without ostentation. His speech was delivered in a well-modulated purr. Richard Branson provided a more flashy model: long hair, no tie, irreverent, slightly foppish and loaded with self-esteem. He performed, and as a performer was mildly entertaining. Margaret Thatcher glowed over him with almost maternal pride. He was a symbol of what she was about: creating a new breed of British entrepreneur, bold and innovative like an eighteenth century buccaneer reincarnated in the twentieth century as a young prince of British capitalism. But even at the conference, the question dangled in the air: was he typical or unique?

In the afternoon the conference broke up into discussion group sessions. I was never quite clear how the discussion groups went, which was mildly disconcerting as at the closing plenary session Lord Young and I were supposed to sum up. Lord Young was detained and Margaret Thatcher stood in for him. For half an hour before the plenary session I sat in a small anteroom in the conference centre with Margaret Thatcher and Bob Hawke, drinking coffee and scribbling notes on the back of an envelope. An official brought in a cable from Australia. It was from the Trade Minister, Michael Duffy. It said, 'Bad luck mate. Ablett suspended for eight weeks.' It turned out to be a complete hoax. It worked. It threw me into a mood of total despair.

Duffy and I enjoyed a friendly rivalry over our respective football teams and Ablett was a star player from my team, Geelong, which looked a certainty for the finals in September. Ablett had in fact been suspended for two weeks, but I didn't find out the truth till later. Bob Hawke saw that I was disconcerted by the contents of the cable so I told him what was in it. He understood my concerns and a few minutes later I heard him explaining the significance of it all to Margaret

Thatcher. She looked puzzled. In the closing session I spoke first: then Margaret Thatcher. She gave a polished off-the-cuff speech. She said, 'I disagree with Senator Button on one point. However, I'm inclined to forgive him as I understand he's very upset by the fate of a Mr Gary Ablett.' I looked at the audience. Some of them were taking notes. I thought these people must think he's Australia's answer to Richard Branson: a new breed of entrepreneur. Perhaps another Alan Bond or Holmes à Court.

Margaret Thatcher was generous with her time and hospitality. There was another dinner at No. 10, this time attended by the Australian ministers and a group of her Cabinet colleagues. I sat between Margaret Thatcher and the wife of the Foreign Secretary, Sir Geoffrey Howe. Lady Howe, a professional social worker and a simpatico conversationalist, made it pretty clear she was not 'one of us', to use McAlpine's phrase. She had my left ear, Mrs Thatcher had the right. Warring messages met in the middle of my head. Our host, the British Prime Minister, handled the conversation like an ikebana flower arrangement, introducing new topics, closing off old ones, giving a word of promise here and a mild reprimand there. She hovered somewhere in the twilight zone between a schoolmistress and a psychotherapist leading a group discussion. There was no doubt who was in charge: who was the master of the ceremony.

Nobody seemed more aware of that than her ministerial colleagues who would begin each conversational point with words like 'as you have observed yourself Prime Minister ...' or 'Prime Minister, I'm sure you'll agree ...' Geoffrey Howe alone amongst the ministers seemed free of this irritating habit. He'd been Foreign Secretary since 1983. He'd had a lot of experience of Margaret Thatcher, and didn't bother to hide his distance from her. It was then less than sixteen months before he resigned from the government. In a scathing speech in the House of Commons he attacked Thatcher's style and the manner in which she dealt with ministerial and Cabinet colleagues. He referred to her 'tragic conflict of loyalties'. Ten days later she lost the prime ministership herself.

A few more things had to be done before the London visit came to an end. The Lord Mayor gave a dinner for Bob Hawke and the Australian delegation at the historic Mansion House in the City of London. The invitation specified white tie and tails so I respectfully declined. I heard that Hawke had asked to be allowed to wear less formal dress, but that his request was politely refused. Shouldering the prime ministerial burden he dressed as required. Australian ministers Kim Beazley and Gareth Evans went in tails. Simon Crean got away with a dinner jacket. I heard that the guests from London high society were prevailed on to sing 'Waltzing Matilda'. It all sounded jovial and somewhat uncomfortable. An Australian newspaper columnist thought I would have found it all rather funny—but I was not to know.

There were a few wrap-up discussions about the conference. It's hard to assess the impact of these events. My guess is that not much happened as a result of it all. We learnt that each country's exports to the other were declining steadily, that the composition of exports from Australia to Britain was changing, and that a number of Australian companies were investing in Britain to try to capture the anticipated benefits of the European Common Market. Not much was discussed or learnt about the outcomes of significant economic change in either country; certainly nothing which could not be read about in a good newspaper. So we were left with the suggestion that to stop the 'drift in the relationship', there should be a series of positive ministerial statements. Somehow I felt sceptical about that. Glendower could 'summon spirits from the vastly deep'. For ministers it's much harder work.

I had a meeting with Kenneth Baker, the Secretary of State for Education and Science, at his Department. We exchanged letters in a formal little ceremony, conducted in a pleasantly informal way. The letters provided for a program of science teacher exchanges, some increased cooperation in environmental sciences and some additional fellowships for university scientists. Maybe this would be the way of future cooperation, a start of the golden age which Kenneth Baker had spoken about with enthusiasm nearly six years before.

On our last day in London, Neil Kinnock, the Leader of the British Labour Party, and some of his shadow ministers came for breakfast as our guests. It was intended as an exchange of information and as a goodwill gesture between representatives of fraternal political parties. It turned out to be a desultory and lacklustre event. In brutal terms, Hawke was a winner and knew it, Kinnock was a loser, and probably knew it. Kinnock and his colleagues were intelligent, sensible people. But they presided over a political party which was apparently incapable of grasping the mood of the times: a party fixed in a straitjacket of the British class structure and ageing images of reality. The occasion pointed out the reasons for Thatcher's success. Political parties which seem to know what they're doing, even if they don't, usually win.

The visit to London was Margaret Thatcher's party. She was an impeccable hostess: cool, poised and hospitable. She went out of her way to entertain the Australian Party and she seemed genuinely interested in the changes taking place in Australia. It was as if, as other doors were closed on her hopes and ambitions, another door had swung open revealing a chink of light. Her Industry Minister Lord Young had chided me on several occasions about the way in which Australian companies were competing with British companies in China. He thought it was getting a bit tough. That's precisely what she liked and respected. In 1989 time was running out for her as Prime Minister of Britain. Time was running out because she and her government had got things wrong. In spite of the heady rhetoric, the iron in the image and her undoubted political skills, Britain continued to decline in influence and wealth. She became the sacrificial lamb, the disposable Prime Minister, the victim of the mistakes of others and herself.

I've not read her own account of her period in government. There is an inevitably self-serving element in books of that kind. She probably regards her finest achievements as the Falklands War, and the subjugation of the British trade unions. The Falklands War was a futile example of recidivist behaviour by an ex-colonial power hankering for a taste of former glory. It got the adrenalin going in all those fossils of the military and civil service establishments, the ersatz county gentry, and the true believers of Britain as a 'land of hope and glory' with which the South of England is cluttered. There were, of course, in the British Government and throughout the country, many doubters. Thatcher had no time for doubters. Like Winston Churchill in the Second World War, she provided 'the roar' of the British Lion and the country enjoyed a few months of euphoria.

One suspects that, at heart, Margaret Thatcher was an incurable romantic, with a romanticism that took the form of a passionate belief in Britain's destiny. 'Thatcherism' emerged as an ideology seeking to get rid of all those things which held Britain back from the fulfilment of that destiny. The check list included unforgivable behaviour from 'lesser breeds' in Africa, the Middle East and Argentina, the unions, sluggish subsidised industries, an overblown public sector, the welfare state, an absence of entrepreneurship and the dubious machinations of the Europeans across the English Channel. The check list dismissed sections of British society, rather than enlisting them. It was the politics of exclusion rather than inclusion. Did she include the debilitating rigidities of the British class structure? If she did, it is not something which she could articulate because of her own lower middle-class origins: a strength in most countries, a burden in England.

In dealing with her check list she displayed a single-minded determination not evident in her limp-wristed predecessors and almost certainly not in those that succeeded her. For a long time she seemed to know where she was going. She won elections. She cajoled and lectured and persuaded. She enjoyed intense admiration and engendered strong animosity. Ultimately the judgement of history for a prime minister turns on the question of whether you leave the job with the country in better shape than when you began. By this criterion Thatcherism was not a success. The remedy failed to produce the results expected of it. There have been a few lasting achievements, but Britain's rigid class structure remains, and is now compounded by deeper divisions of wealth and poverty. Confidence in traditional British institutions has fallen. Internationally Britain continues in relative decline.

With the Falklands War, Margaret Thatcher temporarily re-ignited the spirit of the British people. Sadly, it was the wrong spirit. One suspects that she really wanted a new generation of 'get up and go' Englishmen and women to recapture in the late twentieth century the drive, initiative and flair of the men and women who built the British Empire in the eighteenth and nineteenth century. Like Gorbachev she set herself a hard task. It's no wonder that Lord Young was, for a while, a favoured Cabinet Minister. He believed in entrepreneurs. It's not surprising that Lord McAlpine was a favourite. He was loyal and a commercial visionary who believed in creating wealth. Her admiration for Richard Branson as a youthful buccaneer builder of new businesses seemed unstinted. None of these were old school men. These were the new breed, her sort of people. There just weren't enough of them.

On my last morning in Britain I went to the cricket at Lord's. It was a one-day match between Australia and England. Cricket is a great British institution, somehow also in decline. It seemed a rather dull match. I couldn't quite get into the spirit of the game. After a couple of hours 'Wingco' touched me on the arm. 'Time to go to the airport, Minister.' At the airport he indicated mild disapproval at the fact that I was going to Ireland. Otherwise he seemed totally relaxed and friendly. His responsibilities were finished. The party was over.

Ireland: voices in our past: 1989

The Irish Prime Minister, Charles Haughey, came to Australia in 1988 as part of the bicentennial celebrations, one of many prime ministers and heads of state to visit Australia that year. His visit, however, had a qualitative difference. He came representing a country which, with the exception of Britain, had probably exercised a greater influence on Australian history and culture than any other in the two hundred years of European settlement.

In the course of his visit, he announced a bicentennial gift to Australia from the Republic of Ireland; copy records of the names and particulars of Irish men and women transported to Australia from the time of the First Fleet. There were plenty of them.

Later in 1988 Seamus Brennan, the Irish Trade Minister, brought an Irish business mission to Australia. The mission came to Canberra and held seminars in Melbourne and Sydney. Brennan could talk. Articulate and persuasive, he had the Irish flair for making a case and illustrating it with memorable stories. Ireland, he argued, was the logical base from which Australian companies could do business in the European Community. A common language, the high standard of Irish education and a new dawn of entrepreneurial skills and industrial sophistication made the logic compelling. Even the Japanese, he told us, had something to learn from the born-again Ireland.

He claimed that a Japanese sales representative, marketing a sophisticated machine tool, had explained that the equipment worked to within tolerances of a fraction of a millimetre. 'Aargh,' said the Irish industrialist, 'in Ireland that would not be good enough. Here, it has to be spot on each time.' Nor was the government remiss in the rigorous administration of policy. A taxation amnesty had been provided under which arrears could be paid by a specified date without attracting a penalty. A defaulter apprehended after the expiration of the amnesty period would be sent to gaol. 'It's worked like a charm,' said Brennan. 'We received five hundred million pounds, rather than the eighty million we expected. They've been queuing up outside the tax office with white envelopes in their hands.' He paused, reflectively. 'And Senator, it is a wonderful thing indeed, when I remind you that all this is happening in a Catholic country. You should,' he said, 'bring a return business mission to see all this for yourself.'

The visit of Prime Minister Charles Haughey was an unequivocal success. He got on well with Bob Hawke. They shared common interests in horseracing, a fascination for political power and an appreciation of the history of the Australian–Irish connection. In Ireland, Haughey's political opponents were always accusing him of political and financial skulduggery. In Australia, at Irish Community functions in Sydney, Melbourne and Canberra he charmed his way around the corridors of power.

At a dinner in the Great Hall of Parliament House there was plenty to drink and an Australian folk music performance produced an appropriate mood of sentiment and nostalgia. The two prime ministers made speeches lamenting the fact that the strong connections between Ireland and Australia had been allowed to languish and were not reflected in a more rigorous trading relationship between the two countries. Inevitably, it was decided that there should be an exchange of trade and investment missions between the two countries.

And so, in 1989, I found myself heading for Dublin with a small delegation from Australian businesses.

It was a journey to which I looked forward. I had made only one previous visit to Ireland, in the 1970s. That time I flew to Dublin from Bristol, England, in a small plane. A tough-looking young Irishman, sitting opposite me, had a dotted line tattooed across his throat. Studying him more closely I managed to read above the dotted line the words: 'Cut here, if you're game', like instructions on a Weeties packet. He told me he came from Belfast. I wondered apprehensively if a significant proportion of the Irish population were similarly addicted to macabre invitations of this kind.

In Dublin I stayed in a hotel furnished with all the glitz and gadgets of the 1950s, none of which seemed to work. From there I went out, my head cluttered with images from Irish literature, looking for places introduced to me by Yeats, Joyce and Sean O'Casey. Expecting magic in the limpid waters of the Coode Canal, I found only a stagnant urban drain. O'Connell Street disappointed, Miriam Square struck me as a pale equivalent of the best of Carlton and East Melbourne. I decided that the magic of Dublin was to be found in the literature rather than in reality.

This time I decided to have another go at understanding the place. The Trade and Investment Conference was to begin in Dublin on a Monday. On the Thursday before the conference my son and I flew from London to Shannon Airport on the west coast of Ireland. We intended a quiet anonymous weekend. We planned to hire a car, stay in bed and breakfast accommodation and drive round the coast through County Clare and County Galway. We would visit famous places like the Cliffs of Mohr, the Burra and the Connemara and drive to Clifden on the far West Coast.

At Shannon Airport our planned anonymity began to unravel. We had seriously underestimated Irish hospitality and the fact that it is a small world. The moment we landed we were met by a charming woman from the Shannon Development Board, who sat us up in the airport bar with a large Guinness. She produced maps and tourist brochures and explained them to us as we embarked on a second and third Guinness. Coming out of the bar, I ran into an Australian businessman visiting the county of his forbears. He was on his way to Dublin. It was all the shape of things to come: chance encounters, friendliness, Guinness and charm.

We picked up a hire car at the airport and headed for Limerick and our first experience of an Irish bed and breakfast. The house at No. 15 was a grey, stucco, two-storey building, distinguished from the other houses in the street by a large 'Bed and Breakfast' sign at the front gate. I knocked hesitantly at the front door. Past experience had persuaded me that b and b landladies are sometimes formidable. First impressions, I thought, might be important.

Mrs O'Toole opened the front door herself. She was a big lady—wide rather than tall—with blonded hair and bright-red lips. She seemed to be quivering with excitement. 'Aargh, I've been waitin' for you,' she said, rubbing her hands together. 'It's wonderful, simply wonderful.' She paused; 'Well, it may be terrible for you, but it's wonderful for us.' 'You're very kind,' I mumbled. 'Not at all,' said Mrs O'Toole. 'I know you're important. But I don't know who you are. Who are you now?' Caught off guard I tried to explain. 'Very good, that's very good,' she said. 'Now will you come over here and write it down in my book.' I sat down and wrote a couple of lines in an exercise book on the hall table.

Mrs O'Toole went to the foot of the stairs and called out, 'Brendan, Brendan lad. Bring the camera. We'll go into the back garden and have some photographs.' A few seconds later Brendan, her nineteen-year-old son, came tumbling down the stairs with a camera in his hands. He was followed almost immediately by an American tourist with a large camera bag on his shoulder. 'Ah,' said Mrs O'Toole, 'You'll be wantin'

some photographs too, will you not?' The American appeared
confused. 'No thanks,' he said. 'I'm going out to take some
pictures of Bunratty Castle.' Mrs O'Toole looked at me and
rolled her eyes. Americans have no sense of occasion.

In the small back garden a setting had been arranged with
the unerring skill usually displayed in budget TV productions.
Mrs O'Toole and I sat together on a white garden seat, while
Brendan rearranged the beach umbrella to ensure that the
light was right. Then he went to work with his camera. I
took the opportunity to ask Mrs O'Toole what the exceptional
welcome was about. 'Ah,' she said, 'The *Tao'Iseach* phoned
you this afternoon. He's going to call you back at nine o'clock
in the morning. You must be important if the *Tao'Iseach*
phones.'

We accepted an offer from Mrs O'Toole to take us for a
drive around the city of Limerick. It turned out to be a good
decision. She drove a new white Jaguar which suggested a
good market share of the B and B business. I guessed it was
the only car of its kind in Limerick, where it seemed to enjoy
a degree of respect. Mrs O'Toole was able to drive it slowly
through the narrow streets, holding up the traffic behind her,
while she pointed out various landmarks and historic buildings.
She parked it in churchyards, and on one occasion in the
middle of the road, while we inspected a monument.

Her driving, which engendered an excitement of its own,
was accompanied by a running commentary delivered with
the speed and professionalism of an audio cassette for tourists.
We were told the dates of major events, of poignant moments
in Irish history, about the benign influence of St Patrick and
of the bitter legacy of British landlords. At the end of our
tour we stopped beside a small park to look at a damaged
monument commemorating soldiers killed in the First World
War. 'The IRA blew this monument up,' Mrs O'Toole said.
'Some people say they were wrong to do it. But I don't know.
I just don't know.'

We were having breakfast the following morning when the phone rang. Mrs O'Toole answered it in the kitchen. 'It's for you,' she shouted. 'You'd better take it in the front room.' I picked up the phone in the front room. It was Charles Haughey, the Irish Prime Minister. 'I'm just phoning to welcome you to Ireland,' he said. 'Are you being well looked after?' I assured him I was. He had just fought an election in which he had tried, without success, to obtain a majority in the Parliament. The newspapers were full of stories of endless negotiations between Haughey and his political opponents in an attempt to form a coalition. The future of his government was very much in doubt. I asked him how it was all going. 'It's all a bit difficult,' he said, 'but I suspect it's just a ritual dance.'

An hour later when we said farewell, a small group of neighbours had gathered on the footpath outside the house. Mrs O'Toole formally presented me with a tablemat embroidered with the words:

May you have food and raiment
A soft pillow for your head
May you have forty years in heaven
Before the devil knows you're dead.

As we climbed into the car she leaned forward and said, 'What did the *Tao'Iseach* say again? I want to get it right. Something about a ritual dance?' 'Yes,' I said. 'He told me he was going through a ritual dance.' 'I thought that was it,' she replied. 'I didn't quite hear. That noisy Brendan came into the kitchen in the middle of the conversation. I'll write it down in my book before I forget it.'

And so, with the blessing of Mrs O'Toole and her neighbours, we drove off through County Clare and into County Galway, stopping at the Cliffs of Mohr and a few pubs along the way for a sandwich and a warming Guinness. We drove through the Connemara 'beyond the twelve bens' to Clifden on the West Coast and then back to Dublin.

Arriving in Dublin on a Sunday evening, I was welcomed by Ray Bourke, the Irish Minister for Industry. Having been in London the week before, meeting with uptight Tory politicians and enmeshed in the attendant formalities, Ray Bourke seemed relaxed and down to earth. 'Let's,' he said, 'have a nice and easygoing conference. No fuss. The most important thing is everybody getting to know each other.'

It was an appropriately pragmatic approach. My tactical briefing had warned me that 'the meeting will be more in the nature of a familiarisation exercise on both sides'. There was little of economic and trade substance between the two countries. Irish investment in Australia was $A51 million: Australian investment in Ireland negligible. Irish exports to Australia were $A201 million, glass and alcoholic beverages were significant items. Australian exports to Ireland were $A7 million in total. There was not a great deal on which to build a strong trading relationship. All I could think of was more Guinness and more Fosters.

The Australian business delegation consisted of business-people with some connections with Ireland in banking, insurance, food processing and mining. The Irish delegation was representative of similar interests with the late inclusion of the Director of the Abbey Theatre, who at the last minute refreshingly introduced the issue of cultural exchange to the conference agenda. Ireland was not the land of poets, musicians and playwrights for nothing.

At the opening of the conference Ray Bourke made a speech on the subject of 'Ireland: Ideal partner in Europe', in which he presented Ireland as a base for Australian businesses seeking to operate in the integrated European Market after 1992. In turn I spoke on the even more grandiose topic of 'Australia: a Partner for Cooperation in Europe and the Asia–Pacific Region'. Both delegations worked hard at illustrating the cases advanced by their respective ministers.

Ireland, we were told, was a country of high educational standards and a rapidly developing industrial culture. It offered a skilled workforce, low business taxes and a profitable location for investment in the European Community. Australia, we told them in turn, was the most sophisticated economy in South-East Asia, a gateway between European industry and the markets to Australia's north. Each side listened politely to the other. It all sounded plausible, but confirmed my preliminary view that it was hard to see the building blocks of a stronger economic relationship. The conference broke up into specialist subgroups and reconvened for a lengthy news conference, at which we sought to explain it all to a sceptical Irish press.

The Irish Government hosted a dinner for the Australian delegation at Dublin Castle. For nearly four hundred years until 1922, the Castle was the Vice-Regal residence and seat of the British Administration in Ireland. Walking into the splendid reception hall gave an instant feeling of the heyday of the British Raj. A broad staircase led past rich wall hangings from India and the Far East, to a reception room with a throne presented by William of Orange and classical furniture of the eighteenth and nineteenth centuries. As overseas guests we were given a guided tour of the various state apartments and reception rooms, decorated with glistening chandeliers, gilt mirrors and paintings of viceroys and their ladies.

According to our guide, only the foresight of Eamon de Valera in the 1920s stopped the removal of these trappings of colonial power from Dublin Castle. Our guide gave a detailed explanation as we went along: 'Queen Victoria was the last person to sleep in this room—except for Margaret Thatcher. We put it into working order for her during her state visit to Ireland a few years ago.'

In the last room we were asked to stand in a semicircle around a stain on the gold carpet, just in front of the fireplace.

'Here,' she told us, 'in this spot, the great Irish patriot James Connolly lay wounded for a week before he was taken out and executed by the British. This is where his body was.' She paused and we looked. 'You should know,' she said, studying us closely and with a faint smile, 'that the carpet was not put down until forty years after Connolly's death. And indeed,' she added, 'the carpet has been changed several times since. But the stain always comes back.' There were some sceptical Australian grunts; on balance it seemed to be agreed that one piece of folklore was as good as another.

The good dinner was made better by the storytelling skills of our Irish hosts. The Chairman of the Electricity Authority told us of a visit he made to the south of Ireland to visit a gaoled farmer. He had been sent to prison for refusing to comply with a court order permitting the Authority to put powerlines across his land. Having fasted for several weeks, he announced his intention to fast to death. The Chairman talked to him in his cell for an hour. And then there was a breakthrough. 'I will never agree with you, Mr Moriaty,' said the farmer, 'but you've turned out to be a gentleman, and in honour of that fact I propose to take a small meal.'

There were many such stories, made more fascinating by the richness of the Irish vocabulary. He was an 'artful' man, that farmer, someone observed. True and what a splendid word 'artful' is, but sadly it has disappeared from the vocabulary of conventional English. In Ireland the language and its expression makes everything a little more colourful; a little larger than life. A man at my table, extrapolating on Ireland's position in the European Community, told me I should understand that a certain Irish port was the largest coal port in Europe. It was a categorical statement; until he added, almost as an afterthought; 'If, of course, you cast aside Rotterdam.'

The stories, the descriptions, the droll humour are all the better to an Australian ear for being expressed in an Irish accent which is sometimes easy to imitate but impossible to transpose into print. And within Ireland the accents vary from a softened version of Middle English to the few almost indecipherable English words spoken by the Gaelic speakers of the Connemara.

It was, in Ray Bourke's words, 'a nice and easygoing conference.' We got to know each other better. I am unaware of any tangible outcomes in trade or investment, but hopefully there are some. I left wondering how a small country of three and a half million people had exerted so much influence around the world in countries to which Irish people had migrated. And I wondered about the ease with which Australians and Irish relate to each other.

In a Dublin pub a man asked me 'Have you heard the news?' 'No, I haven't,' I said innocently. 'Well, buy me a "poynt" an' I'll tell you.' Somehow it was a remark which almost made me homesick: the sort of remark one might run across, in different words and accents, anywhere in a hotel in outback Australia. Australians and the Irish share a talent for leg-pulling, scepticism, intolerance of 'tall poppies' and irreverence. The sense of heroic failure is strong in each culture. The Irish recount tales of the Irish King Bryan Barugh with pride, ignoring the fact that he was a glorious failure. Australians do it with Gallipoli and the legendary journey of Burke and Wills. Attempting to identify the Australian character and the Australian sense of humour, most people will do it by referring to qualities which seem also exclusively Irish in origin. The relaxed easygoing scepticism certainly doesn't come from the English.

The history of the Irish in Australia has largely been written in the context of contributions by individuals of Irish extraction to Australian public life and institutions. The history books are studded with accounts of distinguished Irish archbishops, politicians, lawyers, footballers, trade unionists, and sometimes writers and musicians. It is a story which began in 1788, and which continued with the Irish migrants who came to Australia in the early days of European settlement.

But I suspect the Irish contribution to Australia is bigger than that. In one way it can be tested by asking the question 'What makes Australians, in their humour and attitude, different from New Zealanders?' It is hard to find an answer, other than the influence of the Irish, who were here from the beginning of European settlement. There was no significant Irish settlement in New Zealand until the 1920s; perhaps too late to make a real contribution to the literature, the folk music, the language and the humour of Australia's 'Kiwi' cousins. Australia owes much to the Irish legacy.

I left Ireland with the strong feeling that I would like to go back. At Dublin Airport the Australian Ambassador to Ireland, Brian Burke, a man steeped in the tradition of Australian Irish Catholicism, said goodbye to us at the aerobridge. We shook hands. 'It's been good to see you mate,' he said, 'and God bless.'

On the trail of
Ho Chi Minh:
1990

I t's a strange experience filing past the corpse of Ho Chi
Minh. His frail looking body lies on a catafalque in the
mausoleum in Hanoi. A soldier with fixed bayonet stands
motionless at each corner of the catafalque. These are picked
men, powerfully built. The contrast between the frail, ascetic
leader and the loyal, robust followers is an unintended picture
which tells a Vietnamese story. 'The most precious things in
life are liberty and freedom,' Ho used to say. In death, he
wanted to be cremated and his ashes scattered across the
Vietnamese countryside. But he lies there in the mausoleum.
His wishes were not granted. He is too powerful a symbol of
Vietnamese nationalism and the liberation struggle. His body
is working overtime.

The mausoleum is a stark square building of a style which
used to be called 'contemporary Soviet brutal'. Following the
success as a shrine of Moscow's Lenin Mausoleum, the Russians
inflicted a 'mausoleum culture' on China and Vietnam. It
could have spread to other countries. In Russia the embalmer's
art became a science and, from time to time, Ho's body was
flown to Moscow for treatment by Soviet scientists. In 1990
there was a story that the Russians could not pay for this
expensive practice any more and people became concerned
about what the future held.

Ho is much revered. On a normal day there is a queue of
people up to half a kilometre long waiting to go through the

mausoleum. They are said to be mainly peasants from rural Vietnam visiting Hanoi, and the mausoleum is the highlight of the visit. He is a symbol of unity and hope.

Inside, in the dimly lit vaulted chamber, Ho's face looks even more ascetic than in the photographs. His famous beard looks even more wispy. A continuous line of pilgrims shuffle past, outside the guardrail surrounding the catafalque. There is a sprinkling of foreign tourists amongst the Vietnamese. There is no noise; no talking and the silence seems penetrating. It only lasts a couple of minutes before you are out in the broad daylight of contemporary Vietnam. Then, people begin to talk in whispers. From the tourists you catch phrases like 'very impressive', 'what a great man', 'isn't that really something'. They like the abstractions which Ho's life seemed to capture: courage, humility, wisdom, idealism. He seems the very model of an heroic political leader.

A hundred metres or so from the mausoleum you can visit Ho Chi Minh's house. It's a simple two-storey cottage on stilts. Downstairs there's an open conference room with table and chairs and low box-like benches defining the perimeter of the room. There are no walls—the benches are where the children used to sit. Upstairs there is a study and a bedroom, simply furnished with the essential desk, chair and bed. There is a bookcase with a few books, a clothing cupboard, and an ancient and brightly polished phone. For foreign tourists, the place exudes an atmosphere of wisdom and simplicity consistent with the man's image. People like it. Ho, they suspect, was a man who understood what life was all about. At the back of the house there is a concrete air-raid shelter. In the front there is an ornamental lake where Ho used to spend some time each day feeding the fish. When visitors came to see him, he talked and fed the fish at the same time.

I saw the mausoleum and the house for the first time in the middle of 1990. I was on an official visit to Vietnam accompanied by my wife, government officials and a business delegation. We marched in a guided group past the queue of people waiting in the square to see Ho Chi Minh. There was red carpet on the steps leading to the entrance of the mausoleum. A military guard gave me a large wreath with my name on it. Two guards then goosestepped up the steps. I walked up the red-carpeted steps behind them and laid the wreath against the wall. Then we filed into the mausoleum. I've been twice more to the mausoleum on separate visits to Vietnam. I think I go because I like studying the faces of visitors to the mausoleum and listening to their reactions later. Ho Chi Minh is still a very popular leader.

Australia has had a chequered and at times undistinguished history of building relationships with the new nations of Asia. For a long time there probably didn't seem much need. The countries of Asia–Pacific, other than Japan, had their own problems. They were small economies. Our strongest ties of sentiment, culture and trade were with Britain and, to a lesser extent, Europe. Later we developed some dependence on the United States. Conservative governments tended to adopt politically correct attitudes consistent with those in Britain and the United States. We failed to recognise or exploit our most neighbourly qualities: the fact that we were not threatening and had no history of being a colonial power. In our own way we had been a benignly content victim of colonialism ourselves.

In the late 1950s we identified with covert American action in Vietnam and in the early 1960s with increasing military intervention. By the middle of the decade Australia was involved in full-scale military action. Apart from South Korea, we were the only country in the Asian region committing troops and weapons to the United States effort. We were seen as an American client in Asia and we had a lot to lose in addition to the lives of Australian troops.

In Australia opposition to the war increased throughout the 1960s. It was primarily on political and moral grounds. But there was also an underlying feeling that we were at a watershed in our relations with countries of the region. It was time we stopped hanging on other people's coat-tails and the time was ripe to start working out some relationships for ourselves.

The opposition to the war manifested itself dramatically in the moratorium marches in Australia's major cities. The repercussions were felt in Hanoi, and not forgotten. The Whitlam Government, elected in December 1972, ended Australia's involvement in the Vietnam War and moved quickly to recognise the new government in Vietnam. Ho Chi Minh had died in 1969 and was not there to see the fruits of his life's work.

With the withdrawal of the American forces and the end of the civil war, Communist Vietnam retreated into the womb of the Soviet bloc. Russia provided large sums of aid to the fragile and war-damaged Vietnamese economy and Soviet experts and technicians advised on the restructuring of Vietnam. As a news item in Australia, Vietnam went 'off the air'. The Vietnamese story became the story of 'the boat people' and the political and economic refugees, who left Vietnam during the 1970s and early 80s. These were the people who found themselves on the losing side in a bitter civil war, and victims of the recriminations of a totalitarian regime.

In spite of this enforced remoteness, Australia kept in touch with Vietnam through its embassy in Hanoi, its support of aid programs administered by non-government agencies and some business activity by small Australian companies. In the late 80s the Overseas Telecommunications Commission took on the task of rebuilding Vietnam's overseas telecommunications system. It was done effectively and well, and became a symbol of the latent but growing goodwill between the two countries. In 1984 the Vietnamese Foreign Minister, Nguyen Co Thach, visited Canberra and Sydney. Australian Foreign

Minister Bill Hayden had visited Vietnam in 1983 and there were unofficial visits by other Members of Parliament. Low-key dialogue continued.

Throughout the 1980s Vietnam remained a poor country. It still does. Border skirmishes with China, political turbulence and fighting in Cambodia, and the United States economic embargo, which denied the country access to World Bank and International Monetary Fund support, helped ensure that this was so. Average per capita incomes were at the lower end of the spectrum and in spite of rich natural resources it was amongst the world's poorest countries. In the mid-80s part of the Vietnamese population was still subject to periods of near starvation. The country was forced into greater dependence on the Soviet Union. It was not a happy position to be in. Disenchantment with the Soviet system was growing throughout the world. As the decade of the 1980s progressed, the Congress of the Vietnamese Communist Party was beginning to look at alternative models. There were more frequent discussions of the market economy. People explored the idea of a hybrid economic system—called 'market socialism'. At the same time the hegemony of the Soviet empire was beginning to crumble. Russia became increasingly preoccupied with its own problems, and the likelihood of continuing economic aid to Vietnam looked more and more remote.

Our plane landed at Hanoi's Noi Bai Airport at 2.45 p.m. on 13 June 1990. It was an Australian Air Force plane and it was right on time. The passengers comprised fourteen businessmen, seven officials, a number of media representatives, my wife and myself. It was the first large-scale peacetime delegation to Vietnam. At Noi Bai Airport we were met by the Australian Ambassador, Graham Alliband, and a group of smiling Vietnam officials. Alliband spoke the language and understood the country. The airport had an old-fashioned provincial character apart from the MIG fighters lined up along the side of the strip. We drove out of the airport into the 'picturebook' Vietnamese countryside. Buffalo grazed alongside the road: geese honked and flapped their way across in front of the car: one closed one's eyes in anticipation of imminent collisions with bicycles or ancient overladen trucks.

We were to be accommodated at the Le Thach State Guest House in central Hanoi. Our official host, the Minister for Commerce, Mr Hoang Minh Thang, was waiting at the guesthouse to meet us. Thang was sixty-two years of age; short and stocky. His career had followed a pattern fairly typical of Vietnam's ministers and senior officials, except that he had not been educated in the Soviet Union or Eastern Europe. He'd joined the Vietnamese Army when he was sixteen and fought against the French. He had participated in the Battle of Dien Bien Phu in 1954, become a political commissar in his division and then worked his way up through the ranks of the Communist Party and the army. Thirty-five years of his life had been spent in the army: for most of that time Vietnam had been at war.

Thang gave the delegation a warm greeting and we adjourned to a meeting room in the guesthouse for a briefing from the Australian Embassy staff and a discussion about the mission's objectives. It was an interesting delegation, comprising representatives from engineering and construction companies, Telecom, BHP, Pacific Dunlop and the ANZ Bank. Some, like the two men from a small seafood company, the men from OTC and Alan Taylor from a company which operated a coal washery near Haiphong, were old Vietnamese hands. The rest of us were new to it all, anxious to learn, looking for opportunities for collaboration or business.

That night there was a buffet dinner for the delegation at the Australian Embassy's Sundowners Club: round the pool in the embassy compound. An orchestra played Vietnamese music on traditional instruments. It was a beautiful evening and the music and the atmosphere were good. Driving back from the embassy to the guesthouse we had to stop for a minute at a crossroad. A group of children were sitting in the middle of the intersection doing their homework by the light of the central street lamp.

A ministerial and business delegation of this kind has a preordained and inevitable agenda and on this occasion it followed the same pattern. The program began with a round-table discussion at the Ministry for Commerce. The entire Australian delegation attended and a large contingent of Vietnamese officials. We talked about the Vietnamese economy, the prospect of increased trade and investment, the poverty of Vietnam's banking and commercial infrastructure and the small ways in which Australian experts might be of help.

There was an official lunch, followed by the signing of an Agreement on Trade and Economic Cooperation. Mr Thang proposed a toast and kissed me on both cheeks. The delegates clapped: the flamboyant performance was more generous than the contents of the agreement. In the evening the government gave a reception attended by senior ministers, officials and some notables of Vietnamese political history. The following night there was an Australian reception with much the same cast. I attended an official ceremony to hand over a coal washery plant upgraded and operated by an Australian company. We met with the State Committee for Foreign Cooperation and Investment. I visited the OTC satellite station and became the first Australian to use it for a broadcast to Australia from Hanoi.

In between these engagements I had meetings with a number of ministers and officials. They outlined an awesome list of priorities confronted by the government of a country which was one of the ten poorest in the world. Food production came first, then consumer goods for the people, then exports. Infrastructure had to be rebuilt, people trained in technical skills, foreign debt reduced, relations with other countries improved, enterprises given more freedom to operate in the marketplace. The list went on and on. The discussions took place round low tables in a succession of rooms, each dominated by a picture of Ho Chi Minh. Airconditioners groaned away in the corners, trying valiantly to beat back the heat and humidity of the oncoming summer. Lace curtains rustled in the breeze from large fans and attendants refilled cups with tea or Coca-Cola. Australia seemed a long distance away and a very lucky country.

Of the ministers, the Foreign Minister, Nguyen Co Thach, was the most theatrical and ebullient character. He explained the Vietnamese Government's view of events in Cambodia. 'International Affairs,' he explained, 'was like a game of chess. Some countries thought they moved all the pawns, but one pawn in the middle of the board was starting to move by itself. This confused the major players.' The unnamed major players were clearly the United States, China and Japan. Thach had just come from a meeting with Chinese ministers. It seemed he had told them where to go on the Cambodian issue. He paced the floor laughing and gesticulating as he made his point. One day, he said, Vietnam will be a tiger and China is a dragon. Tigers had to try to be nice to dragons, but it was not always easy. He kept saying that China proposals were sometimes 'undercooked'. Thach was warm and cordial towards Australia. He had been a visitor.

There were, in fact, not many places he had not visited in ten years as Foreign Minister; and in his previous overseas service for Vietnam. He had been a diplomatic representative, a participant in numerous international conferences, and a member of the Vietnamese delegation to the Paris peace negotiations in 1972. His life, however, had not been all diplomacy. He had been gaoled by the French for five years at the age of sixteen. He spent nine years as an officer in the army during the war against France. Australia, however, he liked. 'The kangaroo,' he said, 'is an animal which can only jump forward,' and he liked animals which jumped forward. It was a progressive image.

The Prime Minister Do Muoi had also spent five years in a French gaol in the 1940s and later he had worked his way up through the ranks of the Vietnamese Communist Party. He received us in an elegantly furnished and well-proportioned reception room of the presidential palace. We sat under a very large statue of Ho Chi Minh, which dominated one end of the room. Do Muoi spoke warmly about Australia, and was well briefed about Australia's assistance to Vietnam. He embarked on a long discourse, interrupted by translation, about Vietnam's history and the poverty of the country. He anticipated questions. Vietnam had, he said, no bitterness towards Australia arising from our support for the Americans in the war. Australia, he said, had been a puppet and should not be held responsible.

Vietnam wanted to normalise relations with the United States and China. But the United States was obstructing normalisation and this was not in the interests of the United States, Vietnam, nor the world. Vietnam had suffered more than forty years of war. He hoped that there would now be a period of stability and peace. 'Who,' he asked rhetorically, 'runs the United Nations? Countries like Japan, China, the United States, France. We have beaten them in war and now we have to beat them in commerce and trade. That must be our goal for the next period of history.' I was about to raise the issue of human rights in Vietnam. It was in my briefing. Again he anticipated me. 'People come here from Western countries and talk about human rights. Well that's OK. The Americans dropped more bombs on my country than were used in the whole of the Second World War.' His voice rose in anger. 'Where were our human rights then? Now,' he said, 'we have to look to the future. We have to put that behind us and build a new Vietnam.' He smiled and went on to talk about the allegations of human rights breaches in contemporary Vietnam.

Later a senior adviser to Do Muoi came to see me to talk through the issues confronting Vietnam in greater detail. Vietnam, he said, was committed to economic liberalisation. For a long time it had been guided by the Soviet model and in many respects this had been a disaster. He cited, as an example, the heavy industry program introduced in 1975. With the collapse of the Soviet model they had to look elsewhere and they had looked at the Hungarian and Swedish models, from which they had learnt something. But Vietnam had to work out its own destiny. There had been bitterness and difficulty in working out a new market-oriented direction, but the course was now set.

The argument was about detail, with the greatest difficulty being in adjusting pricing policy to market rules. Stability was of overall importance to economic and regional policy. The country had to gamble on stability in the region and there were plans to demob seven hundred thousand soldiers in the next two years. This was not an easy task with five million unemployed people, but it would have to be done. These problems were not helped by Gorbachev's difficulties in the Soviet Union, which would inevitably mean a reduction of Soviet aid. The Communist Party would have to maintain a central role in providing stability, while economic and political liberalisation was proceeding. The legacy of Ho Chi Minh, he said, was still a unifying national force in the country.

At first sight the streets of Hanoi seemed a far cry from the political and economic problems of the government. But life was going on. Hanoi is a city which is rich in history. There are temples and pagodas dating from the eleventh century. A twelfth century pagoda commemorates resistance to invading Chinese armies in 40 AD. Another temple is dedicated to a general who defeated invading Mongols in the thirteenth century. The Temple of Literature, set up in 1070, became the first Vietnamese University in 1076. In the narrow streets of Old Hanoi commerce is carried on as it has been for centuries in Silk Street, Shoe Street, Hat Street and so on. There is a Ho Chi Minh Museum, a Lenin Park, and a Revolutionary Museum, which tells the story of more recent resistance to foreign domination. In the centre of the city there is a gaol known as the 'Hanoi Hilton', where captured American pilots were detained as a deterrent to the bombing of the inner city. The greatest historic legacy, however, is from the period of French colonial rule. There are great boulevards and, in handsome public buildings and villas, fine examples of French colonial architecture. Hanoi bustles with people: a sea of bicycles into which motorbikes and cars increasingly intrude. For the foreigner it is a friendly, law-abiding place. There are plenty of signs of poverty, but the citizens seem a tough, hardworking and proud people.

Saigon, or Ho Chi Minh City, is two thousand kilometres to the south. The largest city in Vietnam, it had been, and was becoming again in 1990, the major commercial centre. We flew there from Hanoi. It had a distinctly different atmosphere from Hanoi: it's like travelling from Melbourne to the Gold Coast. Hanoi is the city of government with a long history and a dignified atmosphere. Saigon has a relatively short history and only began to emerge in the late eighteenth century, starting as a small but important trading centre. Today it buzzes with the lively commerce of the marketplace.

In 1859 it was captured by the French and became the capital of the French Colony of Cochin-China. From then on it began to develop as a prosperous commercial centre. In the Second World War it was captured by the Japanese. Later, Saigon was to become the capital of the Republic of Vietnam until it was captured by North Vietnamese and resistance forces in 1975. Like Hanoi, it has an air of French provincialism with some notable French colonial architecture. There are some grand boulevards and in the old hotels, like the

Continental and the Caravalle, the ghosts of Andre Malraux and Graham Greene linger in the corridors.

I called on the Vice-Chairman of the People's Committee at the town hall, from where the city is run with a degree of autonomy from Hanoi. Later the Australian delegation had a round-table conference with a large delegation from the People's Committee at the former palace of South Vietnam's President. We exchanged information, and listened to the particular problems of Saigon. Appointments continued, one after the other. I opened an Australian seafood plant, visited a clothing factory financed by Taiwanese investment, and had a meeting with an economics adviser to the People's Committee. A man in his sixties, he was full of enthusiasm for the new economic directions. He told me he was studying market economics by candlelight late in the evenings when he had finished the day's work. There was an exchange of friendly receptions: one given by the People's Committee and one by the Australian delegation. I opened the Austrade office. Finally, the Australian delegation met to compare impressions, and talk about what had been achieved in the course of the visit. Everyone liked the country and the people. There was a degree of caution about what was possible in terms of trade and investment. But some of the companies would go back to Vietnam to further explore the possibilities.

I went back to Vietnam several times. In April 1992 Treasurer John Dawkins and I visited Laos and made an official visit to Hanoi. In Hanoi we discussed a new Australian bilateral aid program to be spent on training and infrastructure development and John Dawkins signed an investment protection agreement. We had a lengthy discussion with the new Prime Minister, Vo Van Kiet, and a meeting with the new Foreign Minister, Nguyen Manh Cam. We talked to the Prime Minister and others about BHP's bid for the development of the Dai Hung oil field off the coast of South Vietnam. Later I opened the new Austrade office in Hanoi. Since my first visit Australia had become the third largest foreign investor in Vietnam. There had been regular exchanges of visits by ministers and officials and there was a good relationship between the two countries. In spite of a few fly-by-night Australian businesspeople seeking a quick dollar, the reputation of Australians remained a good one. It was generally recognised that Vietnam was a place where trade and investment involved a long-term approach.

Returning to Vietnam enabled me to better understand and appreciate the history, the culture and the problems of the place. I travelled by train from Saigon to Hanoi, spending time at Nha Trang, Da Nang and the ancient capital of Hue along the route. I visited monasteries, pagodas, and the tombs of Vietnamese kings. I went to the Cu Chi tunnels from where, forty kilometres from Saigon, Vietcong units conducted operations against the forces of the Republic, the Americans and their allies in the years leading up to the capture of the city. The hundreds of kilometres of narrow tunnels are a testimony to what a determined and courageous people can do in circumstances which might well have seemed impossible. I fell victim to the vibrant beauty of the countryside, and the photogenic character of the daily life of peasant agriculture. We made visits to the Ho Chi Minh trail and the famous Ha Long Bay. The language, the climate, bureaucrats and sometimes poor facilities produced difficulties along the way. But I became a convert to the beauty of the place, and the diligence and friendliness of the people.

In 1990 Vietnam was in much the same stage of economic development as a number of Asian countries were fifteen or twenty years ago. Some of these countries are now amongst the impressive strong-growth economies of the region. Fifteen or twenty years ago, Australian politicians and businessmen overflew these countries on their way to Europe and Australia, missed in playing a major role in their development and in establishing a strong commercial presence. We remained aloof and opportunities were not taken.

Vietnam provides a similar, if somewhat more difficult, challenge; but we know a good deal more than we knew two decades ago about relationships with the countries of Asia. Vietnam is a country of nearly seventy million people: the predominant power of Indochina, situated in the middle of the Western Pacific Asian coast. It has poor infrastructure, a low standard of living and problems of political unity. On the other hand it is rich in resources and has a hardworking and well-educated population. Its high literacy rate keeps it out of the list of the world's least developed countries. There are always arguments about possible scenarios for Vietnam. Some think that economic progress will be slow because of poor infrastructure and inadequate managerial skills. Others point to the legacy of Vietnam's political history and the need for greater reconciliation between the North and the South. These concerns have real validity about them.

Vietnam has a host of problems. Sometimes, however, those who linger on the side of pessimism overlook the lessons of history and the influence of will in human affairs. Visiting Vietnam over four years, I have seen huge changes taking place and a commitment to their continuation. The political views of Ho Chi Minh and his colleagues, who embraced Marxism in pursuit of the Vietnamese revolution, will slip quietly into history. If his nationalism, his belief that 'the most precious things in life are liberty and freedom', continues to inspire national sentiment in Vietnam then I think they will make it. They will, as Foreign Minister Thach said, become a 'tiger'.

Australia's relationship with Vietnam has been an exciting and interesting one. In Hanoi in 1993 you could pick up the phone and ring Australia or America on a system installed by OTC. You could read a weekly paper owned fifty–fifty by an Australian group and the Vietnamese Government, or the Vietnamese investment laws translated into English by an

Australian law firm. For banking you could go to the handsome ANZ Bank on the main boulevard round the lake, and you could have a choice of Australian lawyers and accountants to give you advice. If you were hungry and sick of noodles, you could buy a pizza at the pizza parlour of a twenty-four-year-old Perth entrepreneur. There are more examples of the same sort of thing. In Saigon you could have a choice of Australian owned and managed hotels. You could send your children to an Australian school. These are things which add substance to the relationship.

Australians continue to like Vietnam. More Australians are coming to understand the country, and many are working in various capacities to help solve its problems. Compared with other countries of predominantly European population, Australia has been at it for quite some time. There is an old Vietnamese proverb: 'When we eat the fruit we remember those who helped to plant the tree.' In spite of Australia's undistinguished history in cultivating friends in Asia, Vietnam has been a different experience. The tree is now twenty years old and there is a certain satisfaction in watching it grow.

Dropping in on the neighbours

In the 1960s and 1970s Europe, and later America, were the places to go—at least for Australian politicians. As a rule they flew over Asia, with a brief stopover at Singapore or Bangkok dictated by aircraft refuelling requirements rather than a sense of relevance or interest. They headed for Europe to bang their heads against the wall of the Common Agricultural Policy or in search of the security of old allegiances in Britain. In America they looked for keys to the future and the assurances which Big Brothers are sometimes prepared to provide. For a brief period in the early 1970s the Whitlam Government initiated a change of focus. As Opposition Leader, Whitlam made an historic visit to China. His government ended Australia's involvement in the Vietnam War, and worked with mixed success at improving Australia's relationship with Indonesia. China was recognised and diplomatic relations established. Whitlam exchanged acerbic vanities with Singapore's Lee Kuan Yew. One way or another they talked. Whitlam himself was the principal motivator of the new outward orientation. His government was, with one or two exceptions, composed of ministers with a strong and typical inward-looking focus: redressing the perceived wrongs of twenty-three years in Opposition, settling old scores, raising new horizons of domestic indulgence.

The Fraser Government elected in 1975 did little to follow up the directions in which Whitlam's foreign policy initiatives might have taken Australia. It was a government dominated by a bunch of well-to-do farmers. Trade policy was for them essentially about markets for agricultural products, and massaging the buyers of coal and iron ore. The quirky interests of particular ministers produced interesting and sometimes beneficial results. As Trade Minister, Doug Anthony travelled regularly to the Middle East. He enjoyed the hospitality of the Saudi and Gulf States princes; realised the possibility of increased trade in primary products and set about capturing a slice of it for Australia. Malcolm Fraser had a genuine and sympathetic interest in Africa and his publicly expressed views, though painful to some, were in the long term beneficial to Australia. At home the government pursued sensible immigration policies, which were bipartisan in nature and again in Australia's long-term interest. But by and large the country slipped back into introspection and comfortable insularity.

Towards the end of March 1983, I had dinner with Dr Tony Tan, the Singapore Minister for Trade and Industry, at a restaurant in the Canberra suburb of Manuka. I'd been Industry Minister for about two weeks and was tired and a little confused after being submerged in meetings, briefing papers and other official documents. My ignorance was unaccompanied by any concomitant feeling of bliss. The restaurant in Manuka seemed like a sophisticated escape from sandwiches and coffee in Parliament House.

Tony Tan was a thoughtful and unassuming man, who served the Singapore Government in a variety of roles with quiet distinction. He was the first Minister from a foreign country whom I'd met in an official capacity, and I sat down at the dinner table with a feeling of nervous apprehension; like a novice approaching a master of the art of international politics. At the same time I had the feeling that this was the sort of man I had to get to know, to understand and hopefully work with. He asked me some questions about GATT, and the composition of Australian exports and tariffs. I mumbled replies about having to sort out the priorities. He said he thought that was important and that it would be difficult in Australia. He thought we had too many governments, such long distances to travel and so much time taken up with Parliament. 'In Singapore,' he said, 'I am always busy, and our Parliament sits for only six weeks of the year with a maximum of four-hour sessions each day of the sittings. And in reality we have no Opposition.' He manoeuvred a saltcellar back and forth across the table, as if he was contemplating a move in a game of chess. 'I don't envy you,' he said, 'but I wish you well, and I hope you'll come and see me in Singapore.'

Ten months later I took the well-trodden ministerial path to Europe, the United Kingdom and Scandinavia. On the way over I stopped for three days in Bangkok, and on the way back I stopped in Singapore and visited Tony Tan. As we talked about the Singaporean economy and I contemplated Australia's domestic agenda, the contrast seemed stark and Singapore's management simple indeed. A few months later I was in Kuala Lumpur for an ASEAN seminar, and towards the end of 1984 in Indonesia for an Australian–Indonesian business conference. The new focus on the region, encouraged by the Prime Minister, Bob Hawke, meant that relations with ministers and governments in the countries of Asia and the Pacific were no longer simply matters of foreign policy, handled by the Minister for Foreign Affairs. As Industry Minister I'd begun the habit of dropping in on the neighbours. It was sociable and there was plenty to learn.

The relationship between Australia and the modern state of Singapore got off to a shaky start in 1969, when the People's Action Party was elected to government. Nobody in Australia knew much about it. Conservative Australians suspected that it was too radical, left-wing and perhaps even pro-communist. The PAP's Leader and the new Prime Minister was a young lawyer, Lee Kuan Yew, Chinese, Cambridge-educated, and highly articulate. At that time of pervasive Australian ignorance about Asia, it seemed a dangerous mix.

On my first visit to Singapore in 1968 I spent a couple of hours walking in the gardens with George Thompson, an adviser to the PAP and the government. Thompson was from the London School of Economics; a former adviser to British governments and an expert on Malaysia and Singapore. He was an intimate of Lee Kuan Yew, Goh Keng Swee and other members of the talented Singaporean elite. I suspect Thompsons Road in Singapore is named after him. He left me with an impression of a government that knew what it was doing, an impression which remained in spite of some of the unusual and reprehensible methods used to achieve these results.

In 1968 Singapore had the vestiges of a swampy Third World-feeling about it, but they were quickly disappearing. The place was on the way up. Already it was becoming an island emporium for low-cost shopping, a cheap tourist destination and a centre for conventions in good quality hotels.

Singapore's success, and some of its shortcomings, revolve around the complex personality of its long-time Prime Minister, Lee Kuan Yew. He is popularly and correctly identified as the founder of modern Singapore; a description which at times overlooks the contribution of a succession of talented ministers and advisers. But he was always the boss, the articulate and forceful spokesman, and the 'great helmsman' of the island state.

I first met Lee Kuan Yew at Maxim's restaurant in Melbourne in the mid-1970s. It was a small dinner party: Sir Laurence Hartnett; Andrew Peacock; Denis Warner (the foreign correspondent of the Melbourne *Herald*), Lee Kuan Yew and his wife, my wife and I. We talked about the range of happenings in Asia, about Singapore's role and Australia's future. I remember asking him how he replied to the allegations, of concern to people like myself, that he kept a number of his political opponents in gaol. He looked at me with what is perhaps best described as a baleful stare. 'It's quite simple,' he said. 'It's either them or me. These are dangerous men. If I don't keep them in gaol, in a short time they would have me in gaol.'

It was a straightforward, simple and unambiguous answer, which didn't leave much room for argument. But was it correct, or a total exaggeration? Many commentators would disagree with him, arguing that his analysis of the political realities was quite incorrect. At the time I wondered if he believed it himself or whether he was just saying that he had a job to do in building a modern state and couldn't be bothered with the criticisms and diversions of political opponents for whom he had no time.

For me it was my first introduction to an issue which was to constantly crop up in relations between Western countries, including Australia, and the emerging governments of Asia: the extent to which the norms of traditional political democracies should be assumed to apply to governments in former colonies with new and different agendas. From time-to-time it was to be an issue which would bedevil Australia's relations with Indonesia, Malaysia, Vietnam and China. By the early 1990s it had settled down into an ongoing international dialogue on human rights.

Singapore is a small country with no natural resources; its one unique natural advantage being its location. It is an advantage which has been exploited with great skill. Changi Airport has grown with the economy, of which it is an integral part. It is now perhaps the most efficient airport in the world, and Singapore Airlines one of the largest and best. Looking down from a tall building at the Port of Singapore, you might on a busy day count forty or fifty ships lying at anchor. The port is efficient with quick turn-around and a sophisticated distribution system. Singapore has a large number of good hotels. It may be a stopover, but it is also a gateway to Asia, Australasia and the Pacific. From the time of its independence until the present day, Singapore has enjoyed high economic growth with the exception of 1985, when it suffered an aberrant economic downturn.

Singapore has given great emphasis to the development of the human resources of its people. Savings have been encouraged, education at all levels has been a priority and through the agency of the Economic Development Board, a range of incentives offered to encourage overseas firms to establish appropriate businesses and industries. Australians and the rest of the world watched with fascination as Singapore's average per capita income climbed the comparative table, passing New Zealand in the late 1980s and drawing equal with Australia's in the early 1990s. By almost every economic criteria, Singapore has been a stunning success. And it is a clean, well-ordered place.

As success followed success, the Captain of this ship of no fools grew in international stature and repute. At home he kept his hand firmly on the tiller. By the early 1980s he was considered to be becoming increasingly aloof, a prime minister who had begun to take on the role of headmaster. As a headmaster he kept fit, maintained discipline, cajoled, administered and used his national day speech as a vehicle for articulating new visions and old prejudices. He is a fervent non-smoker! In 1986 the national day speech reflected a concern about the maintenance of the intellectual quality of the Singapore elite. Intellectually gifted Singaporeans were to be encouraged by tax incentives to have more children, thereby improving the standard of the gene pool. In the 1987 national day speech, he spoke of the need to match economic growth with advances in 'moral, ethical and aesthetic dimensions', and gave a none too oblique warning about the role of religion in Singaporean society. Religious leaders should not get mixed up in politics and should take off their clerical robes, before they take on anything economic or political.

Catholic priests and Christian pastors were given a special mention in a reference which was believed to apply to some controversy over the security detentions of Catholic lay workers.

Singapore had to continue its 'pursuit of excellence' and be careful of Western attitudes which considered anything superior as 'smacking of elitism'. At other times he talked of the need to attract talented and skilled workers from Hong Kong and the dangers of the 'brain drain' from Singapore to North America, Australia and the United Kingdom. Lee was particularly concerned to preserve the political system which he had created. He tried to encourage talented people into government and his able son, Lee Hsien Loong, had enjoyed a rapid rise through the ministerial ranks. Other ministers complained to me about the decline in quality of the 'cadres' in the PAP. 'Why,' they asked rhetorically, 'should Singaporeans want to go into politics when we have created a society in which they can become rich without the additional effort which politics requires?'

Lee Kuan Yew's habit of handing out admonishments was not confined to Singaporeans. He became an occasional visiting lecturer and a frequent dispenser of 'distant education' to Australians, a role that he assumed quite early in his career and which sometimes gave a touch of ambiguity to an otherwise friendly relationship between the two countries. The fact that he lectured us was not entirely surprising: here we were, right in front of his eyes, an example of 'Western' complacency, indifference, and lack of political will. And so we were chastised about immigration policy, tariffs, laziness, and indulgent freedoms for trade unions and the press. He never went unnoticed. He was such an accomplished performer, and the mixture of the characteristic arrogance of a successful Chinese and the shiny Cambridge polish ensured that people listened. If at times he seemed a bit unfair, the fact that he was largely right, and most Australians knew it, made the whole exercise more worthwhile. And his authority was such that, while Australian politicians were in the 1970s and 1980s prepared to hand out rebukes to a variety of countries for human rights shortcomings, no-one tackled him head on about Singapore's woeful record.

Each time I visited Singapore as a minister in the 1980s the engagements followed a routine pattern. I would call on the Minister for Trade and Industry and, depending on who it was at the particular time, he would talk about the progress of the Singaporean economy and ask a few questions about Australia. I would have the task of trying to improve perceptions of Australia with a briefing typically couched in terms like:

The continued substantial orientation of Singapore to Western Europe and North America is noteworthy. This is partly a function of markets, sources of technology, and the efforts of multinationals. There is a need to develop among Singaporeans more awareness of Australia and the quality and depth of fields such as Australian research, higher education, quality manufacturing, and capacity for innovation.

Persuading a Singaporean minister about that was not always easy, but things improved as time went by. These meetings were always polite and friendly, but at times we were talking about separate agendas and expositions passed like ships in the night.

I would always have meetings with some other ministers, perhaps a meeting with the Science Council of Singapore and on a number of occasions with Philip Yeo, the dynamic and astute Chairman of the Economic Development Board. Inevitably these discussions would be followed by a press conference, attended by journalists from Singapore Broadcasting Corporation television and radio, the *Straits Times* and *Business Times*. The journalists often had an earnestness about them unfamiliar to Australian politicians. The questions were sometimes couched in terms such as 'How can Singapore learn from your mistakes?' and on occasions they were submitted in writing. Then they tended to be big questions:

> Senator Button, as the Minister for Industry, Technology and Commerce, you have been charged with the task of revitalising the Australian industry and to achieve a radical restructuring of Australia's Manufacturing and Service sectors. How did you go about doing it and what were the major obstacles you faced?

There was usually a business lunch at the High Commissioner's residence with a selected group of invited guests. In the early days they were mainly expatriate Australians; representatives of the major Australian banks, Qantas, and big companies like CSR. In later years the guest list included prominent Singaporean businessmen, usually with business interests in Australia. They were interested to exchange views, although mostly they were well informed about economic conditions in Australia. Inevitably there was a meeting with the Australian expatriate community. In the early 80s it took the form of a Friday night 'happy hour' with a small group in a crowded room engaging in some matey backslapping and the ritual drinking of Fosters or Tooheys from pewter tankards. By the 1990s the meetings took place under the aegis of the Singapore–Australia Business Council, usually at a lunch, with a speech from the visiting Minister, questions and a formal response. The numbers had grown to about two hundred or more and there was an air of sophistication lacking in earlier times.

In November 1987 the *International Herald Tribune* celebrated its centenary and marked the event with a conference in Singapore, at which I was invited to speak, together with ministers from Indonesia and Thailand. The conference was opened by Lee Kuan Yew. He entered the auditorium with a phalanx of powerfully built, armed bodyguards, who fanned out around the room in a manner which was impressive if not intimidating. As usual he did it in style. The luncheon address was given by American columnist William Safire, who had the guests laughing so much that the afternoon session began late. Dr Habibie, the Indonesian Science and Technology Minister, spoke after lunch. He began by enjoining us to read in detail the seventy-page speech he had distributed to the audience, and then gave a 'summary' of his speech which lasted well over an hour. By the time I spoke a lot of the audience had left, and I realised the benefits of being a politician in a country where it is easy to command a captive audience. Singapore, except when Lee Kuan Yew or a senior Singaporean minister spoke, was not such a country.

In the late 80s the Singapore Government began to direct additional resources into design. In 1990 a A$30 million design budget was announced, together with the establishment of a design centre and an Institute of Design. The aim was to build up design resources and 'initiate a design culture amongst Singaporeans'. In October 1990 Singapore sponsored an International Design Forum and I was invited to give the keynote address. The forum was attended by several prominent Australian designers. A creditable display of Australian design was included in the exhibition associated with the forum. The elderly and highly respected President of Singapore, Wee Kim Wee, officiated at the conference and presented awards to successful design students. In my address to the conference, reported in the *Straits Times*, I said, 'Design is a discipline concerned with quality. It stems from a deep historical heritage or alternatively must be inculcated in a people from a very young age.' It was a message slow to take root in Australia, but understood and seized on in Singapore. I walked around the exhibition with President Wee, an unassuming, dignified and charming head of state. He kept wandering back to look at a Holden Caprice displayed on the Australian stand. 'It's very nice,' he said. 'I'd like to have one of these.' It made my day. I thought, 'We're getting some things right'.

Apart from brief routine visits, I made my last official trip to Singapore in June 1992 as a guest speaker at the ASEAN Science and Technology Week. Singapore had a new Prime Minister, Go Chok Tong, a more low-key personality than his predecessor with an air of quiet competence about him. Lee Kuan Yew's son was Deputy Prime Minister, a role which sadly he was to relinquish some months later because of ill health. Lee Kuan Yew had become Minister without Portfolio, from where he was able to keep an eye on things and carry out a role as the highly effective roving Ambassador for his country. On television he expressed his confidence in the new Prime Minister and described his view of the relationship between them. Go Chok Tong would be 'in the driving seat'. Lee Kuan Yew would be sitting beside him and if there was any sign of the car running off the road, he would grab the wheel.

The Deputy Prime Minister 'B.G.' Lee opened the conference with a speech which bore the hallmark of the Lee family competence. In my speech I referred to Australia's growing manufactured and services exports to ASEAN countries, and their increasing sophistication in terms of quality and technology. Maybe I imagined things, but I thought people were nodding their heads in agreement. Later at a dinner hosted by the Senior Industry Minister, Lim Boon Heng, and attended by the various Science and Technology ministers from the ASEAN countries, the topic was raised again. Australia, it was implied, was 'lifting its game' and in ASEAN they were beginning to see the results.

Hong Kong is another gateway, but to the landmass and teeming population of China. It is also a convenient transit point for Taiwan, Vietnam, Laos and Cambodia. Like Singapore, it is partly an island with a predominantly Chinese population. Like Singapore, it operates a busy airport and a thriving port, said to be the busiest container port in the world. Physically it is quite different from Singapore, with topographical features which make it an attractive, and to some, a beautiful location. A craggy coastline, 'the Peak' on Hong Kong Island, a rugged hinterland and the bustling harbour have resisted the best efforts of builders and developers to destroy the visual amenity and touch of magic which Hong Kong provides for its visitors. A few spare hours in Hong Kong can be happily occupied with a visit to the New Territories, a ferry ride or a climb to the top of the mountain on the Island.

The economy of Hong Kong is like an externally fitted 'pacemaker', pumping away in rhythm with the huge economy of China. If China slows down, so does Hong Kong. It provides the hotels, the financial services, the contact points, the conferences, the transport and sometimes the experts for people doing business with China. Hong Kong is an open-trading economy with no tariffs or restrictions on foreign investment and low taxes. It is a natural home for multinationals, fast money and high-fliers.

Hong Kong changed as China, in the late 1970s and the 1980s, slowly opened to the world. It used to be a predominantly manufacturing economy with low wages and a myriad of busy factories turning out clothing, footwear, toys and other consumer goods. Australian manufacturers used to regard it as a competitive menace; a constant source of cheap imports. They wondered where it would all end, and how the flood of imports could be held back. Relief was in sight. In Hong Kong the importance of the manufacturing sector of the economy declined as living standards and wages increased and the services sector became predominant. The cheap imports started to come from China, through Hong Kong.

The Government and administration of Hong Kong followed a different pattern from Singapore. When Singapore gained independence it took control of its own destiny. Hong Kong has never had an independent destiny. For the Chinese it was part of China, for the British a useful colony and trading centre. After 1984, the adjustment process from a British colony to a Chinese possession was reflected in the winding down of the British military presence and the move towards some form of representative government.

Australia's relationship with Hong Kong adjusted slowly. Travelling there as a Minister in the 1980s, the changes seemed to be reflected in relationships with the expatriate business community. There was always a pattern about the obligatory appointments in Hong Kong: a call on the Governor, a meeting with the Chief Secretary or other members of the Executive Council, a lunch or dinner with prominent businesspeople, a luncheon address to the Australian Chamber of Commerce. The lunch usually took place at the Hong Kong Jockey Club. In the early 1980s the audience were a disgruntled lot, mainly refugees from the Australian taxation regime and seemingly incapable of understanding why the Australian Government did not have their interests as its highest priority.

Nearly a decade later 'Auscham', as it had now been called, provided a much larger, more professional and sophisticated audience. Australia was more international in outlook, taxes had been significantly reduced, and Australians were doing bigger and better business in Hong Kong. Dinners with the business leaders of the major companies in Hong Kong provided as good an opportunity as any to learn what was happening in the global trade of services from transport to telecommunications. Meetings with officials from the administration were useful in seeking out opportunities for Australian companies to participate in Hong Kong's continuing program of infrastructure building.

In the mid-1980s, on the basis of these contacts and together with other government ministers, I tried my hand at lobbying the Hong Kong administration in favour of an Australian consortium tendering for a contract to build a light rail system in the New Territories. It was a tender fiercely contested by a number of international consortia. The question was continually asked whether in the light of 'Australia's poor industrial relations' the Australian consortium could deliver. A couple of days before the awarding of the contract, I phoned the Under Secretary for Transport in Hong Kong and assured him that the Australian consortium would deliver the system on time. The Australians won the contract and built the system, but a few months after my phone call there was a long strike at the factory where the tramcars were being built. The project was delayed. There were letters from Hong Kong expressing concern. In 1988 I went out to the New Territories to look at the system and ride around it on a Melbourne-built tramcar. Everyone assured me that it was working well, but according to a conductor it was not too popular on the day of my visit. A woman had been knocked over by a tram and killed the day before.

I passed through Hong Kong on my way to Korea in 1992. In retrospect it is hard to differentiate it from other visits. The program said, 'Call on the Governor Lord Wilson, drinks with the directors of the Australian Chamber of Commerce and dinner with senior Hong Kong businesspeople'. There was the usual anxiety about 'events in China' and an air of uncertainty about what the Chinese might do after 1997 when the British colonial regime would finally end. But business seemed to be going well. The per capita GDP had doubled since 1988 and was probably moving ahead of Australia's. At the dinner with 'senior businesspeople' someone told me about a party. It had been arranged by the Hong Kong business community at the famous Peace Hotel in Shanghai, where the great jazz band that played there in the late 1930s was supposedly still playing; $1500 a head plus air fares, accommodation and new outfits for the guests. I must have looked slightly shocked. 'It's good for the Hong Kong economy,' he said. 'Next year we're going to St Petersburg.'

When I first visited Malaysia in the late 1960s, Kuala Lumpur resembled an Australian country town plonked down in the steamy tropics. It had a small Central Business District, a new airport, a university, some golf courses and streets which seemed to ramble off into the lush tropical countryside. It was the first place where I'd seen tough-looking soldiers in armoured personnel carriers patrolling the streets. There had been serious race riots and it was not a happy place. Like Singapore, Hong Kong, Jakarta and Bangkok, Kuala Lumpur changed and got bigger, and managed to do it without falling victim to the worst excesses of rapidly growing urban conglomerates.

Malaysia gained its independence from Britain in 1957. Unlike Singapore and Hong Kong, it was a country well-endowed with natural resources in agriculture and mining and an export economy heavily reliant on rubber, palm oil, tropical timbers and metals. So in the decades following independence it had a similar problem to Australia of overdependence on raw material production. Malaysia lacked major deepwater ports and hard infrastructure. Its manufacturing sector was small. It had a mixed-race population and marked discrepancies in the degree of economic power enjoyed by different racial groups. Inter-ethnic tensions influenced the shape of government policies. Malaysian governments in the 1970s made steady progress in dealing with these issues, although there was mixed success in encouraging the development of manufacturing. In the 1980s the pace was to quicken considerably.

The story of Malaysia in the 1980s and early 90s largely revolves round the personality, vision and energy of its Prime Minister, Dr Mahathir Bin Mohamad. He became Prime Minister in 1981 after a career as a medical practitioner, a bumpy ride in Malaysian politics in the 1960s and service in various ministries in the 1970s. Dr Mahathir ran a successful government. The economy, with occasional blips, had grown steadily with a dramatic improvement in the standard of living. The attraction of cheap labour in the 1980s, plus targeted tax holidays and incentives led to strong foreign investment in manufacturing, employment growth, and much greater diversity of exports. Infrastructure development had proceeded rapidly. As the economic 'pie' grew and was reflected in rising incomes and greater sharing of economic opportunities, ethnic tensions abated. There appeared to be a growing sense of national identity.

Dr Mahathir has never minded a scrap. He's had them in Malaysian politics, with other government leaders in ASEAN, with Britain, the United States. Japan, China and Australia. When I first met him in 1984 at the European Management Forum in Davos, Switzerland in 1984 he was quick to point out the different perspective of a commodity-producing country in Asia from the world of wealthy European countries. In the early years of his government he announced the 'Look East' policy which involved developing stronger links with other Asian economies by implication weaker links with the developed countries of the West. The policy was criticised on trade and economic grounds. Essentially it was considered unfriendly. 'Dr Mahathir,' it was said, was 'a difficult man'.

Western commentators criticised his government on other issues. There were allegations of press censorship, structured racial inequalities, authoritarianism, intolerance, and criticisms of his government's commitment to capital punishment. Malaysian leaders, including the Prime Minister, resented the criticisms, some of which were seen as being based on the 'decadent' values of the West. Perhaps it was again an inevitable debate with no real meeting point and evidence of the risks which follow from attempts to reconcile different views of political and democratic models. In Malaysia's case the sensitivities were probably greater because the criticisms were rarely accompanied by any acknowledgment of the considerable achievements of the Malaysian government. No-one talked much about the Malaysian success story. But given its problems at independence, that is what it has been. And like every political leader, Dr Mahathir, is a creature of his background, his experience and his own vision of what his country is and might become.

Australia has a long history of good relations with Malaysia including defence cooperation, tourism, education of Malaysian students, refugee resettlement, development aid and, more recently, investment. A number of large Australian companies have a substantial presence in Malaysia and amongst Malaysian politicians, civil servants and businesspeople. Australia has a lot of friends. In late 1990 and 1991 relations between the two countries cooled considerably as an alleged result of a television program and criticisms by the Australian press. Australian businesses in Malaysia were said to have been discriminated against. I was asked to lead a business mission to Malaysia in December 1991 to try to sort out the problems and reconcile any differences.

The mission comprised five officials and seventeen others from companies with business interests in Malaysia including representatives of CSIRO and the Universities Vice-Chancellors Committee, with John Gough, the Chairman of Pacific Dunlop, as the 'business leader'. Our host in Malaysia was the Minister for Trade and Industry, Dato Seri Rafidah Aziz, generally referred to as 'Rafidah' and well known in international trade circles for her capacity for blunt speaking, sense of humour and bubbling personality. Rafidah was a charming and hospitable host, and entertained the mission members shortly after our arrival with a banquet at a leading hotel in Kuala Lumpur.

In the course of the three-day stay in Malaysia I had, in addition to talks with the host Minister Rafidah, separate and useful meetings with the ministers for Transport, Education, Science, Environment and Primary Industry. The Education Minister was a bit difficult. He'd been educated in New

Zealand and they seemed to have won his heart and mind. Trade in tropical timber and the effects of logging on the environment were a sensitive issue between the two governments. The acting Minister responsible for the industry, a Chinese, gave me a detailed account of the views of various ministers in the Australian government on this important environmental issue. It was so accurate that I began to suspect he'd been sitting under the table during a Cabinet meeting in Canberra.

A dinner was held at the residence of the Australian High Commissioner for a large group of Australian expatriates in Kuala Lumpur, which was helpful in gaining a feel for the political and business environment. The Malaysia–Australia Business Council gave a well-attended and enthusiastic lunch for the delegation and so did a group of senior Malaysian businessmen. The Malaysia–Australia Business Council lunch was chaired by Tunku Shahabuddin, an Australian-educated businessman married to an Australian and a frequent visitor to this country. He had just been to the Melbourne Cup. I said I'd never been to a Melbourne Cup. He told me that he'd been to nineteen. At the lunch given by Malaysian businessmen the host was the Chief Minister of Sarawak, again a man with strong Australian connections. In the Australian delegation there were a number of people with longstanding associations with Malaysia and a similar situation applied in reverse with the Malaysians. It seemed silly that the good relations between the two countries had been disrupted, and that the obvious personal friendships were not reflected in the political relationships.

In my speech to the Malaysia–Australia Business Council I said: 'In the last year, relations between our two countries have been difficult: but there is a Malay proverb which is applicable now: *Biduk lalu kiambang bertaut*. I understand it means that a boat disturbs the lilies on a quiet river but they quickly come back together when it passes.' I referred to recent visits to Malaysia by Defence Minister Senator Ray and Foreign Affairs Minister Gareth Evans. I said that 'nothing would give me greater pleasure than to complete this visit knowing that there were no longer impediments to our relationship'. I had to make a number of speeches in Malaysia and I referred to the proverb in several of them. In the speech to the lunch I wrote a crude phonetic version in the margin to remind me of the correct pronunciation. That's because on another occasion I hadn't got it quite right, which served as a small reminder of the importance of communication between countries and peoples.

On the second day in Kuala Lumpur the Prime Minister, Dr Mahathir, agreed to see the Australian delegation. I had met him before and I asked to see him on his own, without officials, note takers or anyone else present. We sat in his spacious office and talked for about an hour. For a few minutes he displayed the reserve and diffidence which is sometimes mistaken for arrogance. Then he started to talk about the problems of his country, his own background in politics, and his aspirations for Malaysia—his so-called 20/20 vision, which aimed to have Malaysia a developed country with a high standard of living by the year 2020. 'I suppose,' he said with a laugh, 'that I called it 20/20 vision because I am a doctor.' We talked about the 'freedom of the press' and what it meant. I said that in normal circumstances an Australian government could not and would not try to censor opinions expressed in newspapers or on television.

He said he understood, but sometimes felt that views critical of Malaysia might reflect the views of the Australian Government. It seemed there had to be a formula to resolve this sort of problem. Subsequently Gareth Evans and the Malaysians worked one out. At the end of our discussion he said 'Now I'd like to meet your delegation'. A group of Malaysian officials and the members of the Australian delegation were waiting in a room downstairs. The Prime

Minister walked into the room and gave them what can best be described as a brilliant smile. 'Gentlemen,' he said, 'there has been a period of coolness between our countries. It is now over.' He received a standing ovation and there were smiles all round. Then he sat down and charmed his audience for half an hour. It had been a mission which seemed worthwhile.

I dropped into Jakarta for a two-day visit on 12 December 1991. It was four weeks after the Dili Massacre in East Timor. I had appointments with the Indonesian ministers for Industry, Trade, Finance, Transport, Tourism and Telecommunications, the Deputy Minister for Industry. A meeting with a senior Indonesian businessman and a luncheon address to be given to the Australia–Indonesia Business Council. It seemed like a tight schedule. The Australian Ambassador to Indonesia, Philip Flood, a hardworking and thoughtful diplomat, was at the airport to meet me. A motorcycle police escort guided us at high speed through the traffic on the way to the city. In the car I pondered the growth of Jakarta from a rambling Asian town when I had first visited it twenty-five years before, to a huge modern metropolis.

The Dili Massacre had resulted in a high level of concern in Australia. The Prime Minister Bob Hawke had commented that Australia was 'shocked and distressed by the appalling tragedy in East Timor'. He expressed the belief that events in East Timor 'had shocked and surprised the political leadership in Jakarta'. Welcoming President Suharto's decision to set up a commission of inquiry, he urged that it should be 'comprehensive and credible to Indonesia's international partners'. Press reports in Australia and Indonesia had been full of inconsistencies about what had actually happened in Dili. It was not clear at what level the military had been instructed to act, and allegations and counterallegations were flying back and forth. In Australia there were suspicions that the commission of inquiry would not be genuine. In the car the Ambassador filled me in on the Jakarta perspective of the issues.

We went straight to the Department of Industry for a meeting with Minister Hartarto, who had invited me to visit Indonesia. Hartarto and I had a warm personal relationship, and he was a good friend of Australia. I had first met him in 1984 when he visited Canberra as Industry Minister, and we had met on a number of occasions since. Hartarto was an engineering graduate from the University of New South Wales. He spoke fluent English and understood Australian slang, having worked as a wharfie in Sydney after completing his course at the university. A heavily built, bluff sort of man, he valued frankness rather than political circumspection. In Indonesia he was President of the Australian Alumni Association of Indonesian Graduates of Australian Universities. He showed me, with some pride, his Department's comprehensive data base of Indonesian and overseas companies. We talked for an hour with a group of officials and then I asked to see him on his own, with the Ambassador.

I told him of the depth of concern in Australia about East Timor and expressed the hope that there would be a proper inquiry in the interests of improving understanding and good relations between the two countries. He listened gravely, a man caught on this occasion in the misfortune of understanding two political cultures. He said, 'I will go and talk to the President about it.'

The following day there were a number of journalists at the Australia–Indonesia Business Council lunch. I talked about trade, changes in Australia's industrial performance, the recession and its effects, and finally about East Timor and Australian concerns. There were a number of thoughtful questions about the relationship between Australia and Indonesia; questions based on the assumptions that we were neighbours and ought to know and understand each other better.

Afterwards, talking privately to a group of young Indonesians, I began to understand how little East Timor impacted on the lives of people in Jakarta. Indonesia consists of thousands of islands scattered over a huge area of ocean. Timor was one of them, a long way from Jakarta and few people had been there or knew much about it. The army had the job of keeping order in the far-flung parts of the country and with the experiences of the 1960s in their history, Indonesians have a fear of civil disorder. We talked for half an hour and concluded that there are different perspectives which needed to be talked about again and again.

The Australia–Indonesia Business Council was formed in 1989 and by 1991 was a well-established body. In 1984 I had attended a conference of its predecessor organisation, the Australian Indonesia Business Cooperation Committee, a small body of business pioneers on both sides. The numerical strength and relative sophistication of the AIBC reflected the growth in trade and investment between the two countries, and the expansion of the Australian expatriate community in Jakarta. The strengthening relationship was marked by good commercial relationships, a strong Australian presence in service industries, and the signing of agreements on joint oil production in the Timor Gap, fisheries, and taxation. In 1990–91 thirty thousand Indonesians had visited Australia, six thousand five hundred students were studying in Australia, and the Australia–Indonesia Institute, established in 1989, was promoting exchanges in culture, media, education and sport. Ministers were exchanging regular visits; the relationship was developing on a broad front. When I left Jakarta on a Friday night I was surprised to see Hartarto at the airport. He was dressed in casual clothes and had driven himself out to the airport in his old car to see me off. He wanted to chat and he asked me a few more questions about East Timor.

In October 1992 I went back to Indonesia to the port city of Surabaya to speak at the Conference of the Australia–

Indonesia Business Council. The theme of the conference was 'Neighbours Growing Together' and the focus of the speeches was to be 'Looking towards the year 2000'. Hartarto was there and addressed the conference. There were a number of expert speakers from Australia and Indonesia. There were now over three hundred and fifty Australian members of the AIBC and the conference was well attended.

The hospitality was generous and in the evening we were driven in a cavalcade of cars to the hills, an hour's drive from the city, for a dinner in a chalet hosted by a local businessman. We were entertained with music and dancing. Our host had a number of interests, including the franchise for Holden motor cars which he'd hung onto through lean times. On the way back to Surabaya I shared a car with an adviser to one of the Vice-Presidents. He was a professor of sociology, and he told me that when he'd returned to Indonesia from the United States twenty years before he had been the only trained sociologist in Indonesia. I wondered what advice he gave, and where a sociologist would begin in a society as complex and diverse as Indonesia.

By 1992 cooperation between the Australian and Indonesian governments had reached a point where it was decided to establish a regular ministerial forum. The meeting of the forum took place over three days in November of that year and was attended by five Australian ministers and a number of officials and, in the course of the three days, eight Indonesian ministers. I was Chairman of the Australian side and the Minister for Foreign Affairs, Gareth Evans, co-Chairman. The Coordinating Minister for Economy, Finance and Industry, Radius Prawiro, was Chairman on the Indonesian side, and Ali Alatas, the Indonesian Minister for Foreign Affairs, was co-Chairman. There were numerous officials.

The forum was regarded as 'an important new high-level institution in the bilateral relationship'. The *Jakarta Post* commented that 'political relations between the two countries have been lukewarm over the last few decades and often coloured with suspicion.' The forum, however, took place in an atmosphere of relaxed informality as we discussed a wide range of issues including trade and commerce, tourism, education, industry and resources. Much depended on personal relationships. Prawiro was a charming and friendly host. I knew Hartarto well, and Gareth Evans had a good personal relationship with Alatas. There were other friendships.

Apart from the scheduled sessions of the forum, there were special meetings between ministers and their counterparts, and I had an opportunity to renew my acquaintance with Dr Habibie, the Minister for Science and Technology. Agreements were reached on a number of matters. There were several relaxed and informal lunches and dinners, and a lot of discussion about the ASEAN Free Trade area which was to start in operation in January of 1993. It was probably the most friendly international meeting of its kind which I had attended.

The Australian delegation met with President Suharto at the Presidential Place. He was friendly and astute, displaying both the wisdom of his years and a youthful enthusiasm and interest. I wondered about his long political life in the independence movement, the army and as President. He had reason to be satisfied with most of the great changes in his country's fortunes. He asked after Paul Keating with whom he'd developed a close rapport.

When I left Jakarta I told Hartarto and his wife that I would be retiring from politics in Australia after the next election, which would probably take place in March 1993. Mrs Hartarto thought her husband worked too hard and should retire as well. I told him that I thought I was the longest serving Industry Minister in the world, but we worked it out and found that he had started a month before me in 1983. In 1993, he was to be promoted upwards to the position of Coordinating Minister.

Leaving Jakarta I felt some regrets that it was the last meeting of its kind that I would be attending. I wondered if, and when, I would have time to return privately to Indonesia to try to get a better understanding of our neighbouring country with its huge population, different races, different religions, different cultures and lifestyles. I had gained a smattering of understanding from my visits and from reading. I had begun to understand some of the jokes about the differences in temperament between Sumatrans and Javanese. I had seen some of the dances from the regions and the puppet shows. It was just a taste of a huge and complex country, enough to make me know that in fact I knew very little.

On my vists to Thailand I sometimes used to talk with Mr Snoh Unakul, an old friend from Melbourne University days. He had been Governor of the Reserve Bank, and an economic adviser and was for a time Deputy Prime Minister. We used to talk about various countries in Asia, in between expositions of Thailand's development plans. He used to say that the countries which will do well in Asia are the ones with a 'strong culture'. Culture is a much misused word. It involves tradition and is perhaps conveniently described as a way in which people do things in a particular country. By a 'strong culture' I think he meant countries which are free of racial and religious tension and have a sense of national identity and history. Thailand, he would argue, had a strong culture.

Japan was an obvious example. Hong Kong, an important neighbour of Australia, has no identifiable culture of its own. It has a Chinese culture with a veneer of British colonial efficiency and the values of global business. In Malaysia there is a dominant Malay culture, and Chinese and Indian minorities, which perhaps represent refugee cultures from the countries where those populations originated. Malaysia has been working hard at finding solutions to the mix. Indonesia has a myriad of cultures subsumed in a strong national sentiment. A Singaporean culture seems harder to identify. Lee Kuan Yew has built a society successfully committed to being rich. Sometimes Singaporeans say they want to be like Switzerland: rich and comfortable. I am sure they will succeed. But Switzerland is physically one of the most beautiful countries in the world and Singapore has no such advantage. I cannot imagine people going to Switzerland in search of a fascinating culture. Whether they do it in Singapore remains to be seen.

Australia is the subject of many writings about its cultural identity. We talk a lot about it with a great deal of introspection. Perhaps our culture comes from the land and the continent, and a predominantly European but multiracial community settled in a strange place. I am optimistic enough to think we might be slowly getting it right. Part of this involves getting to know our neighbours and allowing them to know us.